Home Landscaping

Other titles available in the *Home Landscaping* series:

Home Landscaping: California Region

Home Landscaping: Mid-Atlantic Region

Home Landscaping: Northeast Region, including Southeast Canada

Home Landscaping: Northwest Region

Home Landscaping: Southeast Region

CRE▲TIVE
HOMEOWNER®

Home Landscaping
Midwest Region,
including Southern Canada

Roger Holmes & Rita Buchanan

CREATIVE HOMEOWNER®, Upper Saddle River, New Jersey

COPYRIGHT 1999

CRE/\TIVE
HOMEOWNER®

A Division of Federal Marketing Corp.
Upper Saddle River, NJ

Produced by WordWorks.

Editors: Roger Holmes and Rita Buchanan
Assistant editors: Monica Norby and Sarah Disbrow
Copyeditor: Nancy J. Stabile
Design: Deborah Fillion
Layout: Elizabeth Eaton (Portfolio of Designs, Plant
    Profiles); Deborah Fillion (Guide to Installation)
Illustrators: Portfolio of Designs: Warren Cutler,
    Tony Davis (site plans). Guide to Installation:
    Michelle Angle Farrar, Lee Hov, Robert La Pointe, Rick
    Daskam, Teresa Nicole Green.
Indexer: Barbara E. Cohen
Cover design: Michelle Halko
Cover photograph: Larry Lefever, from Grant Heilman

Current Printing (last digit)
20 19 18 17 16 15 14 13 12

Library of Congress Catalog Card Number: 98–84956
ISBN: 1–58011–005–3

CREATIVE HOMEOWNER®
A Division of Federal Marketing Corp.
24 Park Way
Upper Saddle River, NJ 07458
www.creativehomeowner.com

Safety First

Though all concepts and methods in this book have been reviewed for safety, it is not possible to overstate the importance of using the safest working methods possible. What follows are reminders—do's and don'ts for yard work and landscaping. They are not substitutes for your own common sense.

▲ *Always* use caution, care, and good judgment when following the procedures described in this book.

▲ *Always* determine locations of underground utility lines before you dig, and then avoid them by a safe distance. Buried lines may be for gas, electricity, communications, or water. Start research by contacting your local building officials. Also contact local utility companies; they will often send a representative free of charge to help you map their lines. In addition, there are private utility locator firms that may be listed in your Yellow Pages. *Note*: Previous owners may have installed underground drainage, sprinkler, and lighting lines without mapping them.

▲ *Always* read and heed the manufacturer's instructions for using a tool, especially the warnings.

▲ *Always* ensure that the electrical setup is safe; be sure that no circuit is overloaded and that all power tools and electrical outlets are properly grounded and protected by a ground-fault circuit interrupter (GFCI). Do not use power tools in wet locations.

▲ *Always* wear eye protection when using chemicals, sawing wood, pruning trees and shrubs, using power tools, and striking metal onto metal or concrete.

▲ *Always* read labels on chemicals, solvents, and other products; provide ventilation; heed warnings.

▲ *Always* wear heavy rubber gloves rated for chemicals, not mere household rubber gloves, when handling toxins.

▲ *Always* wear appropriate gloves in situations in which your hands could be injured by rough surfaces, sharp edges, thorns, or poisonous plants.

▲ *Always* wear a disposable face mask or a special filtering respirator when creating sawdust or working with toxic gardening substances.

▲ *Always* keep your hands and other body parts away from the business ends of blades, cutters, and bits.

▲ *Always* obtain approval from local building officials before undertaking construction of permanent structures.

▲ *Never* work with power tools when you are tired or under the influence of alcohol or drugs.

▲ *Never* carry sharp or pointed tools, such as knives or saws, in your pockets. If you carry such tools, use special-purpose tool scabbards.

The Landscape Designers

Carter Lee Clapsadle is landscape horticulturist with the College of St. Catherine, St. Paul, Minn. Trained at the University of Minnesota in horticulture and plant biology, Mr. Clapsadle has many years' experience as a nurseryman and garden designer in Oregon, Alaska, and Minnesota. He currently maintains 110 acres of college land, managing the greenhouse and designing and implementing garden displays. Mr. Clapsadle teaches design classes at the University of Minnesota through the Practical Scholar Program. He has received awards for urban beautification, garden tours, and landscaping from the city of Anchorage and the state of Alaska. His designs appear on pp. 28–31, 36–39, 40–43, 72–75, 96–99, and 104–107.

Larry Giblock came to horticulture in the early 1980s from a career in fashion design. He assisted with field studies of native plants at the Cleveland Natural History Museum and was instrumental in forming the Native Plant Society of Ohio. In 1988 the Cleveland Botanical Garden hired him to develop and oversee their Wildflower Garden, and in 1993 care of the Japanese Garden was added to his responsibilities. Mr. Giblock's residential garden designs draw on gardening traditions of Eastern as well as Western cultures and emphasize native plants, local materials, and the work of local craftspeople. His designs appear on pp. 44–47, 64–67, 76–79, 84–87, and 88–91.

Jan Little is manager of horticultural education at the Morton Arboretum in Lisle, Ill. A registered landscape architect, she has worked on a wide range of projects, including residential and commercial landscapes, woodland restoration, public gardens, and urban renovations. Ms. Little's public beautification projects for Geneva, Ill. (where she lives and works), have received several landscape design awards. Her designs appear on pp. 24–27, 32–35, 60–63, 68–71, 92–95, and 108–111.

Michael Schroeder, a University of Minnesota graduate, has practiced landscape architecture and urban design in the region since 1985. He works for Hoisington Koegler Group, Inc., in Minneapolis, where he has done award-winning work helping communities develop their own design strategies. Mr. Schroeder teaches a class in landscape design for homeowners at the Minnesota Landscape Arboretum. Residential landscape design is his avocation, and he enjoys trying out ideas on his own property in Edina, Minn. His designs appear on pp. 20–23, 48–51, 52–55, 56–59, 80–83, and 100–103.

Contents

PORTFOLIO OF DESIGNS

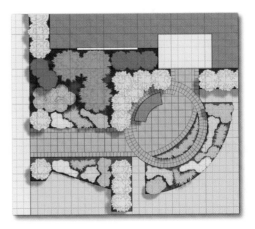

GUIDE TO INSTALLATION

PLANT PROFILES

About This Book

Of all the home improvement projects homeowners tackle, few offer greater rewards than landscaping. Paths, patios, fences, arbors, and, most of all, plantings can enhance home life in countless ways, large and small, functional and pleasurable, every day of the year. At the main entrance, an attractive brick walkway flanked by eye-catching shrubs and perennials provides a cheerful send-off in the morning and welcomes you home from work in the evening. A carefully placed grouping of small trees, shrubs, and fence panels creates privacy on the patio or screens a nearby eyesore from view. An island bed showcases your favorite plants, while dividing the backyard into areas for several different activities.

Unlike with some home improvements, the rewards of landscaping can lie as much in the activity as in the result. Planting and caring for lovely shrubs, perennials, and other plants can afford years of enjoyment. And for those who like to build things, outdoor construction projects can be a special treat.

While the installation and maintenance of plants and outdoor structures are within the means and abilities of most people, few of us are as comfortable determining exactly which plants or structures to use and how best to combine them. It's one thing to decide to dress up the front entrance or patio, another to come up with a design for doing so.

That's where this book comes in. Here, in the Portfolio of Designs, you'll find designs for nearly two dozen common home landscaping situations, created by landscape professionals who live and work in the Midwest region. Drawing on years of experience, they balance functional requirements and aesthetic possibilities, choosing the right plant or structure for the task, confident of its proven performance in similar situations.

Complementing the Portfolio of Designs is the Guide to Installation, the book's second section, which will help you install and maintain the plants and structures called for in the designs. The third section, Plant Profiles, gives information on all the plants used in the book. The discussions that follow take a closer look at each section; we've also printed representative pages of the sections on pp. 9 and 10 and pointed out their features.

Portfolio of Designs

This section is the heart of the book, providing examples of landscaping situations and solutions that are at once inspiring and accessible. Some are simple, others more complex, but each one can be installed in a few weekends by homeowners with no special training or experience.

For each situation, we present two designs, the second a variation of the first. As the sample pages on the facing page show, the first design is displayed on a two-page spread. A perspective illustration (called a "rendering") shows what the design will look like several years after installation, when the perennials and many of the shrubs have reached mature size. The rendering also shows the planting as it will appear at a particular time of year. (For more on how plantings change over the course of a year, see "Seasons in Your Landscape," pp. 12–15.) A site plan shows the positions of the plants and structures on a scaled grid. Text introduces the situation and the design and describes the plants and projects used.

The second design, presented on the second two-page spread, addresses the same situation as the first but differs in one or more important aspects. It might show a planting suited for a shady rather than a sunny site, or it might incorporate different structures or kinds of plants (adding annuals to a perennial border, for example). As for the first design, we present a rendering, site plan, and written information, but in briefer form. The second spread also includes photographs of a selection of the plants featured in the two designs. The photos showcase noteworthy qualities—lovely flowers, handsome foliage, or striking form—that these plants contribute to the designs.

Installed exactly as shown here, these designs will provide years of enjoyment. But individual needs and properties will differ, and we encourage you to alter the designs to suit your site and desires. Many types of alterations are easy to make. You can add or remove plants and adjust the sizes of paths, patios, and fences to accommodate larger or smaller sites. You can rearrange groupings and substitute favorite plants to suit your taste. Or you can integrate the design with your existing landscaping. If you are uncertain about how to solve specific problems or about the effects of changes you'd like to make, consult with staff at a local nursery or with a landscape designer in your area.

Guide to Installation

In this section you'll find detailed instructions and illustrations covering all the techniques you'll need to install any design from start to finish. Here we explain how to think your way through a landscaping project and anticipate the various steps. Then you'll learn how to do each part of the job: readying the site; laying out the design; choosing materials; building paths, trellises, or other structures; preparing the soil for planting; buying the recommended plants and putting them in place; and car-

Portfolio of Designs

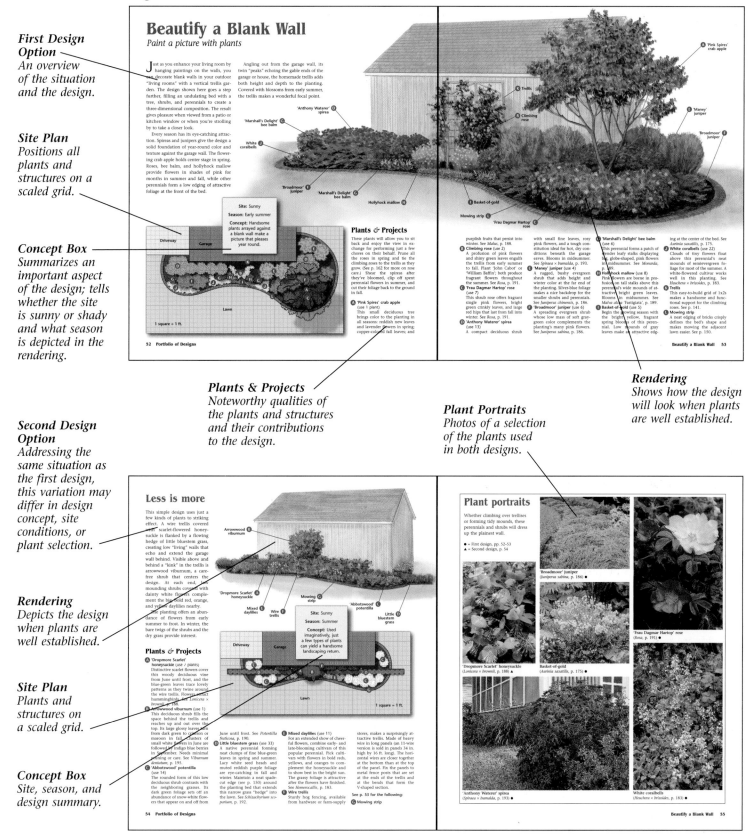

First Design Option
An overview of the situation and the design.

Site Plan
Positions all plants and structures on a scaled grid.

Concept Box
Summarizes an important aspect of the design; tells whether the site is sunny or shady and what season is depicted in the rendering.

Plants & Projects
Noteworthy qualities of the plants and structures and their contributions to the design.

Plant Portraits
Photos of a selection of the plants used in both designs.

Rendering
Shows how the design will look when plants are well established.

Second Design Option
Addressing the same situation as the first design, this variation may differ in design concept, site conditions, or plant selection.

Rendering
Depicts the design when plants are well established.

Site Plan
Plants and structures on a scaled grid.

Concept Box
Site, season, and design summary.

Guide to Installation

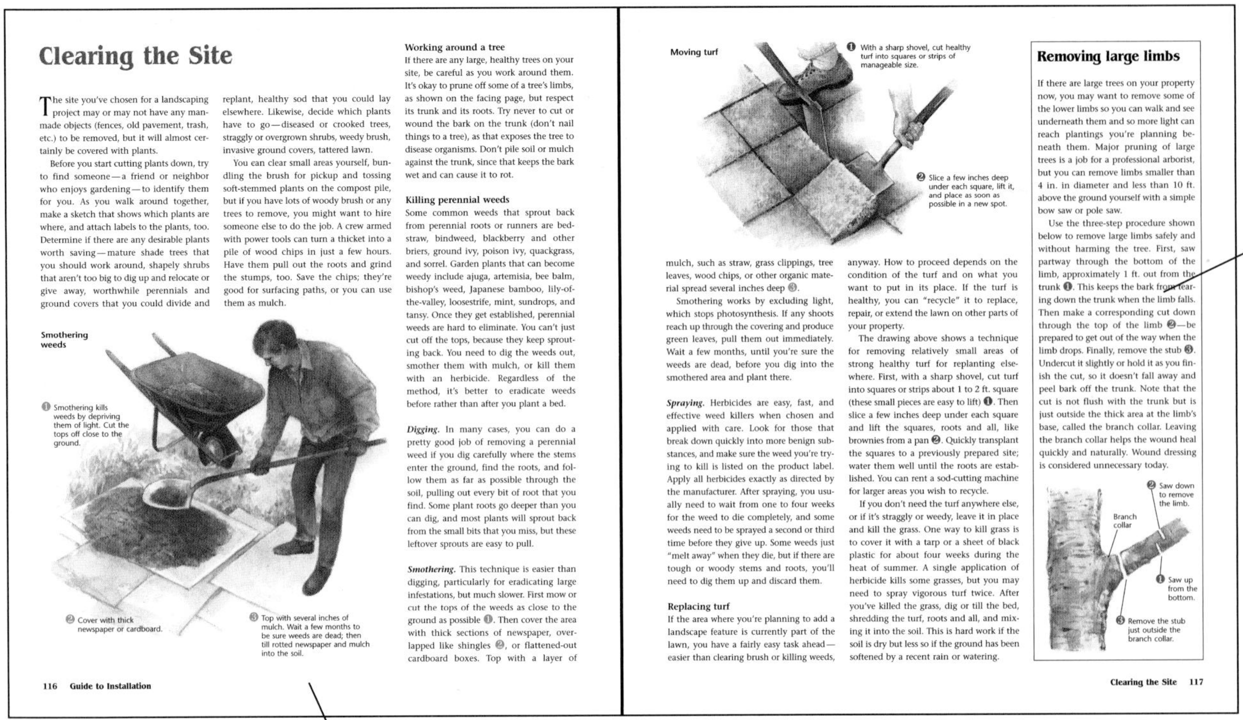

Clearing the Site

The site you've chosen for a landscaping project may or may not have any man-made objects (fences, old pavement, trash, etc.) to be removed, but it will almost certainly be covered with plants.

Before you start cutting plants down, try to find someone—a friend or neighbor who enjoys gardening—to identify them for you. As you walk around together, make a sketch that shows which plants are where, and attach labels to the plants, too. Determine if there are any desirable plants worth saving—mature shade trees that you should work around, shapely shrubs that aren't too big to dig up and relocate or give away, worthwhile perennials and ground covers that you could divide and replant, healthy sod that you could lay elsewhere. Likewise, decide which plants have to go—diseased or crooked trees, straggly or overgrown shrubs, weedy brush, invasive ground covers, tattered lawn.

You can clear small areas yourself, bundling the brush for pickup and tossing soft-stemmed plants on the compost pile, but if you have lots of woody brush or any trees to remove, you might want to hire someone else to do the job. A crew armed with power tools can turn a thicket into a pile of wood chips in just a few hours. Have them pull out the roots and grind the stumps, too. Save the chips; they're good for surfacing paths, or you can use them as mulch.

Smothering weeds

1 Smothering kills weeds by depriving them of light. Cut the tops off close to the ground.

2 Cover with thick newspaper or cardboard.

3 Top with several inches of mulch. Wait a few months to be sure weeds are dead; then till rotted newspaper and mulch into the soil.

Working around a tree

If there are any large, healthy trees on your site, be careful as you work around them. It's okay to prune off some of a tree's limbs, as shown on the facing page, but respect its trunk and its roots. Try never to cut or wound the bark on the trunk (don't nail things to a tree), as that exposes the tree to disease organisms. Don't pile soil or mulch against the trunk, since that keeps the bark wet and can cause it to rot.

Killing perennial weeds

Some common weeds that sprout back from perennial roots or runners are bedstraw, bindweed, blackberry and other briers, ground ivy, poison ivy, quackgrass, and sorrel. Garden plants that can become weedy include ajuga, artemisia, bee balm, bishop's weed, Japanese bamboo, lily-of-the-valley, loosestrife, mint, sundrops, and tansy. Once they get established, perennial weeds are hard to eliminate. You can't just cut off the tops, because they keep sprouting back. You need to dig the weeds out, smother them with mulch, or kill them with an herbicide. Regardless of the method, it's better to eradicate weeds before rather than after you plant a bed.

Digging. In many cases, you can do a pretty good job of removing a perennial weed if you dig carefully where the stems enter the ground, find the roots, and follow them as far as possible through the soil, pulling out every bit of root that you find. Some plant roots go deeper than you can dig, and most plants will sprout back from the small bits that you miss, but these leftover sprouts are easy to pull.

Smothering. This technique is easier than digging, particularly for eradicating large infestations, but much slower. First mow or cut the tops of the weeds as close to the ground as possible 1. Then cover the area with thick sections of newspaper, overlapped like shingles 2, or flattened-out cardboard boxes. Top with a layer of mulch, such as straw, grass clippings, tree leaves, wood chips, or other organic material spread several inches deep 3.

Smothering works by excluding light, which stops photosynthesis. If any shoots reach up through the covering and produce green leaves, pull them out immediately. Wait a few months, until you're sure the weeds are dead, before you dig into the smothered area and plant there.

Spraying. Herbicides are easy, fast, and effective weed killers when chosen and applied with care. Look for those that break down quickly into more benign substances, and make sure the weed you're trying to kill is listed on the product label. Apply all herbicides exactly as directed by the manufacturer. After spraying, you usually need to wait from one to four weeks for the weed to die completely, and some weeds need to be sprayed a second or third time before they give up. Some weeds just "melt away" when they die, but if there are tough or woody stems and roots, you'll need to dig them up and discard them.

Replacing turf

If the area where you're planning to add a landscape feature is currently part of the lawn, you have a fairly easy task ahead—easier than clearing brush or killing weeds, anyway. How to proceed depends on the condition of the turf and on what you want to put in its place. If the turf is healthy, you can "recycle" it to replace, repair, or extend the lawn on other parts of your property.

The drawing above shows a technique for removing relatively small areas of strong healthy turf for replanting elsewhere. First, with a sharp shovel, cut turf into squares or strips about 1 to 2 ft. square (these small pieces are easy to lift) 1. Then slice a few inches deep under each square and lift the squares, roots and all, like brownies from a pan 2. Quickly transplant the squares to a previously prepared site; water them well until the roots are established. You can rent a sod-cutting machine for larger areas you wish to recycle.

If you don't need the turf anywhere else, or if it's straggly or weedy, leave it in place and kill the grass. One way to kill grass is to cover it with a tarp or a sheet of black plastic for about four weeks during the heat of summer. A single application of herbicide kills some grasses, but you may need to spray vigorous turf twice. After you've killed the grass, dig or till the bed, shredding the turf, roots and all, and mixing it into the soil. This is hard work if the soil is dry but less so if the ground has been softened by a recent rain or watering.

Moving turf

1 With a sharp shovel, cut healthy turf into squares or strips of manageable size.

2 Slice a few inches deep under each square, lift it, and place as soon as possible in a new spot.

Removing large limbs

If there are large trees on your property now, you may want to remove some of the lower limbs so you can walk and see underneath them and so more light can reach plantings you're planning beneath them. Major pruning of large trees is a job for a professional arborist, but you can remove limbs smaller than 4 in. in diameter and less than 10 ft. above the ground yourself with a simple bow saw or pole saw.

Use the three-step procedure shown below to remove large limbs safely and without harming the tree. First, saw partway through the bottom of the limb, approximately 1 ft. out from the trunk 1. This keeps the bark from tearing down the trunk when the limb falls. Then make a corresponding cut down through the top of the limb 2—be prepared to get out of the way when the limb drops. Finally, remove the stub 3. Undercut it slightly or hold it as you finish the cut, so it doesn't fall away and peel bark off the trunk. Note that the cut is not flush with the trunk but is just outside the thick area at the limb's base, called the branch collar. Leaving the branch collar helps the wound heal quickly and naturally. Wound dressing is considered unnecessary today.

2 Saw down to remove the limb.

Branch collar

1 Saw up from the bottom.

3 Remove the stub just outside the branch collar.

116 Guide to Installation

Clearing the Site 117

"Sidebars"
Detailed information on special topics, set within ruled boxes.

Step-by-Step
Illustrations show process; steps are keyed by number to discussion in the main text.

Choices
Selections here help you choose from the many varieties of certain popular plants.

Plant Profiles

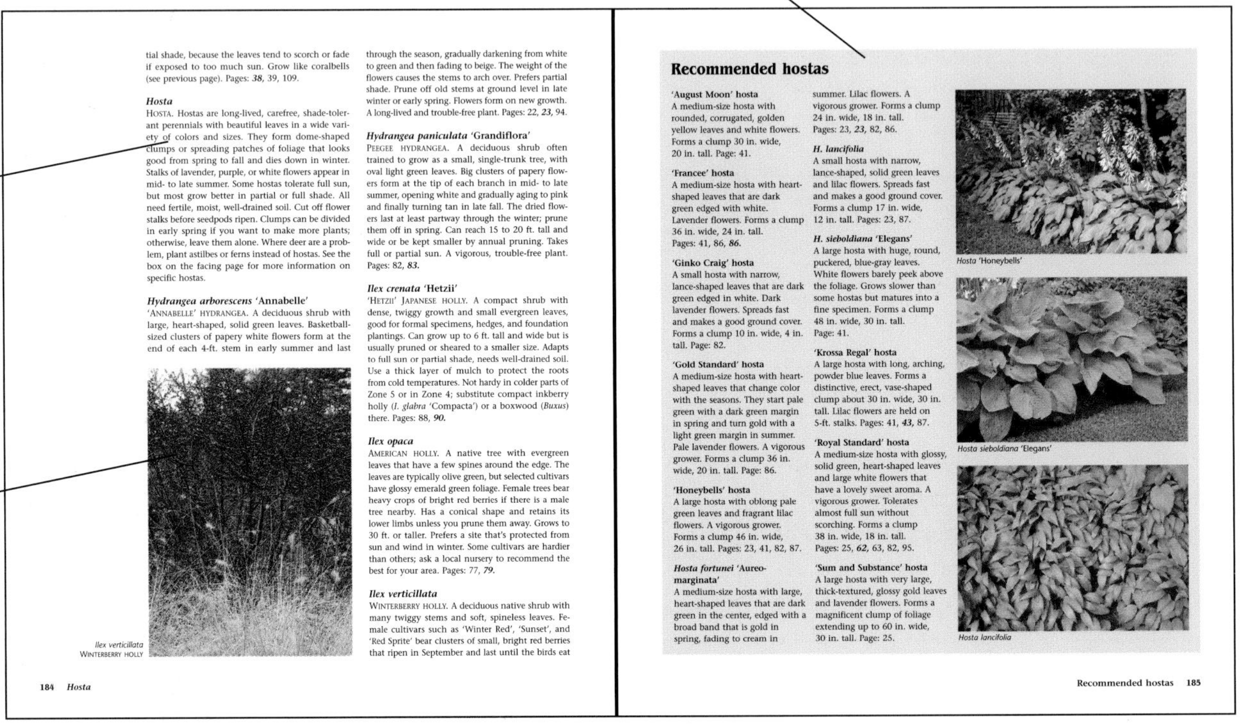

tial shade, because the leaves tend to scorch or fade if exposed to too much sun. Grow like coralbells (see previous page). Pages: ***38***, 39, 109.

Hosta

HOSTA. Hostas are long-lived, carefree, shade-tolerant perennials with beautiful leaves in a wide variety of colors and sizes. They form dome-shaped clumps or spreading patches of foliage that looks good from spring to fall and dies down in winter. Stalks of lavender, purple, or white flowers appear in mid- to late summer. Some hostas tolerate full sun, but most grow better in partial or full shade. All need fertile, moist, well-drained soil. Cut off flower stalks before seedpods ripen. Clumps can be divided in early spring if you want to make more plants; otherwise, leave them alone. Where deer are a problem, plant astilbes or ferns instead of hostas. See the box on the facing page for more information on specific hostas.

***Hydrangea arborescens* 'Annabelle'**

'ANNABELLE' HYDRANGEA. A deciduous shrub with large, heart-shaped, solid green leaves. Basketball-sized clusters of papery white flowers form at the end of each 4-ft. stem in early summer and last through the season, gradually darkening from white to green and then fading to beige. The weight of the flowers causes the stems to arch over. Prefers partial shade. Prune off old stems at ground level in late winter or early spring. Flowers form on new growth. A long-lived and trouble-free plant. Pages: 22, ***23***, 94.

***Hydrangea paniculata* 'Grandiflora'**

PEEGEE HYDRANGEA. A deciduous shrub often trained to grow as a small, single-trunk tree, with oval light green leaves. Big clusters of papery flowers form at the tip of each branch in mid- to late summer, opening white and gradually aging to pink and finally turning tan in late fall. The dried flowers last at least partway through the winter; prune them off in spring. Can reach 15 to 20 ft. tall and wide or be kept smaller by annual pruning. Takes full or partial sun. A vigorous, trouble-free plant. Pages: 82, ***83***.

***Ilex crenata* 'Hetzii'**

'HETZII' JAPANESE HOLLY. A compact shrub with dense, twiggy growth and small evergreen leaves, good for formal specimens, hedges, and foundation plantings. Can grow up to 6 ft. tall and wide but is usually pruned or sheared to a smaller size. Adapts to full sun or partial shade, needs well-drained soil. Use a thick layer of mulch to protect the roots from cold temperatures. Not hardy in colder parts of Zone 5 or in Zone 4; substitute compact inkberry holly (*I. glabra* 'Compacta') or a boxwood (*Buxus*) there. Pages: 88, ***90***.

Ilex opaca

AMERICAN HOLLY. A native tree with evergreen leaves that have a few spines around the edge. The leaves are typically olive green, but selected cultivars have glossy emerald green foliage. Female trees bear heavy crops of bright red berries if there is a male tree nearby. Has a conical shape and retains its lower limbs unless you prune them away. Grows to 30 ft. or taller. Prefers a site that's protected from sun and wind in winter. Some cultivars are hardier than others; ask a local nursery to recommend the best for your area. Pages: 77, ***79***.

Ilex verticillata

WINTERBERRY HOLLY. A deciduous native shrub with many twiggy stems and soft, spineless leaves. Female cultivars such as 'Winter Red', 'Sunset', and 'Red Sprite' bear clusters of small, bright red berries that ripen in September and last until the birds eat

Ilex verticillata
WINTERBERRY HOLLY

Recommended hostas

'August Moon' hosta
A medium-size hosta with rounded, corrugated, golden yellow leaves and white flowers. Forms a clump 30 in. wide, 20 in. tall. Page: 41.

'Francee' hosta
A medium-size hosta with heart-shaped leaves that are dark green edged with white. Lavender flowers. Forms a clump 36 in. wide, 24 in. tall. Pages: 41, 86, ***86***.

'Ginko Craig' hosta
A small hosta with narrow, lance-shaped leaves that are dark green edged in white. Dark lavender flowers. Spreads fast and makes a good ground cover. Forms a clump 10 in. wide, 4 in. tall. Page: 82.

'Gold Standard' hosta
A medium-size hosta with heart-shaped leaves that change color with the seasons. They start pale green with a dark green margin in spring and turn gold with a light green margin in summer. Pale lavender flowers. A vigorous grower. Forms a clump 36 in. wide, 20 in. tall. Page: 86.

'Honeybells' hosta
A large hosta with oblong pale green leaves and fragrant lilac flowers. A vigorous grower. Forms a clump 46 in. wide, 26 in. tall. Pages: 23, 41, 82, 87.

***Hosta fortunei* 'Aureo-marginata'**
A medium-size hosta with large, heart-shaped leaves that are dark green in the center, edged with a broad band that is gold in spring, fading to cream in summer. Lilac flowers. A vigorous grower. Forms a clump 24 in. wide, 18 in. tall. Pages: 23, ***23***, 82, 86.

H. lancifolia
A small hosta with narrow, lance-shaped, solid green leaves and lilac flowers. Spreads fast and makes a good ground cover. Forms a clump 17 in. wide, 12 in. tall. Pages: 23, 87.

***H. sieboldiana* 'Elegans'**
A large hosta with huge, round, puckered, blue-gray leaves. White flowers barely peek above the foliage. Grows slower than some hostas but matures into a fine specimen. Forms a clump 48 in. wide, 30 in. tall. Page: 41.

'Krossa Regal' hosta
A large hosta with long, arching, powder blue leaves. Forms a distinctive, erect, vase-shaped clump about 30 in. wide, 30 in. tall. Lilac flowers are held on 5-ft. stalks. Pages: 41, ***43***, 87.

'Royal Standard' hosta
A medium-size hosta with glossy, solid green, heart-shaped leaves and large white flowers that have a lovely sweet aroma. A vigorous grower. Tolerates almost full sun without scorching. Forms a clump 38 in. wide, 18 in. tall. Pages: 25, ***62***, 63, 82, 95.

'Sum and Substance' hosta
A large hosta with very large, thick-textured, glossy gold leaves and lavender flowers. Forms a magnificent clump of foliage extending up to 60 in. wide, 30 in. tall. Page: 25.

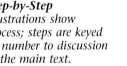

Hosta 'Honeybells'

Hosta sieboldiana 'Elegans'

Hosta lancifolia

184 *Hosta*

Recommended hostas 185

Detailed Plant Information
Descriptions of each plant's noteworthy qualities and requirements for planting and care.

Plant Portraits
Photos of selected plants.

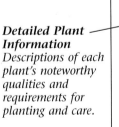

ing for the plants to keep them healthy and attractive year after year.

We've taken care to make installation of built elements simple and straightforward. The paths, trellises, fences, and arbors all use basic, readily available materials, and they can be assembled by people who have no special skills or tools beyond those commonly used for home maintenance. The designs can easily be adapted to meet specific needs or to fit in with the style of your house or other landscaping features.

Installing different designs requires different techniques. You can find the techniques that you need by following the cross-references in the Portfolio to pages in the Guide to Installation, or by skimming the Guide. You'll find that many basic techniques are reused from one project to the next. You might want to start with one of the smaller, simpler designs. Gradually you'll develop the skills and confidence to do any project you choose.

Most of the designs in this book can be installed in a weekend or two; some will take a little longer. Digging planting beds and erecting fences and arbors can be strenuous work. If you lack energy for such tasks, consider hiring a neighborhood teenager to help out; local landscaping services can provide more comprehensive help.

Plant Profiles

The final section of the book includes a description of each of the plants featured in the Portfolio. These profiles outline the plants' basic preferences for environmental conditions, such as soil, moisture, and sun or shade, and provide advice about planting and ongoing care.

Working with the book's landscape designers, we selected plants carefully, following a few simple guidelines: Every plant should be a proven performer in the region; once established, it should thrive without pampering. All plants should be available from a major local nursery or garden center; if they're not in stock, they could be ordered, or you could ask the nursery staff to recommend suitable substitutes.

In the Portfolio section, you'll note that plants are referred to by their common name but are cross-referenced to the Plant Profiles section by their Latin, or scientific, name. While common names are familiar to many people, they can be confusing. Distinctly different plants can share the same common name, or one plant can have several different common names. Latin names, therefore, ensure greatest accuracy and are more appropriate for a reference section such as this. Although you can confidently purchase most of the plants in this book from local nurseries using the common name, knowing the Latin name allows you to make sure that the plant you're ordering is actually the one that is shown in our design.

Midwest Hardiness Zones

The map here, based on one developed by the U.S. Department of Agriculture, divides the region according to minimum winter temperatures and assigns "zone" numbers to those temperature bands. All but a handful of plants in this book will survive the lowest temperatures in Zones 4, 5, and 6. (Alternatives for those that don't are usually provided in the Plant Profiles.) If you live in Zone 3, however, you should ask at a local nursery for advice about suitable substitutes for those plants not reliably hardy in your zone.

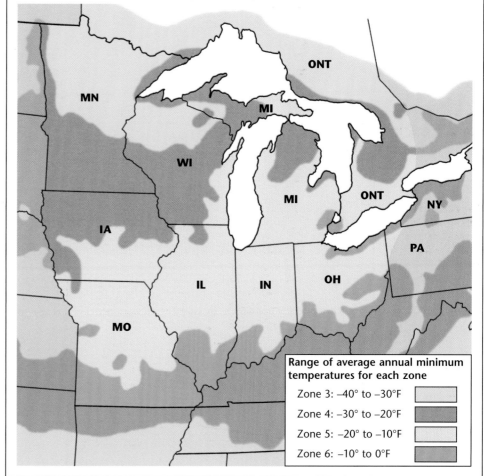

Range of average annual minimum temperatures for each zone

Zone 3: –40° to –30°F	
Zone 4: –30° to –20°F	
Zone 5: –20° to –10°F	
Zone 6: –10° to 0°F	

Seasons in Your Landscape

One of the rewards of landscaping is watching how plants change through the seasons. During the dark winter months, you look forward to the bright, fresh flowers of spring. Then the lush green foliage of summer is transformed into the blazing colors of fall. Perennials that rest underground in winter can grow head-high by midsummer, and hence a flower bed that looks flat and bare in December becomes a jungle in July.

To illustrate typical seasonal changes, we've chosen one of the designs from this book (see p. 68) and shown here how it would look in spring, summer, fall, and winter. As you can see, this planting looks quite different from one season to the next, but it always remains interesting. Try to remember this example of transformation as you look at the other designs in this book. There we show how the planting will appear in one season and call attention to any plants that will stand out at other times of the year.

The task of tending a landscape also changes with the seasons. Below we've noted the most important seasonal jobs in the annual work cycle.

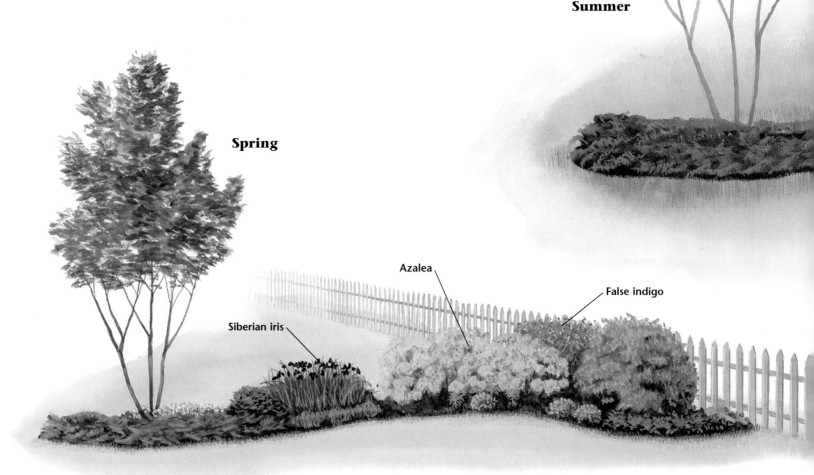

Summer

Spring

Azalea

False indigo

Siberian iris

Summer

In summer, flowering perennials such as the white and purple coneflowers, lilies, and coreopsis shown here add spots of color to the otherwise green landscape. To coax as many flowers as possible from these plants and to keep the garden tidy, cut or shear off older blossoms as they fade. Summer weather is typically hot and humid throughout this region, but droughts are not uncommon. Water new plantings at least once a week during dry spells, and water older plants, too, if the soil gets so dry that they wilt. Pull any weeds that sprout up through the mulch; this is easiest when the soil is moist from rain or watering.

White coneflower

Coreopsis

Lily

Purple coneflower

Spring

Crocuses, daffodils, and other spring bulbs start blooming in April in the Midwest region, a welcome sign of the end of a long winter. Soon it's time to start mowing the lawn, and by the end of May all the trees have fresh new leaves. Many shrubs and perennials, such as the yellow azalea, blue false indigo, and purple Siberian iris shown here, bloom in spring. Others that will bloom in summer or fall are just low mounds of foliage now.

Do a thorough garden cleanup about the time the bulbs bloom. Remove last year's perennial flower stalks and tattered foliage, cut ornamental grasses to the ground, prune shrubs and trees as needed, renew the mulch, and neaten the edges between lawn and beds.

Fall

Fall foliage season lasts for a month or so in the Midwest region, starting in mid- to late September. Trees and shrubs such as the serviceberry, burning bush, and azalea shown here paint the landscape in shades of red, orange, pink, purple, gold, and yellow. Meanwhile, fall-blooming perennials such as asters and chrysanthemums, or the Japanese anemones and October plants shown here, produce colorful flowers that stay fresh-looking for weeks in the cool, crisp autumn weather.

Sometime in October, the first hard frost will kill tender plants to the ground, signaling the time for fall cleanup. Toss frosted annuals on the compost pile. You can cut perennials and grasses down now or wait until spring. Rake fallen leaves into a pile or bin and save them to use as mulch in spring.

Fall

Serviceberry

Azalea

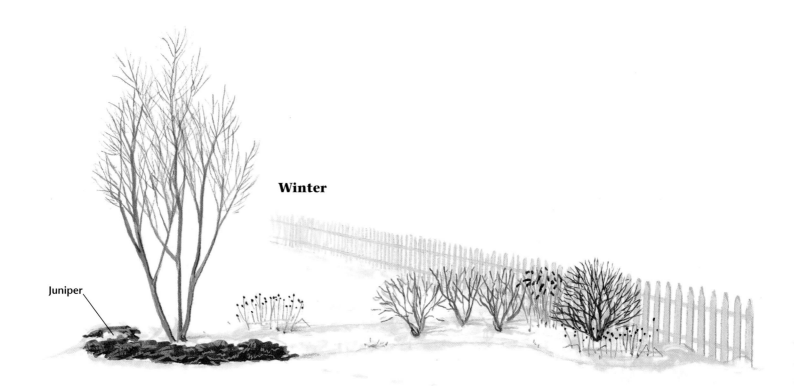

Winter

Juniper

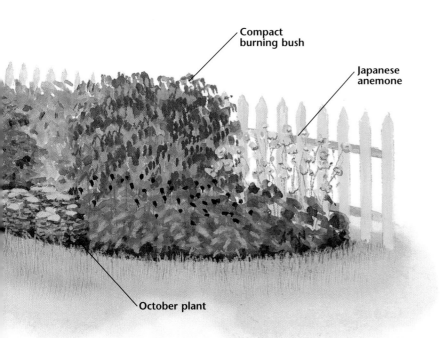

Compact burning bush

Japanese anemone

October plant

Winter

In winter, when plants are dormant and snow covers the ground, you appreciate the evergreen foliage of conifers such as the juniper shown here, and the twigs and bark of deciduous trees and shrubs. Clumps of rustling grass or shrubs and trees with bright berries are welcome in winter, too.

Spray broad-leaved evergreens with antidesiccant before the weather gets too cold, and build burlap shelters around any young or exposed evergreens that need extra protection. Once the ground freezes, spread some pine boughs or coarse mulch over newly planted perennials to keep them from frost-heaving. During the winter, if a heavy snow or an ice storm snaps or crushes some shrubs, you can trim away the broken parts as soon as convenient, but if plants get frozen during a severe cold spell, wait until spring to assess the damage before deciding how far to cut them back.

As Your Landscape Grows

Landscapes change over the years. As plants grow, the overall look evolves from sparse to lush. Trees cast cool shade where the sun used to shine. Shrubs and hedges grow tall and dense enough to provide privacy. Perennials and ground covers spread to form colorful patches of foliage and flowers. Meanwhile, paths, arbors, fences, and other structures gain the comfortable patina of age.

Constant change over the years—sometimes rapid and dramatic, sometimes slow and subtle—is one of the joys of landscaping. It is also one of the challenges. Anticipating how fast plants will grow and how big they will eventually get is difficult, even for professional designers, and was a major concern in formulating the designs for this book.

To illustrate the kinds of changes to expect in a planting, these pages show one of the designs at three different "ages." Even though a new planting may look sparse at first, it will soon fill in. And because of careful spacing, the planting will look as good in 10 to 15 years as it does after 3 to 5. It will, of course, look different, but that's part of the fun.

At Planting

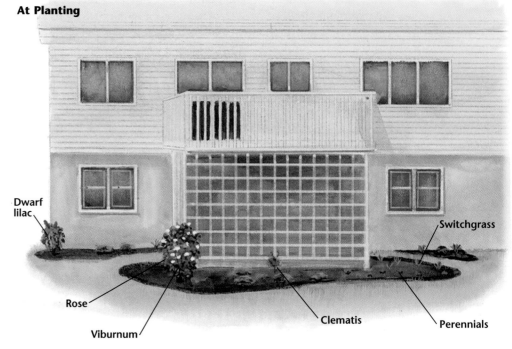

Three to Five Years

At Planting—Here's how the deck planting (pp. 92–93) might appear in late spring immediately after planting. The rose and clematis haven't begun to climb the new lattice trellis. The viburnum and lilac, usually sold in 2- to 5-gal. cans, start blooming as young plants and may have flowers when you buy them, but there will be enough space that you may want to plant some short annuals around them for the first few growing seasons. You can put short annuals between the new little junipers, too. The switchgrass and perennials, transplanted from quart- or gallon-size containers, are just low tufts of foliage now, but they grow fast enough to produce a few flowers the first summer.

Three to Five Years—As shown here in midsummer, the rose and clematis now reach most of the way up the supports. Although they aren't mature yet, the lilac, viburnum, and junipers look nice and bushy, and they're big enough that you don't need to fill around them with annuals. So far, the vines and shrubs have needed only minimal pruning. Most grasses and perennials reach full size about three to five years after planting; after that, they need to be divided and replanted in freshly amended soil to keep them healthy and vigorous.

Ten to Fifteen Years—Shown again in summer, the rose and clematis now cover their supports, and the lilac and viburnum are as tall as they'll get. To maintain all of these plants, you'll need to start pruning out some of the older stems every year in early spring. The junipers have spread sideways to form a solid mass; prune them as needed along the edge of the lawn and pathways. When the junipers crowd them out, move the daylilies to another part of your property, or move them to the front of the bed to replace the other perennials, as shown here.

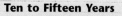

Ten to Fifteen Years

Portfolio of Designs

This section presents designs for nearly two dozen situations common in home landscapes. You'll find designs to enhance entrances, decks, and patios. There are gardens of colorful perennials and shrubs, as well as structures and plantings that create shady hideaways, dress up nondescript walls, and even make a centerpiece of a lowly mailbox. Large color illustrations show what the designs will look like, and site plans delineate the layout and planting scheme. Texts explain the designs and describe the plants and projects appearing in them. Installed as shown or adapted to meet your site and personal preferences, these designs can make your property more attractive, more useful, and—most important—more enjoyable for you, your family, and your friends.

First Impressions

Make a pleasant passage to your front door

Why wait until a visitor reaches the front door to extend a cordial greeting? Well-chosen plants and a revamped walkway not only make the short journey a pleasant one, they can also enhance your home's most public face and help settle it comfortably in its surroundings.

The curved walk in this design offers visitors a friendly welcome and a helpful "Please come this way." The first stage of the journey passes between two clipped shrub roses into a handsome garden "room" with larger shrubs near the house and smaller, colorful perennials by the walk. An opening in a hedge of long-blooming shrub roses then leads to a wider paved area that functions as an outdoor foyer. There you can greet guests or relax on the bench and enjoy the plantings that open out onto the lawn. A double course of pavers intersects the walk and an adjacent planting bed, and the circle it describes contrasts nicely with the rectilinear lines of the house and hedge.

Site: Sunny

Season: Summer

Concept: A distinctive walkway and colorful plantings make an enticing entry to your home.

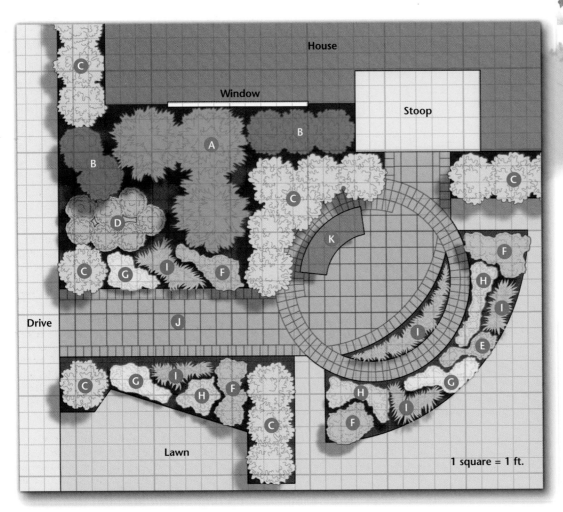

C 'Frau Dagmar Hartop' rose

J Walk

'Frau Dagmar Hartop' C rose

House

Window

Stoop

C

B

A

B

C

D

C

G

I

F

K

F

H

I

I

E

Drive

J

G

C

G

I

H

F

H

I

F

C

I

G

Lawn

1 square = 1 ft.

Plants & Projects

Mixing shrubs and perennials, this planting offers colorful flowers and attractive foliage from spring through fall. The shrubs provide structure through the winter and are handsome when covered with new snow. The perennials are dormant in winter; cut them to the ground to make room for snow shoveled off the walk. Maintenance involves pruning the shrubs and clipping spent flowers to keep everything tidy.

A **'Sea Green' juniper**
(use 3 plants)
This rugged evergreen shrub anchors a corner of the first garden "room" with arching branches that provide year-

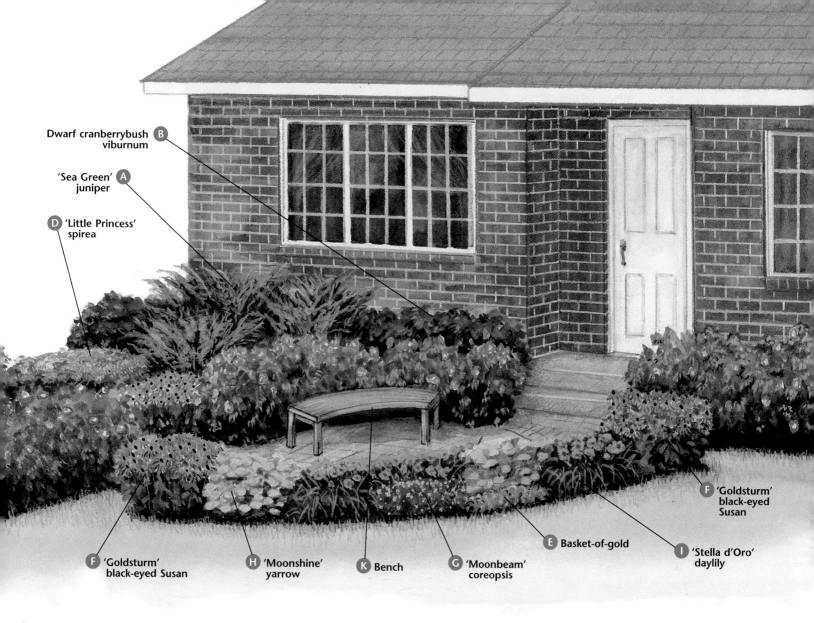

Dwarf cranberrybush viburnum **B**

'Sea Green' juniper **A**

D 'Little Princess' spirea

F 'Goldsturm' black-eyed Susan

H 'Moonshine' yarrow

K Bench

G 'Moonbeam' coreopsis

E Basket-of-gold

F 'Goldsturm' black-eyed Susan

I 'Stella d'Oro' daylily

round pale green color. See *Juniperus chinensis,* p. 186.

B Dwarf cranberrybush viburnum (use 5)
This small deciduous shrub has a dense, bushy habit and dark green, maplelike leaves that turn shades of red in fall. It won't outgrow its place beneath the windows. See *Viburnum opulus* 'Nanum', p. 195.

C 'Frau Dagmar Hartop' rose (use 18 or more)
With its crinkly bright green leaves, fragrant single pink flowers, and colorful red hips from autumn into winter, this easy-to-grow deciduous shrub puts on quite a show. Flowers all summer; forms a dense

"natural-looking" hedge. Extend the planting along the house as needed. See *Rosa,* p. 191.

D 'Little Princess' spirea (use 7)
Another compact deciduous shrub, with dainty twigs and leaves. Bears clear pink flowers in June and July. See *Spiraea japonica,* p. 193.

E Basket-of-gold (use 4)
The planting's first flowers appear on this perennial in spring. After the fragrant yellow blooms fade, the low mounds of gray leaves look good through late fall. See *Aurinia saxatilis,* p. 175.

F 'Goldsturm' black-eyed Susan (use 20)
A popular prairie perennial,

this bears large golden yellow flowers (each with a dark "eye" in the center) that are a cheerful sight in late summer. See *Rudbeckia fulgida,* p. 192.

G 'Moonbeam' coreopsis (use 22)
For months during the summer, this perennial features masses of tiny pale yellow flowers on neat mounds of lacy dark green foliage. See *Coreopsis verticillata,* p. 179.

H 'Moonshine' yarrow (use 17)
A perennial offering flat heads of sulphur yellow flowers for much of the summer. The fine gray-green leaves contrast nicely with surrounding foliage. See *Achillea,* p. 172.

I 'Stella d'Oro' daylily (use 30)
Distinctive golden yellow flowers hover over this perennial's attractive grassy foliage from mid-June until fall. See *Hemerocallis,* p. 183.

J Walk
Made of precast concrete pavers, the walk and decorative edgings require careful layout and installation. Consider renting a mason's saw to ensure accuracy when cutting pavers. See p. 118.

K Bench
A nursery or garden center can usually order a simple curved bench like the one shown here, although a straight bench will do, too.

A shady welcome

If your entry is shady, receiving less than six hours of sunlight a day, try this design. Near the drive, the walk is framed by a small tree and a selection of attractive shrubs and perennials. The wider paving here and near the door provides room to gather for hellos and good-byes.

The path to the door curves gently around a small garden featuring a selection of hostas and ferns that enliven the shady site with striking foliage. A steppingstone path through the planting invites visitors to take a closer look or, in spring, to better enjoy the fragrant flowers of the azaleas.

Plants & Projects

A Serviceberry (use 1 plant)
A multistemmed specimen of this small, deciduous tree is perfect here. It offers white flowers in early spring, berry-like fruits in summer, showy foliage in fall, and an attractive form in winter. See *Amelanchier × grandiflora*, p. 173.

B 'Annabelle' hydrangea (use 1)
Big, rounded clusters of papery flowers perch at the ends of long stems through the summer, changing from white to green to beige. This deciduous shrub's large green leaves are also attractive. See *Hydrangea arborescens*, p. 184.

C 'Golden Lights' azalea (use 6)
A hardy deciduous shrub, it brightens the entry garden with fragrant large yellow flow-

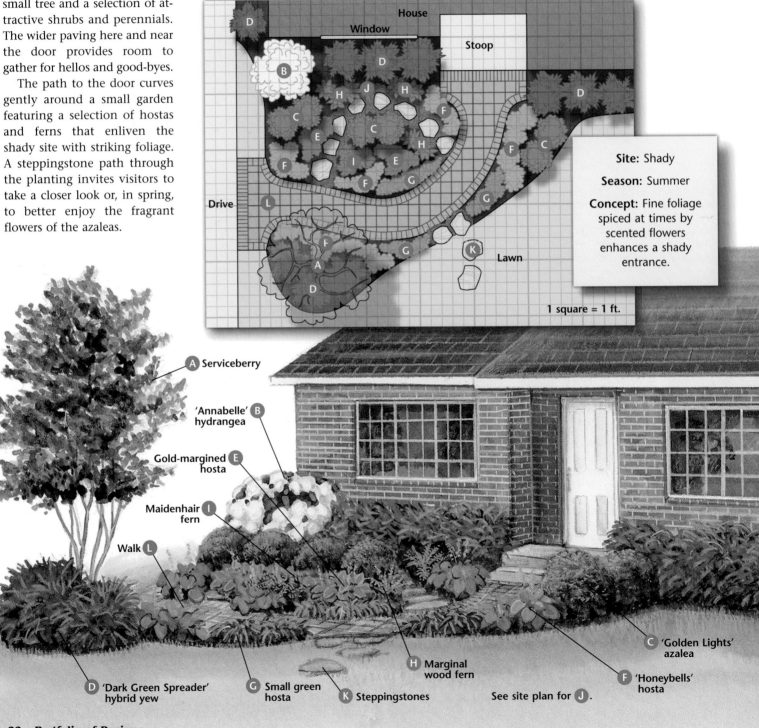

Site: Shady

Season: Summer

Concept: Fine foliage spiced at times by scented flowers enhances a shady entrance.

1 square = 1 ft.

A Serviceberry

'Annabelle' B hydrangea

Gold-margined E hosta

Maidenhair I fern

Walk L

D 'Dark Green Spreader' hybrid yew

G Small green hosta

K Steppingstones

H Marginal wood fern

See site plan for J.

C 'Golden Lights' azalea

F 'Honeybells' hosta

ers in late spring. See *Rhododendron, p. 190.*

D **'Dark Green Spreader' hybrid yew** (use 8 or more)
This spreading evergreen shrub makes a good mass of color year round next to the house and beneath the serviceberry. Extend them along the foundation of the house as needed. See *Taxus × media, p. 193.*

E **Gold-margined hosta** (use 6)
This easy-to-grow perennial's large, gold-edged green leaves draw the eye to the center of the planting from spring until frost. Stalks of lilac-colored flowers are a bonus in summer. See *Hosta fortunei* 'Aureo-marginata', p. 184.

F **'Honeybells' hosta** (use 24)
The pale green leaves of this perennial are an attractive edging along the walk. In late summer its fragrant lilac-colored flowers make a stroll to the door particularly pleasant. See *Hosta*, p. 184.

G **Small green hosta** (use 20)
The small, narrow green leaves of this perennial are a nice contrast to its large-leaved cousins nearby; its flowers are also lilac colored but are unscented. See *Hosta lancifolia*, p. 184.

H **Marginal wood fern** (use 7)
A native perennial whose lustrous, finely divided evergreen fronds add a woodland touch to the planting. See Ferns: *Dryopteris marginalis*, p. 181.

I **Maidenhair fern** (use 3)
One of the most elegant ferns, with bright green lacy fronds on shiny black stems; a lovely contrast to the hostas. Also perennial, but its foliage dies back in winter. See Ferns: *Adiantum pedatum*, p. 181.

J **Carpet bugle** (use about 30)
This perennial ground cover will quickly fill in between the steppingstones on both sides of the walk, making a green carpet studded with small bluish purple flowers in early summer. See *Ajuga reptans*, p. 172.

K **Steppingstones**
Choose flagstones in colors to complement the house and walk. See p. 123.

See p. 21 for the following:

L Walk

Plant portraits

Pretty flowers and colorful foliage brighten an entrance in sun or shade and welcome guests over a long season.

● = First design, pp. 20–21
▲ = Second design, pp. 22–23

Dwarf cranberrybush viburnum
(*Viburnum opulus* 'Nanum', p. 195) ●

Gold-margined hosta
(*Hosta fortunei* 'Aureo-marginata', p. 184) ▲

'Moonshine' yarrow
(*Achillea*, p. 172) ●

Carpet bugle
(*Ajuga reptans*, p. 172) ▲

'Annabelle' hydrangea
(*Hydrangea arborescens*, p. 184) ▲

A Step Up
Plant a foundation garden

Homes on raised foundations are seldom without foundation plantings. These simple skirtings of greenery hide unattractive concrete-block underpinnings and help overcome the impression that the house is hovering a few feet above the ground. Useful as these plantings are, they are too often just monochromatic expanses of clipped junipers, dull as dishwater. But as this design shows, a durable, low-maintenance foundation planting can be more varied, more colorful, and more fun.

This design makes a front porch an even more welcome haven on a hot summer's day. Chosen for a shady site, the plants include evergreen shrubs and perennials that combine handsome foliage and pretty flowers. Hanging planters filled with annuals extend the garden right onto the porch.

The plants are arranged to provide interest when viewed from the porch as well as from the street or entry walk. The bed sweeps out in a graceful curve to connect with the steps and entry walk, making an attractive setting for visitors.

Site: Shady

Season: Summer

Concept: A planting to be enjoyed from the street or while sitting on the cool shady porch.

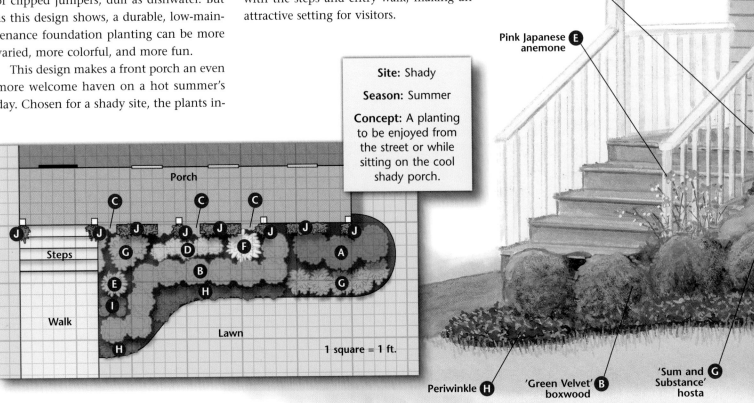

1 square = 1 ft.

Porch · Steps · Walk · Lawn

See site plan for **I**.

Hanging boxes and baskets **J**

'Emerald Gaiety' euonymus **C**

Pink Japanese anemone **E**

Periwinkle **H**

'Green Velvet' boxwood **B**

'Sum and Substance' hosta **G**

Plants & Projects

A foundation planting should look good in each season. Rhododendron blossoms in spring give way to a summer display of hosta, astilbe, and anemone flowers in shades of pink and white. Once the perennials have died back, they reveal the vining euonymus covering the base of the porch. Along with the other evergreens, it carries the planting through fall and winter. Other than tending the planters, care involves a minimum of seasonal cleanup. The shrubs' natural forms are tidy, so pruning is an infrequent chore.

A 'Olga Mezitt' rhododendron (use 3 plants)
An evergreen shrub with striking clusters of pink flowers in early spring and dark green foliage that turns maroon in winter. See *Rhododendron*, p. 191.

B 'Green Velvet' boxwood (use 10)
These tidy little evergreen shrubs will form an informal hedge (with minimal pruning) at the front of the planting. The foliage stays green through the winter. See *Buxus*, p. 176.

C 'Emerald Gaiety' euonymus (use 6)
This evergreen vine quickly covers lattice panels beneath the porch. Dark green leaves are edged with white and may turn pink in the winter. See *Euonymus fortunei*, p. 180.

D 'Ostrich Plume' astilbe (use 5)
The cascading, pink plumes of this perennial are eye-catching from the porch or the street. Shiny, dark green, divided foliage looks good long after the midsummer bloom has faded. See *Astilbe × arendsii*, p. 174.

D 'Ostrich Plume' astilbe

H Periwinkle

F 'Royal Standard' hosta

'Sum and Substance' **G** hosta

'Olga Mezitt' **A** rhododendron

E **Pink Japanese anemone**
(use 1)
Lovely mauve-pink flowers rise well above the handsome dark green lobed leaves of this perennial in late summer and fall. See *Anemone vitifolia* 'Robustissima', p. 173.

F **'Royal Standard' hosta** (use 3)
This perennial's fragrant white flowers rise above a mound of big green leaves in late summer, perfuming the porch with a sweet scent. See *Hosta*, p. 184.

G **'Sum and Substance' hosta**
(use 8)
Huge, glossy gold, textured leaves form large showy mounds at each end of the planting. Although it bears lavender flowers in late summer, some people remove them to showcase the foliage. See *Hosta*, p. 184.

H **Periwinkle** (use 18)
Dark green shiny leaves and blue spring flowers of this perennial ground cover form a clean, evergreen edge in front of the boxwoods. See *Vinca minor*, p. 197.

I **Sweet woodruff** (use 5)
Tucked between a boxwood and the anemone, this perennial ground cover is a pleasant surprise to visitors approaching the steps. Bears tiny white flowers in spring. See *Galium odoratum*, p. 181.

J **Hanging boxes and baskets**
(as desired)
Hang window boxes from the railing and baskets from the porch roof and plant them with shade-tolerant annuals, such as the trailing ivy, impatiens, begonias, coleus, and vinca vine we've shown here.

On the sunny side

If your site is sunny, try this design. (It can easily be adapted to a house with a covered porch.) The backbone of the planting is a selection of deciduous and evergreen shrubs chosen for their attractive foliage and pleasing natural forms—no fussy shearing needed here. Perennials flesh out the design, adding color and contrasting foliage textures.

Here, evergreens provide color and deciduous shrubs add structure in winter. Scented blossoms appear in spring. Accented by colorful flowers in summer, handsome foliage puts on a brilliant show in fall.

If your site allows, you can repeat or adapt elements of the design to extend the planting to the other side of the stoop.

The shrubs need little pruning to look their best. Just remove dead or diseased wood and clip a branch or two as needed to enhance the plants' natural form.

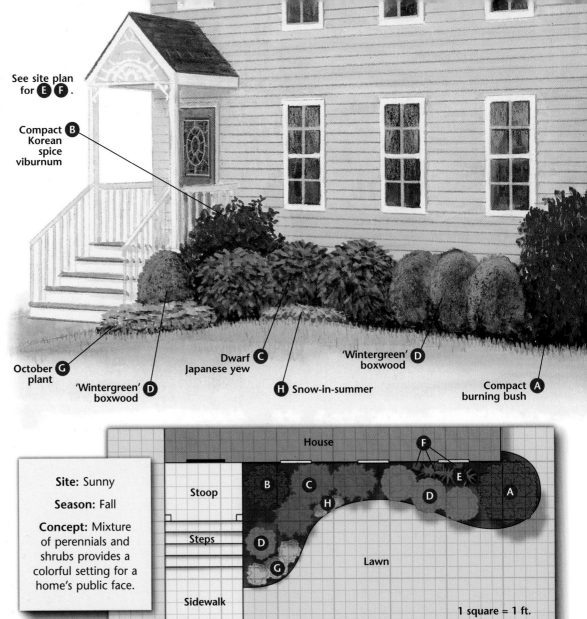

See site plan for **E** **F** .

Compact **B** Korean spice viburnum

October **G** plant

'Wintergreen' **D** boxwood

Dwarf **C** Japanese yew

'Wintergreen' **D** boxwood

Snow-in-summer **H**

Compact **A** burning bush

Site: Sunny

Season: Fall

Concept: Mixture of perennials and shrubs provides a colorful setting for a home's public face.

House

Stoop

Steps

Sidewalk

Lawn

1 square = 1 ft.

Plants & Projects

A Compact burning bush
(use 1 plant)
Dark green leaves and orderly layered branches make this deciduous shrub a handsome presence at the corner of the house in summer and winter. In fall, its fiery mass of brilliant crimson foliage makes it a showstopper. See *Euonymus alatus* 'Compactus', p. 180.

B Compact Korean spice viburnum (use 1)
The delicious spicy scent of this deciduous shrub's white flowers greets visitors at the door in May. Foliage is attractive through summer and fall; pretty pink flower buds emerge in early spring. See *Viburnum carlesii* 'Compactum', p. 195.

C Dwarf Japanese yew (use 3)
With spreading dark green branches, this tough, slow-growing evergreen shrub is appealing in all four seasons. See *Taxus cuspidata* 'Nana', p. 193.

D 'Wintergreen' boxwood (use 4)
The small evergreen leaves of this compact shrub hold their bright green color through the winter. Little pruning required to maintain the soft, mounded form. See *Buxus*, p. 176.

E Siberian iris (use 3)
Enjoy this perennial's elegant flowers in early summer and its graceful clumps of slender arching foliage for the rest of the season. Flowers come in shades of blue, yellow, or white. See *Iris sibirica*, p. 186.

F 'Stargazer' lily (use 3)
Planted among the irises, these regal perennials will scent the entire planting in late summer with the rich perfume of their white-edged crimson flowers. See *Lilium*, p. 187.

G October plant (use 3)
This perennial's fleshy blue-gray foliage contrasts with the nearby evergreens, and its rosy pink flowers add color in fall. See *Sedum sieboldii*, p. 193.

H Snow-in-summer (use 3)
Star-shaped white flowers blanket this perennial in early spring. After flowering, its spreading mat of silvery gray evergreen leaves shines at the foot of the yews. See *Cerastium tomentosum*, p. 177.

Plant portraits

These shrubs and perennials will dress up even the most nondescript foundation, while requiring just the minimum of care.

● = First design, pp. 24–25
▲ = Second design, p. 26

October plant
(*Sedum sieboldii*, p. 193) ▲

Sweet woodruff
(*Galium odoratum*, p. 181) ●

'Emerald Gaiety' euonymus
(*Euonymus fortunei*, p. 180) ●

Snow-in-summer
(*Cerastium tomentosum*, p. 177) ▲

'Stargazer' lily
(*Lilium*, p. 187) ▲

Up Front and Formal
Garden geometry transforms a small front yard

Formal gardens have a special appeal. Their simple geometry is soothing in a hectic world, and their look is timeless, never going out of style. Traditional two-story homes with symmetrical facades are especially suited to the clean lines and balanced features shown here.

The design creates a small courtyard at the center of four rectangular beds defined by evergreen hedges and flagstone walkways. Inside the hedges, carefree perennial catmint makes a colorful floral carpet during the summer. The flagstone paving reinforces the design's geometry, while providing access to the front door from the sidewalk. (If a driveway runs along one side of the property, the crosswalk could extend to it through an opening in the hedge.) At the center of the compositon, the paving widens to accommodate a planter filled with annuals, a pleasant setting for greetings or good-byes. A bench at one end of the crosswalk provides a spot for longer chats or restful moments enjoying the plantings or, perhaps, contemplating a garden ornament at the other end.

Loose, informal hedges soften the rigid geometry. Deciduous shrubs change with the seasons, offering flowers in the spring and brilliant fall foliage, while the evergreens are a dependably colorful presence year round.

'Nigra' arborvitae Ⓐ

'Techny' Ⓑ
arborvitae

Garden Ⓘ
ornament

'Blue Wonder' Ⓕ
catmint

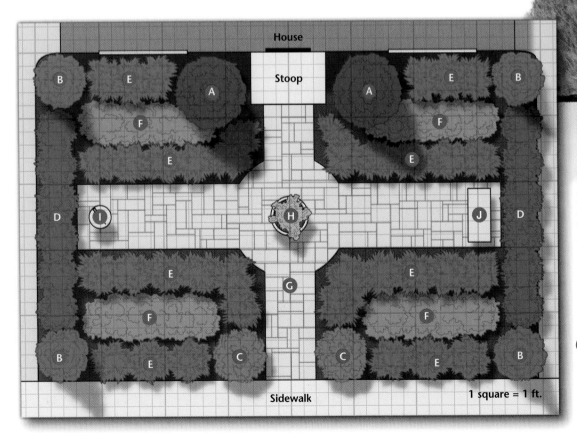

Plants & Projects

Precise layout is important in a simple design such as this. Start with the flagstone walks; they aren't difficult to build but require some time and muscle. The hedge shrubs are chosen for their compact forms. You'll need to clip the lilacs annually to maintain their shape, but the junipers will require little pruning over the years.

Ⓐ **'Nigra' arborvitae**
(use 2 plants)
These upright, pyramidal evergreen trees stand like sentinels at the front door, where their scented foliage greets visitors.

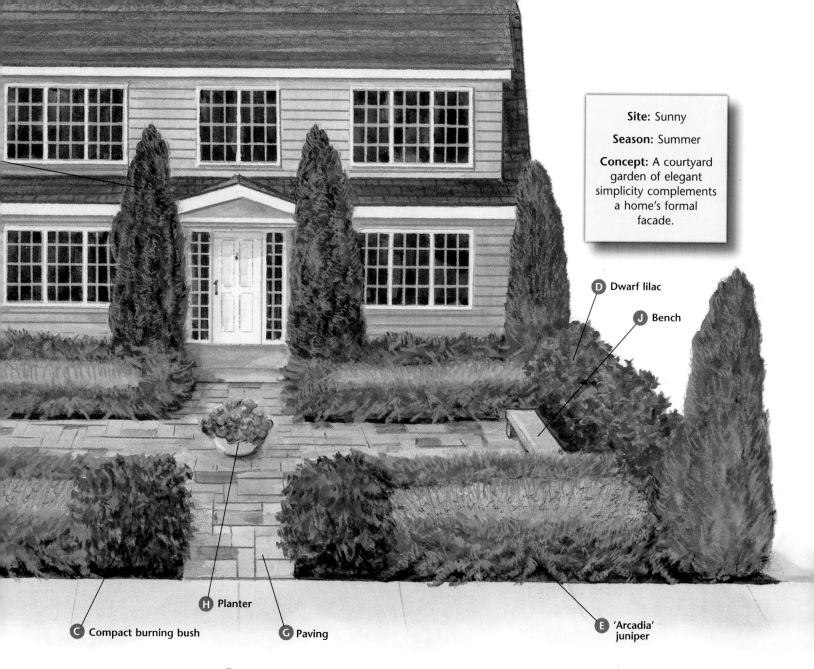

Site: Sunny

Season: Summer

Concept: A courtyard garden of elegant simplicity complements a home's formal facade.

D Dwarf lilac

J Bench

H Planter

C Compact burning bush

G Paving

E 'Arcadia' juniper

Prune to keep their height in scale with the house. See *Thuja occidentalis*, p. 194.

B **'Techny' arborvitae** (use 4)
Marking the corners of the design, this evergreen tree forms a shorter, broader cone than its cousin by the door. See *Thuja occidentalis*, p. 194.

C **Compact burning bush** (use 2)
A deciduous shrub forming a neat globe of green foliage, it turns an attention-grabbing crimson in fall. An excellent choice to mark the property's entrance. See *Euonymus alatus* 'Compactus', p. 180.

D **Dwarf lilac** (use 12)
This compact deciduous shrub makes an attractive loose hedge offering fragrant spring-time flowers and glossy green foliage that has a purplish cast in fall. See *Syringa meyeri* 'Palibin', p. 193.

E **'Arcadia' juniper** (use 36)
The arching branches of this spreading evergreen shrub line the walks with bright green color through four seasons. See *Juniperus sabina*, p. 186.

F **'Blue Wonder' catmint** (use 40)
Loose spikes of misty blue flowers rise above the silvery, aromatic foliage of this perennial in June, filling the beds with color. Blooms continue or repeat through the summer. See *Nepeta × faassenii*, p. 189.

G **Paving**
Rectangular flagstones in random sizes suit the style of this house; brick or precast pavers work with other house styles. See p. 118.

H **Planter**
Nurseries and garden centers offer a range of planters that are suitable for formal settings. Choose one that complements

the style of your house and fill it with colorful annuals such as the geraniums in the round stone planter shown here. If you're ambitious, change the plantings with the seasons.

I **Garden ornament**
Place a sundial (shown here), reflecting ball, statue, or other ornament as a focal point at the end of the crosswalk.

J **Bench**
A stone bench is a nice companion for the planter and sundial here, but wood or metal benches can also work well in formal settings.

Formal and fresh

This design gives a formal feel to a front yard without requiring a complete makeover. Two neat rectangular lawns flank a central "courtyard" and its large planter full of colorful annuals. Borders are once again formed by lilac and juniper hedges, which provide the same varied seasonal interest as in the previous design. But here the enclosure is completed by a striking edging of sumac and ornamental grass along the walk.

The planting offers flowers in spring and lots of healthy foliage in summer. But it comes into its own in fall, the season shown here. Deciduous trees and shrubs provide colorful accents. The 7-ft.-tall seed heads of the moor grass can make an airy corridor of the walk. Or you can trim off the stalks, as shown here, and enjoy a lower edging of golden yellow foliage.

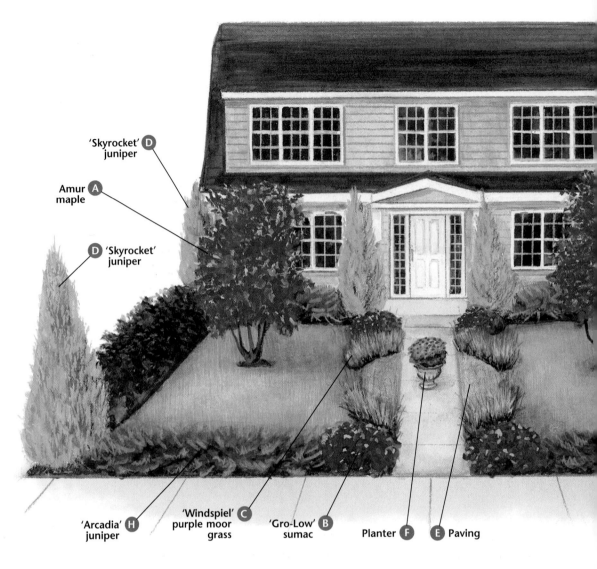

'Skyrocket' juniper **D**

Amur **A** maple

'Skyrocket' **D** juniper

'Arcadia' **H** juniper

'Windspiel' **C** purple moor grass

'Gro-Low' **B** sumac

Planter **F**

E Paving

Plants & Projects

A **Amur maple** (use 2 plants)
This small, deciduous, often multitrunked tree produces attractive flowers in spring, red fruits in summer, and blazing clear red foliage in fall. See *Acer ginnala*, p. 172.

B **'Gro-Low' sumac** (use 4)
A deciduous shrub that spreads to form a low mound of glossy dark green foliage that turns scarlet in fall. The bare stems are interesting in winter, too. See *Rhus aromatica*, p. 191.

C **'Windspiel' purple moor grass** (use 16)
The dark green tufts of this perennial grass turn golden yellow in fall, when they are topped with stalks up to 7 ft. tall bearing yellow seed heads.

Site: Sunny

Season: Fall

Concept:
Unexpected plants add zip to a design of low-key formality.

Foliage and stalks break off at ground level in late fall, making room for you to pile snow shoveled off the walk. See *Molinia arundinacea*, p. 189.

D **'Skyrocket' juniper** (use 6)
These tall, narrow evergreen shrubs frame the door like two

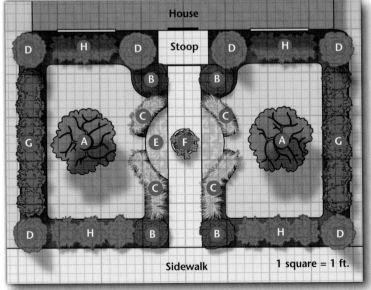

House

Stoop

Sidewalk

1 square = 1 ft.

D 'Skyrocket' juniper

G Dwarf lilac

H 'Arcadia' juniper

blue-green columns. Use 'Pathfinder' if you want a wider, pyramidal shrub. See *Juniperus scopulorum,* p. 186.

E Paving
To create the central "courtyard" using an existing cement sidewalk, you can add arcs of well-tamped crushed rock (as shown here; see p. 118) or pour cement pads.

F Planter
Choose an urn to match the house and fill it with annuals. A seasonal planting of chrysanthemums is shown here.

See p. 29 for the following:

G Dwarf lilac (use 12)

H 'Arcadia' juniper (use 12)

Plant portraits

These plants add character to the simple lines and geometric shapes of a formal front yard.

● = First design, pp. 28–29
▲ = Second design, pp. 30–31

Compact burning bush
(*Euonymus alatus* 'Compactus', p. 180) ●

'Techny' arborvitae
(*Thuja occidentalis,* p. 194) ●

Dwarf lilac
(*Syringa meyeri* 'Palibin', p. 193) ● ▲

'Blue Wonder' catmint
(*Nepeta* × *faassenii,* p. 189) ●

Amur maple
(*Acer ginnala,* p. 172) ▲

'Skyrocket' juniper
(*Juniperus scopulorum,* p. 186) ▲

Angle of Repose
Make a back-door garden in a sheltered niche

Many homes offer the opportunity to tuck a garden into a protected corner. In the front yard, such spots are ideal for an entry garden or a landscaping display that enhances the view of your house from the sidewalk or the street. If the niche is in the backyard, like the site shown here, the planting can be more intimate, part of a comfortable outdoor room you can stroll through at leisure or enjoy from a nearby terrace or window.

This planting has been specially designed with spring in mind, so we're showing that season here. (For a look at the planting later on, when perennials and shrubs take over the show, see p. 34.) Dozens of spring bulbs light up the corner from February through May, assisted by the spring blossoms on the rhododendrons and Korean spice viburnum.

Early flowers aren't the only pleasures of spring, though. Step along the path to appreciate the magic of spring at closer range. Watch buds burst into leaf on the burning bush and cotoneaster, and mark the progress of the season as new, succulent shoots of summer perennials emerge.

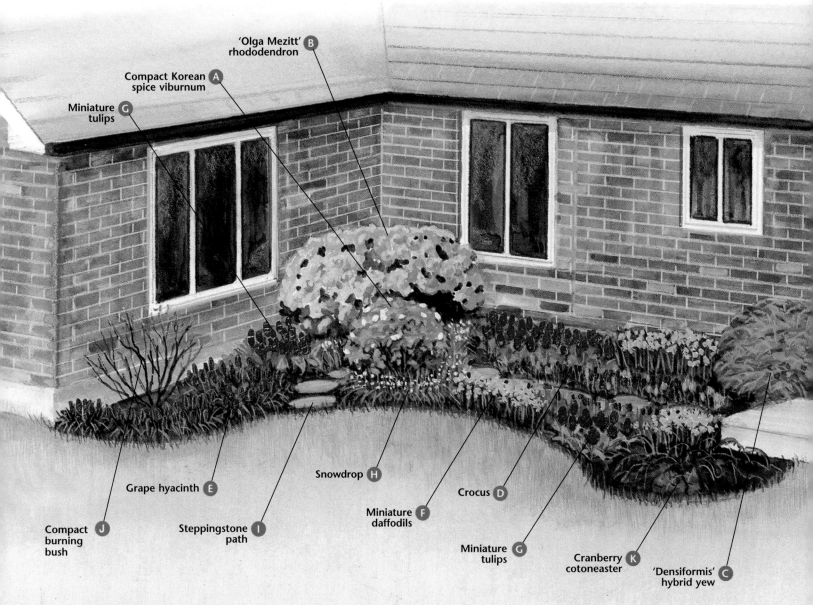

'Olga Mezitt' rhododendron **B**

Compact Korean spice viburnum **A**

Miniature tulips **G**

Grape hyacinth **E**

Compact burning bush **J**

Steppingstone path **I**

Snowdrop **H**

Miniature daffodils **F**

Crocus **D**

Miniature tulips **G**

Cranberry cotoneaster **K**

'Densiformis' hybrid yew **C**

Plants & Projects

Interplant generous drifts and clumps of bulbs among the perennials. Once planted, bulbs require little care beyond clipping off spent flowers. After they bloom, their foliage is hidden by the emerging perennials. Divide the bulbs every few years if the patches become crowded or if you want to plant some elsewhere.

A **Compact Korean spice viburnum** (use 1 plant)
The fragrant white flower clusters of this spring-blooming deciduous shrub invite you down the path. Foliage is attractive summer and fall. See *Viburnum carlesii* 'Compactum', p. 195.

B **'Olga Mezitt' rhododendron** (use 3)
This evergreen shrub is covered with clear pink flowers for weeks from early spring. The small dark green leaves (which turn maroon in fall) make a fine backdrop for the perennials. See *Rhododendron*, p. 191.

C **'Densiformis' hybrid yew** (use 1)
An evergreen shrub, it makes a low, spreading mound of fine-textured dark green foliage. See *Taxus × media*, p. 193.

D **Crocus** (use 50)
Cup-shaped flowers on short stalks in early spring. Plant 6 or 8 per square foot along the path. A mix of purple- and gold-flowered types will go well with the other bulbs. See Bulbs: *Crocus*, p. 176.

E **Grape hyacinth** (use 25)
Grassy foliage and fragrant purple flowers resembling grape clusters make a pretty spring carpet beneath the burning bush. See Bulbs: *Muscari armeniacum*, p. 176.

F **Miniature daffodils** (use 25)
A spring planting isn't complete without these cheerful favorites. 'February Gold', 'Baby Moon', and 'Tête-à-Tête' offer small, early yellow flowers and low foliage that is easily covered by the perennials. See Bulbs: *Narcissus*, p. 176.

G **Miniature tulips** (use 20)
Shorter than "ordinary" tulips, but just as colorful, 'Red Riding Hood' and 'Lilac Wonder' are good choices here. See Bulbs: *Tulipa*, p. 176.

H **Snowdrop** (use 25)
One of the first flowers of spring, the nodding, snowy white blooms beckon above slender, grassy foliage at the bend in the path. See Bulbs: *Galanthus nivalis*, p. 176.

I **Steppingstone path**
Precast pavers, 2 ft. in diameter, can be installed after you've prepared the planting bed. Tamp down the soil along the path, set the pavers in place, and spread mulch between them. See p. 118.

See p. 34 for the following:

J **Compact burning bush** (use 1)

K **Cranberry cotoneaster** (use 1)

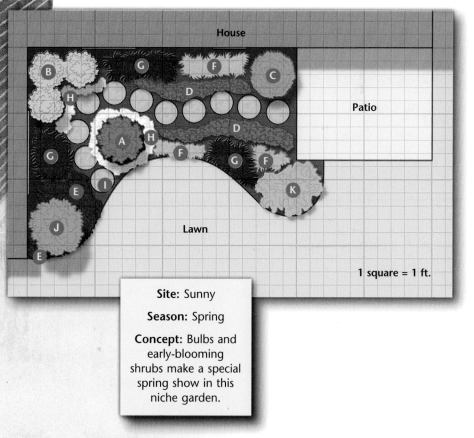

House

Patio

Lawn

1 square = 1 ft.

Site: Sunny

Season: Spring

Concept: Bulbs and early-blooming shrubs make a special spring show in this niche garden.

The scene in summer

There's no drop-off in interest or enjoyment as this planting moves from spring (shown on the previous pages) to summer and fall. Now perennials join shrubs in a tapestry of colorful foliage and flowers.

Summer flowers come in shades of red, pink, and blue, with mounds of yellow coreopsis as accents. The foliage is equally attractive. Defining the back corners are contrasting evergreens, one broad-leaved, one coniferous. At the front corners, two deciduous shrubs provide a fiery fall display. Tall arching grasses add height; in fall and winter, their dry leaves and seed heads rustle and sway in the breeze.

Plants & Projects

A Compact burning bush (use 1 plant)
Green in summer, this deciduous shrub turns first copper and then an eye-popping crimson in fall. See *Euonymus alatus* 'Compactus', p. 180.

B Cranberry cotoneaster (use 1)
A deciduous shrub whose glossy green leaves turn bright red in fall. Bears small pink flowers in spring and cranberry red fruits in fall. See *Cotoneaster apiculatus*, p. 179.

C Maiden grass (use 2)
Arching clumps of this perennial's silvery green leaves are topped in fall by fluffy seed heads, which are attractive in winter. See *Miscanthus sinensis* 'Gracillimus', p. 189.

D 'Stargazer' lily (use 3)
The fragrance of this perennial's lovely pink flowers will entice you down the path in August. See *Lilium*, p. 187.

E Purple coneflower (use 5)
In July and August, this perennial bears large daisylike flowers on stiff stalks above coarse green leaves. Mix pink- and white-flowered cultivars here. See *Echinacea purpurea*, p. 180.

F 'Kobold' blazing star (use 3)
This perennial produces spikes of magenta flowers on leafy stalks in July and August. See *Liatris spicata*, p. 187.

G 'Sunny Border Blue' veronica (use 3)
Spikes of bright blue flowers top mats of lustrous green leaves. This perennial blooms all summer if you keep clipping off spent flower spikes. See *Veronica*, p. 195.

H 'Blue Clips' Carpathian bellflower (use 6)
This perennial also blooms most of the summer, displaying cuplike blue flowers above clumps of delicate leaves. See *Campanula carpatica*, p. 177.

I 'Moonbeam' coreopsis (use 3)
Masses of small yellow flowers cover this perennial's mounds of lacy green foliage from midsummer into fall. See *Coreopsis verticillata*, p. 179.

See p. 33 for the following:

J Compact Korean spice viburnum

K 'Olga Mezitt' rhododendron

L 'Densiformis' hybrid yew

M Steppingstone path

Site: Sunny

Season: Summer

Concept: Colorful perennials and shrubs pick up where spring bulbs leave off.

1 square = 1 ft.

Plant portraits

Distinctive shrubs combine with spring-flowering bulbs and summer-flowering perennials to provide months of enjoyment.

● = Spring, pp. 32–33
▲ = Summer, p. 34

'Densiformis' hybrid yew
(*Taxus × media*, p. 193) ● ▲

Purple coneflower
(*Echinacea purpurea*, p. 180) ▲

'Kobold' blazing star
(*Liatris spicata*, p. 187) ▲

'Olga Mezitt' rhododendron
(*Rhododendron*, p. 191) ● ▲

Cranberry cotoneaster
(*Cotoneaster apiculatus*, p. 179) ● ▲

A Neighborly Corner

Beautify a boundary with easy-care plants

The corner where your property meets your neighbor's and the sidewalk can be a kind of grassy no-man's-land. This design defines the boundary with a planting that can be enjoyed by both property owners. Good gardens make good neighbors, so we've used well-behaved low-maintenance plants that won't make extra work for the person next door—or for you.

Because of its exposed location, remote from the house and close to the street, this is a less personal planting than those in other more private and frequently used parts of your property. This design is meant, therefore, to be appreciated from a distance. It showcases five handsome shrubs, arranged in blocks, rather like a patchwork quilt, beneath a fine multitrunked tree.

(An existing fence on the property line, like the one shown here, can help frame the composition.)

Although several of these plants offer attractive flowers, it is their foliage that makes this planting special. As the seasons progress you'll see blues, greens, reds, and yellows, culminating in an eye-popping display of fiery autumn leaves.

Plants & Projects

For the first few years, mulch the planting well to retain moisture and to keep down weeds until the shrubs fill in. This is a very easy planting to maintain if you choose to prune only to maintain the natural shapes of the shrubs, which soften the geometry imposed by the planting plan.

A **Amur maple** (use 1 plant)
A small but fast-growing deciduous tree; pick one that has multiple trunks. Bears pale flowers in spring, green leaves and red fruits in summer, and crimson foliage in autumn. See *Acer ginnala*, p. 172.

B **'Gro-Low' sumac** (use 4)
These tough deciduous shrubs spread to form low mounds beneath the maple. Shiny green leaves turn scarlet in fall. See *Rhus aromatica*, p. 191.

C **'Anthony Waterer' spirea** (use 3)
Small, fine blue-green leaves set off the rosy pink flowers of this compact deciduous shrub. Blooms in summer. See *Spiraea × bumalda*, p. 193.

D **'Blue Star' juniper** (use 7)
The prickly, rich blue foliage of this low evergreen shrub makes a striking contrast with its neighbors. See *Juniperus squamata*, p. 186.

E **'Crimson Pygmy' Japanese barberry** (use 3)
The small, deep purple leaves of this deciduous shrub are as eye-catching in summer as in fall, when they turn a rich crimson. The low, rounded mounds are set off by the colors of the nearby juniper and sumac. See *Berberis thunbergii*, p. 175.

F **'Goldflame' spirea** (use 4)
The leaves of this small deciduous shrub have a different look in each season: gold in spring, chartreuse in summer, and orange-red in fall. Bears pale pink flowers in summer. See *Spiraea × bumalda*, p. 193.

C 'Anthony Waterer' spirea

D 'Blue Star' juniper

Fence

C

A

D

E

B   Sidewalk

F

Lawn

1 square = 1 ft.

Site: Sunny

Season: Summer

Concept: Enhance the property line with a low-care, neighbor-friendly planting of trees and shrubs.

A Amur maple

B 'Gro-Low' sumac

F 'Goldflame' spirea

E 'Crimson Pygmy' Japanese barberry

Plant portraits

Whether it's with flowers or foliage, these durable shrubs and perennials will add months of eye-catching color to your corner.

● = First design, pp. 36–37
▲ = Second design, p. 39

'Dr. Merrill' magnolia
(*Magnolia × loebneri*, p. 188) ▲

'Crimson Pygmy' Japanese barberry
(*Berberis thunbergii*, p. 175) ●

Blue oat grass
(*Helictotrichon sempervirens*, p. 182) ▲

'Zagreb' coreopsis
(*Coreopsis verticillata*, p. 179) ▲

'Gro-Low' sumac
(*Rhus aromatica*, p. 191) ●

'Palace Purple' heuchera
(*Heuchera micrantha*, p. 183) ▲

A patchwork of perennials

This design places colorful, easy-care perennials in a block pattern similar to that in the first design. The result is an equally striking quilt of herbaceous plants. The peak season here is summer, when patches of flowers and foliage in yellows, blues, and purple play off one another. The foliage of the flowering plants is also attractive when these perennials are not in bloom.

If a mix of perennials and shrubs appeals to you, consider combining favorite plants from each design. This is easy to do and still maintain the color scheme. For example, you could substitute the Japanese barberry in the first design for the heuchera here. Or use the 'Blue Star' juniper instead of the blue oat grass. Shrubs give the planting a presence in winter, when the perennials are dormant.

A 'Dr. Merrill' magnolia

B 'Mary Todd' daylily

F 'Palace Purple' heuchera

G 'Blue Wonder' catmint

Blue oat grass **C**

'Zagreb' coreopsis **D**

Rue **E**

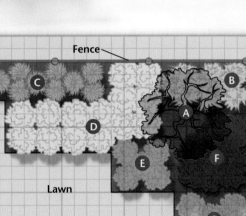

Fence

C

D

A

B

E

F

G

Lawn

Sidewalk

1 square = 1 ft.

Site: Sunny

Season: Summer

Concept: Replacing shrubs with perennials creates a colorful summertime display of flowers and foliage.

Plants & Projects

A **'Dr. Merrill' magnolia** (use 1 plant)
This small deciduous tree is enveloped in a fragrant cloud of white flowers in spring. Smooth bark and large fuzzy buds look good in winter. Prune off lower limbs to get a better view of the daylilies. See *Magnolia × loebneri*, p. 188.

B **'Mary Todd' daylily** (use 9)
The yellow flowers of this perennial brighten the corner in July, and the grassy leaves are attractive for months. 'Hyperion' is a good substitute. See *Hemerocallis*, p. 183.

C **Blue oat grass** (use 11)
This perennial's bristly mound of narrow blue leaves looks good year round. See *Helictotrichon sempervirens*, p. 182.

D **'Zagreb' coreopsis** (use 14)
Cheerful golden yellow flowers cover this perennial's mound of lacy foliage from July through September. See *Coreopsis verticillata*, p. 179.

E **Rue** (use 5)
This perennial bears small yellow flowers for two to three weeks in midsummer, and its fine-textured blue-gray foliage is handsome from spring to fall. See *Ruta graveolens*, p. 192.

F **'Palace Purple' heuchera** (use 22)
Another perennial grown primarily for its foliage. Its low, tidy mounds of deep purple leaves add season-long color next to the sidewalk. See *Heuchera micrantha*, p. 183.

G **'Blue Wonder' catmint** (use 5)
The silvery, aromatic foliage of this perennial is topped with misty blue flower spikes from early summer to fall if you keep removing spent blossoms. See *Nepeta × faassenii*, p. 189.

Streetwise and Stylish

Give your curbside strip a new look

Homeowners seldom think much about the strip that runs between the sidewalk and street. At best it is a tidy patch of lawn; at worst, a weed-choked eyesore. Yet this is one of the most public parts of your property. Planting this strip attractively can give pleasure to passersby and to visitors who park next to the curb, as well as enhancing the streetscape you view from the house. (This property is usually city-owned, so check local ordinances for restrictions before you start a remake.)

In older neighborhoods, mature trees lining the street create more shade than most grass can tolerate. The design shown here replaces thinning turf in a shady site with a lush planting of hostas, ferns, and ground covers. Leaves in a pleasing variety of sizes, shapes, and colors make an inviting display from spring through fall.

It might help to think of this curbside strip as an island bed between two defined boundaries: the street and the sidewalk. The beds are divided by a pedestrian walkway, providing room for visitors to get in and out of their cars. You can expand the beds to fill a longer strip, or plant lawn next to them. This design, or a variation, would also work nicely in a shady location along a patio, property line, or foundation.

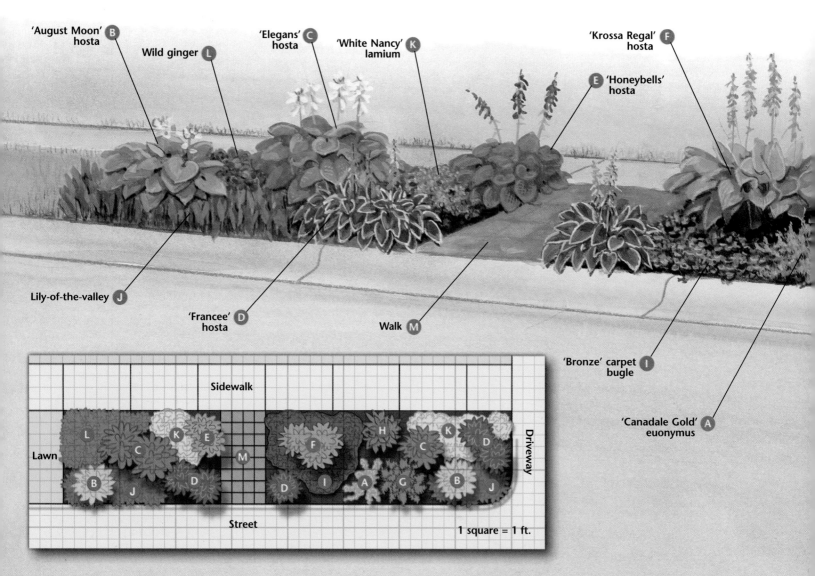

Plants & Projects

This can be a difficult site. Summer drought and shade, winter road salt, pedestrian and car traffic, and errant dogs are usual conditions along the street. Plants have to be tough to perform well here, but they need not look tough. The ones used here make a dramatic impact during the growing season. Then all but the sturdy low-growing euonymus die back in winter, so piles of snow won't hurt them. To help provide adequate moisture, add plenty of organic matter to the soil when you prepare the beds.

Site: Shady

Season: Summer

Concept: Striking foliage gives a lush look to a shady curbside planting.

A **'Canadale Gold' euonymus** (use 1 plant)
A broad-leaved evergreen, this shrub forms a low, spreading mound. The small rounded leaves have yellow margins and contrast attractively with the large-leaved hostas. See *Euonymus fortunei*, p. 180.

B **'August Moon' hosta** (use 2)
A perennial (like all hostas), this cultivar forms a broad clump of textured golden yellow leaves. Thin stalks bear white flowers in mid- to late summer. See *Hosta*, p. 184.

C **'Elegans' hosta** (use 3)
This hosta's huge blue, textured leaves form imposing mounds at the center of each bed. White flowers in summer. See *Hosta sieboldiana*, p. 184.

D **'Francee' hosta** (use 5)
This hosta's dark green heart-shaped leaves are edged with white, and its flowers are lavender. See *Hosta*, p. 184.

E **'Honeybells' hosta** (use 2)
Forms a large, broad clump of pale green oblong leaves. The lilac flowers are scented. See *Hosta*, p. 184.

F **'Krossa Regal' hosta** (use 3)
Long, powder blue leaves form a large mound, more erect than the other hostas in the planting. Lilac flowers dangle well above the foliage on tall, thin stalks. See *Hosta*, p. 184.

G **Japanese painted fern** (use 6)
This elegant perennial is a subtle accent for the planting, with its fronds delicately painted in glowing tones of green, silver, and maroon. See Ferns: *Athyrium goeringianum* 'Pictum', p. 181.

H **Maidenhair fern** (use 5)
This perennial forms a dainty mass of lacy green fronds on wiry black stems; looks great with the blue hostas. See Ferns: *Adiantum pedatum*, p. 181.

I **'Bronze' carpet bugle** (use 22)
The dark bronze-green leaves of this fast-spreading perennial ground cover set off the hostas and ferns handsomely. Small bluish purple flowers add color in late spring and early summer. See *Ajuga reptans*, p. 172.

J **Lily-of-the-valley** (use 32)
A perennial ground cover, it quickly forms a patch of large erect leaves. In spring, tiny white bell-shaped flowers dangle from slender stalks and produce a wonderful sweet scent. See *Convallaria majalis*, p. 179.

K **'White Nancy' lamium** (use 26)
This perennial ground cover's small silvery leaves edged with green practically shine in the shade. Bears white flowers in early summer. See *Lamium maculatum*, p. 187.

L **Wild ginger** (use 12)
Another perennial ground cover, this produces fuzzy heart-shaped leaves that create a beautiful dull green carpet beneath the blue hosta leaves. See *Asarum canadense*, p. 174.

M **Walk**
Use brick, flagstone, or the simple cement pavers shown here. Choose a color to match your house. See p. 118.

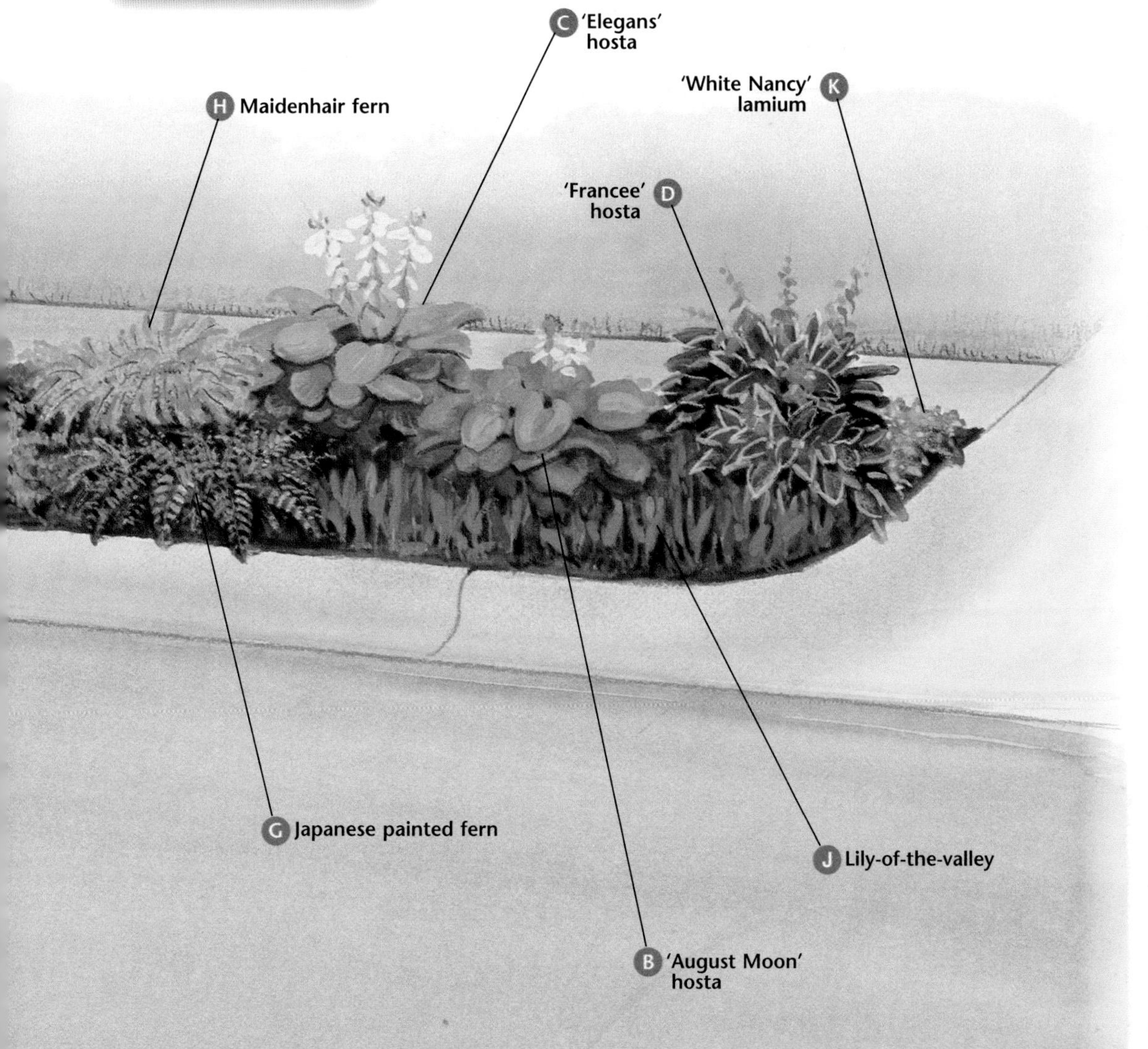

C 'Elegans' hosta

H Maidenhair fern

'White Nancy' lamium K

'Francee' hosta D

G Japanese painted fern

J Lily-of-the-valley

B 'August Moon' hosta

On the sunny side

If your streetside property is in full sun, try this durable mixture of grasses and perennials. Planted in masses on both sides of a walkway, they make a striking sight for many months every year.

The spring and early-summer display offers contrasting foliage textures in a palette of greens. From midsummer to frost, flowers and leaves create a patchwork of rusty red, purple, tan, yellows, and golds. The seed heads and dry foliage of the grasses and sedums are eye-catching through the winter, even when half buried in snow.

Planting in "blocks" gives the design an interesting geometry, softened at the edges as the plants reach full height each year. Spacing plants tightly in a mass also reduces the need for weeding. The only maintenance required is cutting all the plants nearly to the ground in late winter or early spring.

Plants & Projects

A **'Karl Foerster' feather reed grass** (use 18 plants)
Tall, slim flower spikes appear above the slender green leaves of this perennial grass in mid-summer, rising 5 ft. tall and changing from gold to silver as they mature. The foliage and seed heads look good through the winter. See *Calamagrostis × acutiflora*, p. 176.

B **Little bluestem grass** (use 60)
The fine dark blue-green leaves of this perennial grass grow in dense clumps. In the fall, the foliage turns a beautiful muted reddish purple, topped with dancing seed heads that look good through the winter. See *Schizachyrium scoparius*, p. 192.

C **'Autumn Joy' sedum** (use 16)
This perennial's neat mound of fleshy gray-green foliage provides a pleasing contrast to the slender grasses. Flat clusters of tiny flowers are pale in late summer, turning pink and then rust-colored by fall. See *Sedum*, p. 193.

D **'Goldsturm' black-eyed Susan** (use 25)
An improved version of a familiar perennial. In summer it bears golden yellow daisylike flowers with dark central "eyes" that persist (as shown here) after the petals have dropped. See *Rudbeckia fulgida*, p. 192.

E **'Purple Dome' New England aster** (use 12)
A compact perennial whose tidy mounds of dark foliage are blanketed by deep purple flowers in early fall. See *Aster novae-angliae*, p. 174.

See p. 41 for the following:

F **Walk**

Site: Sunny

Season: Early fall

Concept: Attractive massed planting adapted to extreme streetside conditions.

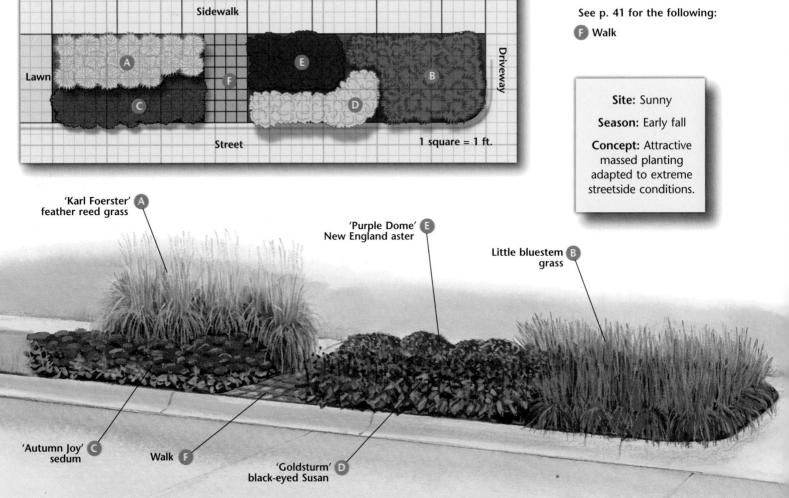

'Karl Foerster' **A** feather reed grass

'Purple Dome' **E** New England aster

Little bluestem **B** grass

'Autumn Joy' **C** sedum

Walk **F**

'Goldsturm' **D** black-eyed Susan

Plant portraits

The fine foliage and flowers of these plants belie their tough nature. They withstand the rigors of the street all year long.

● = First design, pp. 40–41
▲ = Second design, p. 42

'Krossa Regal' hosta
(*Hosta*, p. 184) ●

Little bluestem grass
(*Schizachyrium scoparius*, p. 192) ▲

Japanese painted fern
(Ferns: *Athyrium goeringianum* 'Pictum', p. 181) ●

'Goldsturm' black-eyed Susan
(*Rudbeckia fulgida*, p. 192) ▲

'White Nancy' lamium
(*Lamium maculatum*, p. 187) ●

Maidenhair fern
(Ferns: *Adiantum pedatum*, p. 181) ●

Landscaping a Low Wall

A colorful two-tier garden replaces a bland slope

Some things may not love a wall, but plants and gardeners do. For plants, walls offer warmth for an early start in spring and good drainage for roots. Gardeners appreciate the rich visual potential of composing a garden on two levels, as well as the practical advantage of working on two relatively flat surfaces instead of a single sloping one.

This design places two complementary perennial borders above and below a wall bounded at one end by a set of stairs. While each bed is relatively narrow, when viewed from the lower level they combine to form a border almost 10 ft. deep, with plants rising to eye level or more. The planting can be extended farther along the wall with the same or similar plants.

Building the wall that makes this impressive sight possible doesn't require the time or skill it once did. Nor is it necessary to scour the countryside for tons of fieldstone or to hire an expensive contractor. Thanks to precast retaining-wall systems, anyone with a healthy back (or access to energetic teenagers) can install a knee-high do-it-yourself wall in as little as a weekend.

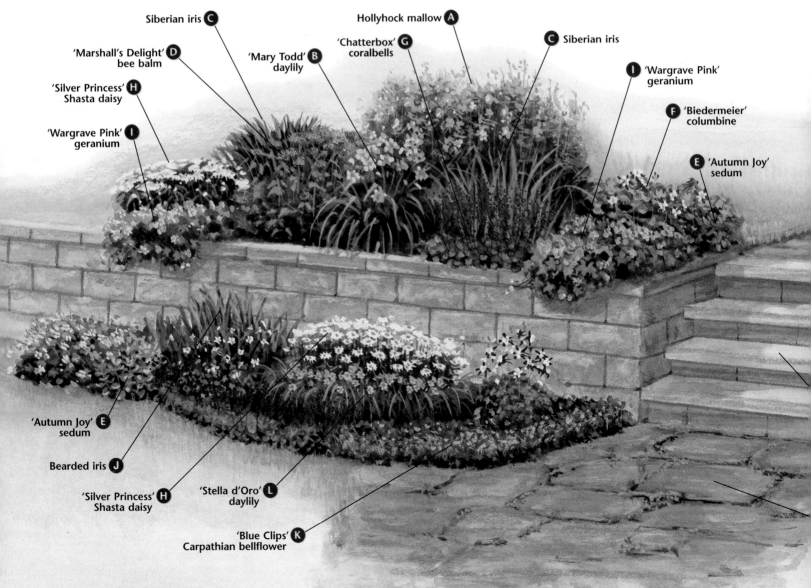

Siberian iris **C**

'Marshall's Delight' **D**
bee balm

'Silver Princess' **H**
Shasta daisy

'Wargrave Pink' **I**
geranium

'Mary Todd' **B**
daylily

Hollyhock mallow **A**

'Chatterbox' **G**
coralbells

C Siberian iris

I 'Wargrave Pink'
geranium

F 'Biedermeier'
columbine

E 'Autumn Joy'
sedum

'Autumn Joy' **E**
sedum

Bearded iris **J**

'Silver Princess' **H**
Shasta daisy

'Stella d'Oro' **L**
daylily

'Blue Clips' **K**
Carpathian bellflower

Plants & Projects

Composed of durable perennials, this planting offers a summer-long display of flowers in pinks, blues, and whites, with splashes of golden yellow and a hint of violet and purple. Extend the show in spring by planting crocuses in groups of a dozen or more all through the bed. Mulch to control weeds and to conserve moisture; snip off spent blooms to keep things tidy; and cut plants to the ground in late fall or early spring.

Site: Sunny

Season: Summer

Concept: Low retaining wall creates easy-to-maintain beds for a distinctive two-level planting of perennials.

A **Hollyhock mallow**
(use 3 plants)
In midsummer, this perennial sends up dozens of tall stems, each covered with lovely soft pink flowers. The low mound of bright green foliage looks good the rest of the season. See *Malva alcea* 'Fastigiata', p. 189.

B **'Mary Todd' daylily** (use 3)
Large, textured yellow flowers of this perennial rise on tall stalks from a handsome clump of grassy foliage, making a striking midsummer center-piece for the upper bed. See *Hemerocallis*, p. 183.

C **Siberian iris** (use 2)
The slender upright leaves of this perennial are attractive all season, and the graceful flowers add brilliant June color. Use any cultivar with blue flowers here. See *Iris sibirica*, p. 186.

D **'Marshall's Delight' bee balm**
(use 2)
Big, globe-shaped, pink flowers perch atop this perennial's tall leafy stalks in July and August. Spreads to form a loose clump; flowers attract hummingbirds. See *Monarda*, p. 189.

E **'Autumn Joy' sedum** (use 4)
This perennial forms a vase-shaped clump of distinctive, fleshy, gray-green leaves. Flat-topped flower clusters appear in August, turning from pale pink to rusty red by October. See *Sedum*, p. 193.

F **'Biedermeier' columbine**
(use 8)
Tucked in several places in the planting, this compact peren-nial bears lovely blue, pink, or white flowers that dance above mounds of delicate green leaves from late spring into summer. See *Aquilegia*, p. 173.

G **'Chatterbox' coralbells** (use 8)
This low-growing perennial's neat mounds of semievergreen leaves edge the top of the wall and the front of the bed nicely. Tiny red flowers on wiry stems hover above the foliage for much of the summer. See *Heuchera sanguinea*, p. 183.

H **'Silver Princess' Shasta daisy**
(use 7)
A low-growing form of an al-ways popular perennial. In July, large white daisies are borne about a foot above a low mat of shiny foliage that looks good all season. See *Chrysanthemum × superbum*, p. 177.

I **'Wargrave Pink' geranium**
(use 8)
The bright pink flowers and handsome divided leaves of this perennial create a cheerful, informal effect as they spill over the wall. Blooms heavily in early summer, then off and on until fall. See *Geranium endressii*, p. 182.

J **Bearded iris** (use 3)
The elegant flowers of this perennial last only a week or two, but they are worth every minute. Flat sprays of stiff, swordlike leaves accent the base of the wall. The white-flowered cultivar 'Immortality' (recommended here) blooms in early summer and again in fall. See *Iris*, p. 186.

K **'Blue Clips' Carpathian bellflower** (use 10)
A perennial offering small spreading mounds of delicate glossy green leaves covered for most of the summer with pretty blue flowers. A perfect edging for the lower path. See *Campanula carpatica*, p. 177.

L **'Stella d'Oro' daylily** (use 4)
This extraordinary perennial produces a fresh batch of golden yellow flowers each day from mid-June until fall. See *Hemerocallis*, p. 183.

M **Retaining wall and steps**
The low, precast retaining wall shown here is typical of those available at home and garden centers and local landscaping suppliers. See p. 130.

N **Walk**
The flagstone walk drifts into the lower bed as if inviting strollers to stop and enjoy the view. You can plant thyme in the gaps between the flagstones to further mingle the walk and beds. See p. 118.

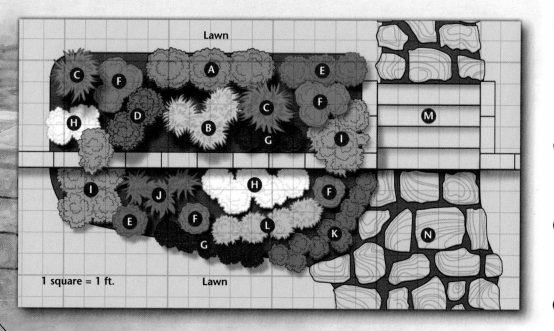

1 square = 1 ft.

M Retaining wall and steps

N Walk

Plant portraits

These perennials thrive in the sunny warmth of a two-tiered garden and provide months of vibrant color.

● = First design, pp. 44–45
▲ = Second design, pp. 46–47

'Marshall's Delight' bee balm
(*Monarda*, p. 189) ●

Dwarf fountain grass
(*Pennisetum alopecuroides* 'Hameln', p. 190) ▲

'The Fairy' rose
(*Rosa*, p. 191) ▲

'Wargrave Pink' geranium
(*Geranium endressii*, p. 182) ●

'Brilliant' maiden pink
(*Dianthus deltoides*, p. 180) ▲

Hollyhock mallow
(*Malva alcea* 'Fastigiata', p. 189) ●

Mix in shrubs

A small but handsome selection of shrubs and perennials give this wall planting a decidedly different but equally pleasing look. Viewed from above, a gently curving low hedge serves as an edging for lawn or an entertainment area on the top level. Viewed from below, the hedge joins the wall as a backdrop for a planting featuring long-blooming flowers in pink and blue set among ground covers with striking silvery foliage.

The symmetrical layout of the beds and the uniformity of the walk's crushed-stone surface give this design a more formal feel than the one on the preceding pages, but the cascade of roses lends a note of interesting unruliness to the scene. It's easy to expand the design for a longer wall by repeating the planting pattern.

Plants & Projects

Ⓐ **'Green Mound' alpine currant** (use 6 plants)
These deciduous shrubs have small, bright green leaves and a compact rounded habit that requires no pruning to form the loose, informal hedge shown in this design. See *Ribes alpinum*, p. 191.

Ⓑ **'The Fairy' rose** (use 3)
Small, double pink blossoms cover this deciduous shrub's low, spreading foliage from summer's beginning until frost. The plant in the top bed will cascade over the wall to mingle with the two in the lower bed. See *Rosa*, p. 191.

Ⓒ **Dwarf fountain grass** (use 2)
This perennial grass anchors the ends of the hedge with low

'Green Mound' **A** alpine currant

'The Fairy' **B** rose

'Blue Queen' **D** salvia

Retaining wall **H** and steps

C Dwarf fountain grass

E 'Brilliant' maiden pink

'Silver Brocade' **F** beach wormwood

'Brilliant' **E** maiden pink

mounds of arching foliage that turns from green to gold or tan in fall. Fluffy flower and seed heads nod above the foliage from midsummer on. See *Pennisetum alopecuroides* 'Hameln', p. 190.

D 'Blue Queen' salvia (use 6)
This perennial produces masses of color in front of the wall. Numerous spikes of tiny, vivid blue flowers bloom in June and continue until fall if you remove spent flowers. See *Salvia superba*, p. 192.

E 'Brilliant' maiden pink (use 12)
The rose-red flowers of this perennial rise from a spreading mat of slender blue-green semievergreen leaves in early summer. Remove spent flowers to

extend bloom until autumn. See *Dianthus deltoides*, p. 180.

F 'Silver Brocade' beach wormwood (use 9)
The large, coarse, silver-gray leaves of this perennial ground cover are an excellent foil for the flowers and foliage of the other plants. Spreads softly over the wall and along the front edge of the lower bed. See *Artemisia stelleriana*, p. 174.

G Walk
A well-compacted crushed-stone walk is tidy and easy to maintain. For an even more formal look, try square precast pavers. See p. 118.

See p. 45 for the following:

H Retaining wall and steps

Site: Sunny

Season: Summer

Concept: A simple mixture of shrubs and perennials in a loosely formal but high-impact design.

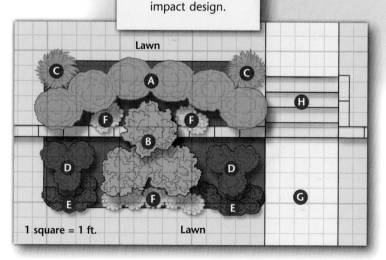

G Walk

Lawn

1 square = 1 ft. Lawn

"Around Back"

Dress up the family's day-to-day entrance

When it comes to landscaping, the most-used parts of a property are often the most neglected. The walk from the garage or driveway to the back door of the house is just such a spot. You make the journey numerous times each day, so why not make it as pleasant a trip as possible? A simple design such as the one shown here can transform this space, making it at once more inviting and more functional.

In a high-traffic area frequented by ball-bouncing, bicycle-riding children as well as by busy adults, delicate, fussy plants have no place. These tough, easy-care plants provide a pleasing mix of foliage and flowers throughout the growing season.

Dense, upright arborvitae form a narrow meandering hedge, a living wall that links the house and garage, while screening the more private backyard from the busy driveway. A wide opening in the hedge creates an informal gate to the backyard. Golden yellow daylilies and white phlox edge the drive and walk for months in the summer. Bulbs scattered among the daylilies will enliven the spring and are followed by a blizzard of small white flowers on the spirea—a special treat, perhaps, for those enjoying the early-summer sun on a backyard patio. In fall, a large clump of boltonia brightens the view from the drive with another dazzling display of white flowers.

'Marshall's Delight' D
bee balm

'Holmstrup' A
arborvitae

'Stella d'Oro' F
daylily

'Miss Lingard' E
phlox

'Snowbank' C
boltonia

'Marshall's Delight' D
bee balm

Plants & Projects

Durable shrubs and perennials bring color and texture to the area between your house and garage without adding to your weekend chores. You can integrate the spireas and arborvitae with existing foundation plantings or extend the design shown here to create a foundation planting. These plants are easy to maintain. Just cut back the perennials' faded flowers in summer and remove dead foliage in fall or spring. Every few years in early spring you'll need to divide crowded perennials and rejuvenate the spireas by cutting them to the ground.

A **'Holmstrup' arborvitae** (use 8 plants)
The compact, upright forms of these slow-growing evergreen shrubs make an attractive hedge without additional pruning to shape. Fragrant glossy green foliage adds color and structure to the planting through the winter. See *Thuja occidentalis*, p. 194.

B **'Snowmound' spirea** (use 14)
In May or early June the profusion of white flowers covering the arching branches of this deciduous shrub truly do make it look like a mound of snow. Small blue-green leaves and a neat form make it an excellent foundation planting through the rest of the year. See *Spiraea nipponica*, p. 193.

C **'Snowbank' boltonia** (use 1)
Finely cut blue-green foliage of this rugged perennial looks good all season and forms an upright clump that spreads slowly. In autumn, clouds of small white flowers are a treat near the driveway. See *Boltonia asteroides*, p. 175.

D **'Marshall's Delight' bee balm** (use 6)
Big, globe-shaped, pink flowers of this perennial bloom in mid-summer, their bright hues blending beautifully with the white phlox nearby. Forms a clump of erect stems bearing fragrant mintlike foliage. See *Monarda*, p. 189.

E **'Miss Lingard' phlox** (use 6)
This longtime favorite perennial bears fragrant pure white flowers on long stalks in mid-summer. Foliage is attractive all growing season. See *Phlox carolina*, p. 190.

F **'Stella d'Oro' daylily** (use 18)
This perennial produces golden yellow flowers from early June until late fall (a remarkable feat, given that each flower lasts for only one day). Its bright flowers and grassy foliage are set off beautifully by the dark backdrop of arborvitae. For additional spring color, plant crocuses, grape hyacinth, snowdrop, small tulips, or dwarf daffodils (see Bulbs, p. 176) among the daylilies, whose emerging foliage will cover the leaves of fading bulbs. See *Hemerocallis*, p. 183.

B 'Snowmound' spirea

Site: Sunny

Season: Summer

Concept: A design to beautify a much-used passageway and to separate backyard and driveway activities.

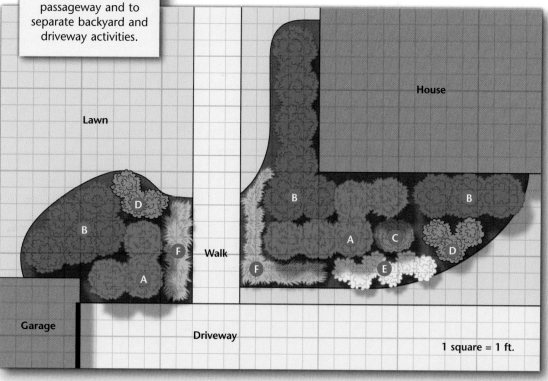

Lawn

House

Walk

Garage

Driveway

1 square = 1 ft.

Fence and flora

If you can't wait for a hedge to mature, try the fence shown in this design. It looks good and provides enclosure right away. Lined with daylilies and shrubs, the fence, like the arborvitae hedge in the previous design, helps separate activities on the driveway from those in the backyard. And as the trees mature, they will form a leafy screen at eye level and above.

Spring, shown here, is the most colorful season for this planting, with bulbs, spireas, and crab apples all in flower. Attractive foliage fills out the summer and fall, garnished with a many-colored edging of cheerful daylilies.

Other than a little fall and spring cleanup and a spot of routine pruning every couple of years, this planting will make few demands on your time.

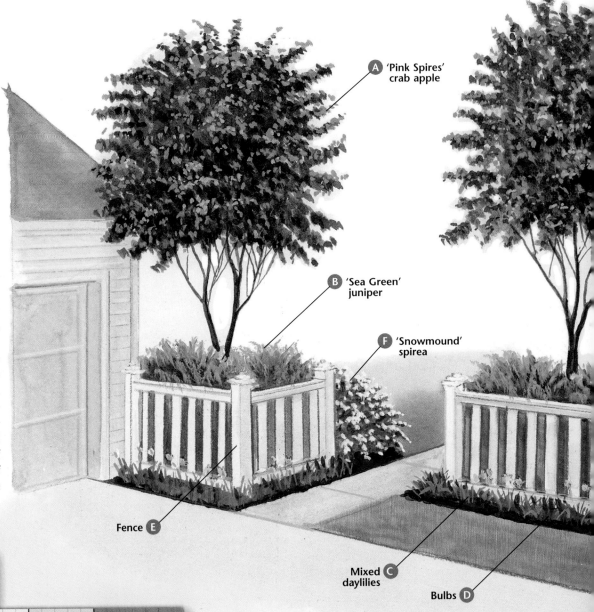

A 'Pink Spires' crab apple

B 'Sea Green' juniper

F 'Snowmound' spirea

Fence **E**

Mixed daylilies **C**

Bulbs **D**

Site: Sunny

Season: Late spring

Concept: Simple fence creates an instant enclosure; attractive trees and shrubs enhance the scene as they mature.

House

Lawn

Walk

Garage

Driveway

1 square = 1 ft.

Plants & Projects

A **'Pink Spires' crab apple** (use 2 plants)
These small deciduous trees bring four seasons of beauty to the back walk. In spring, limbs bear reddish new leaves and lavender-pink flowers. Summer sees healthy green foliage that turns copper-colored in fall. Small purple-red fruits dangle from bare branches through the winter. See *Malus*, p. 188.

B **'Sea Green' juniper** (use 4)
This tough evergreen shrub can handle hot, dry summers and piles of snow with equal ease. Its arching dark green foliage is a colorful anchor to the planting year round. See *Juniperus chinensis*, p. 186.

C **Mixed daylilies** (use 19)
For an extended show of lovely flowers, combine early- and late-blooming cultivars of this useful perennial. Its grassy leaves hide the spent foliage of earlier-blooming bulbs. Foliage and cheerful flowers make a bright, informal edging for the fence. See *Hemerocallis*, p. 183.

Plant portraits

These back-door plants have front-door style, with attractive foliage, pretty flowers, and little need for maintenance.

● = First design, pp. 48–49
▲ = Second design, pp. 50–51

'Sea Green' juniper
(*Juniperus chinensis*, p. 186) ▲

'Miss Lingard' phlox
(*Phlox carolina*, p. 190) ●

'Pink Spires' crab apple
(*Malus*, p. 188) ▲

'Holmstrup' arborvitae
(*Thuja occidentalis*, p. 194) ●

D Bulbs (as needed)
Plant handfuls of your favorite small bulbs in clumps among the daylilies for a spring show. We've shown dwarf daffodils and grape hyacinths here. See Bulbs, p. 176.

E Fence
This variation on the classic picket fence makes a nice backdrop for the shrubs and daylilies. See p. 140.

See p. 49 for the following:

F 'Snowmound' spirea (use 8)

'Snowmound' spirea
(*Spiraea nipponica*, p. 193) ● ▲

Beautify a Blank Wall
Paint a picture with plants

Just as you enhance your living room by hanging paintings on the walls, you can decorate blank walls in your outdoor "living rooms" with a vertical trellis garden. The design shown here goes a step further, filling an undulating bed with a tree, shrubs, and perennials to create a three-dimensional composition. The result gives pleasure when viewed from a patio or kitchen window or when you're strolling by to take a closer look.

Every season has its eye-catching attraction. Spireas and junipers give the design a solid foundation of year-round color and texture against the garage wall. The flowering crab apple holds center stage in spring. Roses, bee balm, and hollyhock mallow provide flowers in shades of pink for months in summer and fall, while other perennials form a low edging of attractive foliage at the front of the bed.

Angling out from the garage wall, its twin "peaks" echoing the gable ends of the garage or house, the homemade trellis adds both height and depth to the planting. Covered with blossoms from early summer, the trellis makes a wonderful focal point.

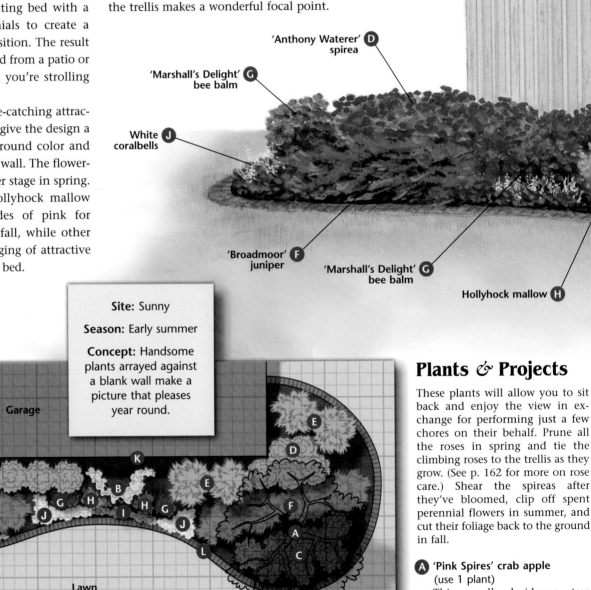

'Anthony Waterer' **D** spirea

'Marshall's Delight' **G** bee balm

White **J** coralbells

'Broadmoor' **F** juniper

'Marshall's Delight' **G** bee balm

Hollyhock mallow **H**

Site: Sunny

Season: Early summer

Concept: Handsome plants arrayed against a blank wall make a picture that pleases year round.

Driveway

Garage

Lawn

1 square = 1 ft.

Plants & Projects

These plants will allow you to sit back and enjoy the view in exchange for performing just a few chores on their behalf. Prune all the roses in spring and tie the climbing roses to the trellis as they grow. (See p. 162 for more on rose care.) Shear the spireas after they've bloomed, clip off spent perennial flowers in summer, and cut their foliage back to the ground in fall.

A 'Pink Spires' crab apple
(use 1 plant)
This small deciduous tree brings color to the planting in all seasons: reddish new leaves and lavender flowers in spring; copper-colored fall leaves; and

'Pink Spires' crab apple — A

Trellis — K

Climbing rose — B

'Maney' juniper — E

'Broadmoor' juniper — F

Basket-of-gold — I

Mowing strip — L

'Frau Dagmar Hartop' rose — C

purplish fruits that persist into winter. See *Malus*, p. 188.

B Climbing rose (use 2)
A profusion of pink flowers and shiny green leaves engulfs the trellis from early summer to fall. Plant 'John Cabot' or 'William Baffin'; both produce fragrant flowers throughout the summer. See *Rosa*, p. 191.

C 'Frau Dagmar Hartop' rose (use 7)
This shrub rose offers fragrant single pink flowers, bright green crinkly leaves, and large red hips that last from fall into winter. See *Rosa*, p. 191.

D 'Anthony Waterer' spirea (use 13)
A compact deciduous shrub

with small fine leaves, rosy pink flowers, and a tough constitution ideal for hot, dry conditions beneath the garage eaves. Blooms in midsummer. See *Spiraea × bumalda*, p. 193.

E 'Maney' juniper (use 4)
A rugged, bushy evergreen shrub that adds height and winter color at the far end of the planting. Silver-blue foliage makes a nice backdrop for the smaller shrubs and perennials. See *Juniperus chinensis*, p. 186.

F 'Broadmoor' juniper (use 6)
A spreading evergreen shrub whose low mass of soft gray-green color complements the planting's many pink flowers. See *Juniperus sabina*, p. 186.

G 'Marshall's Delight' bee balm (use 6)
This perennial forms a patch of slender leafy stalks displaying big, globe-shaped, pink flowers in midsummer. See *Monarda*, p. 189.

H Hollyhock mallow (use 8)
Pink flowers are borne in profusion on tall stalks above this perennial's wide mounds of attractive bright green leaves. Blooms in midsummer. See *Malva alcea* 'Fastigiata', p. 189.

I Basket-of-gold (use 5)
Begin the growing season with the bright yellow, fragrant spring blooms of this perennial. Low mounds of gray leaves make an attractive edg-

ing at the center of the bed. See *Aurinia saxatilis*, p. 175.

J White coralbells (use 22)
Clouds of tiny flowers float above this perennial's neat mounds of semievergreen foliage for most of the summer. A white-flowered cultivar works well in this planting. See *Heuchera × brizoides*, p. 183.

K Trellis
This easy-to-build grid of 1x2s makes a handsome and functional support for the climbing roses. See p. 141.

L Mowing strip
A neat edging of bricks crisply defines the bed's shape and makes mowing the adjacent lawn easier. See p. 150.

Less is more

This simple design uses just a few kinds of plants to striking effect. A wire trellis covered with scarlet-flowered honeysuckle is flanked by a flowing hedge of little bluestem grass, creating low "living" walls that echo and extend the garage wall behind. Visible above and behind a "kink" in the trellis is arrowwood viburnum, a carefree shrub that centers the design. At each end, low mounding shrubs covered with dainty white flowers complement the big, bold red, orange, and yellow daylilies nearby.

The planting offers an abundance of flowers from early summer to frost. In winter, the bare twigs of the shrubs and the dry grass provide interest.

Plants & Projects

A 'Dropmore Scarlet' honeysuckle (use 7 plants)
Distinctive scarlet flowers cover this woody deciduous vine from June until frost, and the blue-green leaves trace lovely patterns as they twine around the wire trellis. Flowers attract hummingbirds. See *Lonicera × brownii*, p. 188.

B Arrowwood viburnum (use 1)
This deciduous shrub fills the space behind the trellis and reaches up and out over the top. Its large glossy leaves turn from dark green to crimson or maroon in fall. Clusters of small white flowers in June are followed by indigo blue berries in September. Needs minimal pruning or care. See *Viburnum dentatum*, p. 195.

C 'Abbotswood' potentilla (use 14)
The rounded form of this low deciduous shrub contrasts with the neighboring grasses. Its dark green foliage sets off an abundance of snow-white flowers that appear on and off from

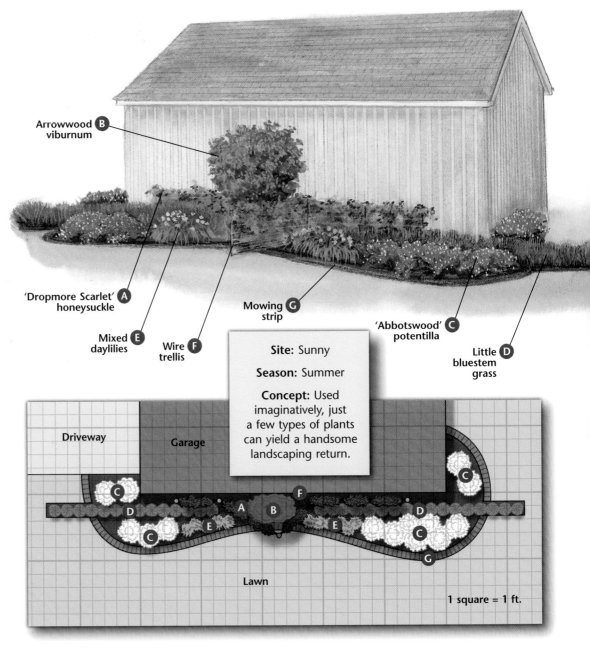

Arrowwood viburnum **B**

'Dropmore Scarlet' honeysuckle **A**

Mixed daylilies **E**

Wire trellis **F**

Mowing strip **G**

'Abbotswood' potentilla **C**

Little bluestem grass **D**

Site: Sunny

Season: Summer

Concept: Used imaginatively, just a few types of plants can yield a handsome landscaping return.

Driveway

Garage

Lawn

1 square = 1 ft.

June until frost. See *Potentilla fruticosa*, p. 190.

D Little bluestem grass (use 33)
A native perennial forming neat clumps of fine blue-green leaves in spring and summer. Lacy white seed heads and muted reddish purple foliage are eye-catching in fall and winter. Maintain a neat spade-cut edge (see p. 150) around the planting bed that extends this narrow grass "hedge" into the lawn. See *Schizachyrium scoparium*, p. 192.

E Mixed daylilies (use 11)
For an extended show of cheerful flowers, combine early- and late-blooming cultivars of this popular perennial. Pick cultivars with flowers in bold reds, yellows, and oranges to complement the honeysuckle and to show best in the bright sun. The grassy foliage is attractive after the flowers have finished. See *Hemerocallis*, p. 183.

F Wire trellis
Sturdy hog fencing, available from hardware or farm-supply

stores, makes a surprisingly attractive trellis. Made of heavy wire in long panels (an 11-wire version is sold in panels 34 in. high by 16 ft. long). The horizontal wires are closer together at the bottom than at the top of the panel. Fix the panels to metal fence posts that are set at the ends of the trellis and at the bends that form the V-shaped section.

See p. 53 for the following:

G Mowing strip

Plant portraits

Whether climbing over trellises
or forming tidy mounds, these
perennials and shrubs will dress
up the plainest wall.

● = First design, pp. 52–53
▲ = Second design, p. 54

'Broadmoor' juniper
(*Juniperus sabina*, p. 186) ●

'Frau Dagmar Hartop' rose
(*Rosa*, p. 191) ●

'Dropmore Scarlet' honeysuckle
(*Lonicera* × *brownii*, p. 188) ▲

Basket-of-gold
(*Aurinia saxatilis*, p. 175) ●

'Anthony Waterer' spirea
(*Spiraea* × *bumalda*, p. 193) ●

White coralbells
(*Heuchera* × *brizoides*, p. 183) ●

A Shady Hideaway

Build a cozy retreat in a corner of your yard

One of life's little pleasures is sitting in a shady spot reading a book or newspaper or just looking out onto your garden, relishing the fruit of your labors. If your property is long on lawn and short on shade, a bench under a leafy arbor can provide a cool respite from the heat or the cares of the day. Tucked into a corner of the property and set among attractive shrubs, vines, and perennials, the arbor shown here is a desirable destination even when the day isn't sizzling.

Honeysuckle and evergreen arborvitae create a cozy enclosure screened from neighboring properties, while affording a clear view of your own. Plantings in front of the arbor and extending along the property lines integrate the hideaway with the lawn and make a handsome scene when viewed from your house.

Flowers and foliage contribute color and fragrance in and around the arbor throughout the growing season. Scarlet honeysuckle and pink-and-white roses bloom for months, joined in late spring by fragrant pink peonies and in midsummer by cheerful daisies. Swaths of green, blue-gray, and silver foliage provide background and balance to the floral display and are eye-catching in their own right.

Site: Sunny

Season: Summer

Concept: Enjoy colorful, fragrant plants while you relax under a shady arbor or stroll beside the plantings.

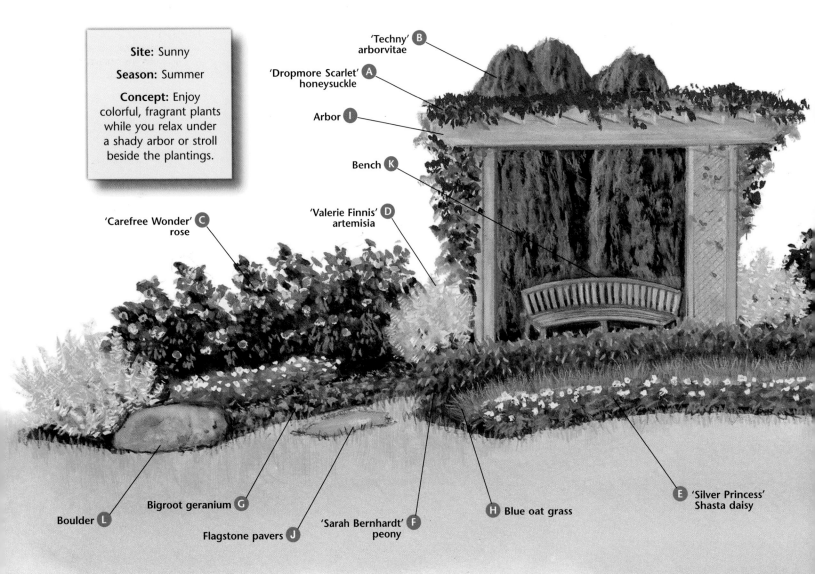

'Techny' arborvitae **B**

'Dropmore Scarlet' honeysuckle **A**

Arbor **I**

Bench **K**

'Valerie Finnis' artemisia **D**

'Carefree Wonder' rose **C**

'Silver Princess' Shasta daisy **E**

Boulder **L**

Bigroot geranium **G**

Flagstone pavers **J**

'Sarah Bernhardt' peony **F**

Blue oat grass **H**

Plants & Projects

The arbor, flagstones, and plants can be installed in a few weekends. You'll need to train the honeysuckle during the first year (see p. 165). Maintenance sessions spring and fall to prune the roses (see p. 162) and the honeysuckle and to clean up or divide the perennials should keep the planting looking good for years.

A **'Dropmore Scarlet' honeysuckle** (use 4 plants)
The woody stems and blue-green leaves of this deciduous climbing vine will cover the arbor in just a few years. Scarlet flowers bloom from early summer until frost. See *Lonicera × brownii*, p. 188.

B **'Techny' arborvitae** (use 3)
Forming broad cones, these evergreen trees create a handsome backdrop and privacy screen for the arbor. Bench sitters will also enjoy the pleasing scent of the rich green, fine-textured foliage. See *Thuja occidentalis*, p. 194.

C **'Carefree Wonder' rose** (use 12)
True to its name, this deciduous shrub rose blooms happily all summer long with little care from you. Fragrant double pink-and-white flowers cover knee-high massed plantings on either side of the arbor. See *Rosa*, p. 191.

D **'Valerie Finnis' artemisia** (use 20)
A perennial that is valued for its gleaming silvery white foliage and tough disposition. Grouped near the arbor and at the ends of the beds, it sets off the foliage and flowers of the other plants beautifully. See *Artemisia ludoviciana*, p. 174.

E **'Silver Princess' Shasta daisy** (use 33)
In July, low sturdy stalks bear large white daisies with yellow centers. This perennial's dark green foliage is attractive for months. See *Chrysanthemum × superbum*, p. 177.

F **'Sarah Bernhardt' peony** (use 8)
A sentimental favorite, this perennial offers large fragrant pink flowers in May or early June. Forms a clump of attractive foliage that turns purple or gold in fall. See *Paeonia*, p. 189.

G **Bigroot geranium** (use 30)
An ideal edging plant, this perennial forms a low mound of deeply lobed, aromatic leaves covered with pink flowers for weeks in June. See *Geranium macrorrhizum*, p. 182.

H **Blue oat grass** (use 8)
This perennial grass makes a tidy mound of slender, striking blue-gray leaves. Provides a handsome contrast in shape, color, and texture to the neighboring peonies and daisies. Leaves hold their shape and color year round (if the winter isn't harsh). See *Helictotrichon sempervirens*, p. 182.

I **Arbor**
Creating a large, comfortable garden "room," this arbor is simple to build. See p. 142.

J **Flagstone pavers**
Laid individually in the lawn (see p. 123), flagstones make an informal path to the arbor. Under the arbor, stones laid on a sand-and-gravel base (see p. 124) form a small patio-like surface.

K **Bench**
There is space for one large bench (like the gently curved version shown here) or several small benches under the arbor.

L **Boulders**
Large stones anchor the ends of the beds and mark the beginning of the path.

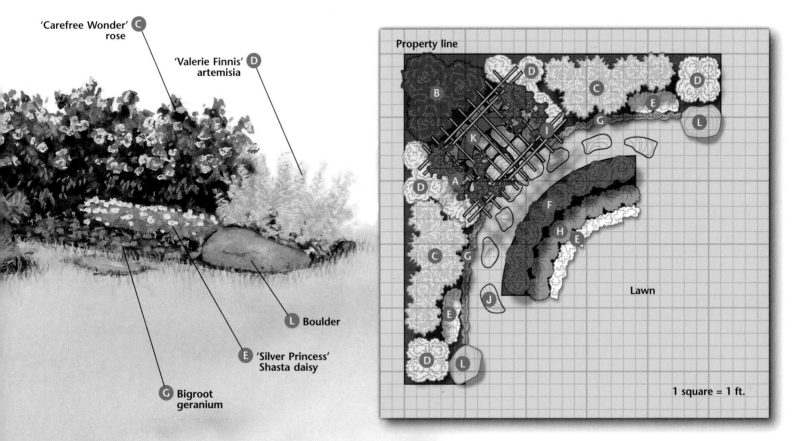

'Carefree Wonder' **C** rose

'Valerie Finnis' **D** artemisia

L Boulder

E 'Silver Princess' Shasta daisy

G Bigroot geranium

Property line

Lawn

1 square = 1 ft.

Plant portraits

Privacy, shade, flowers, foliage, and fragrance—these plants provide all the necessities for a backyard retreat.

● = First design, pp. 56–57
▲ = Second design, pp. 58–59

'Sarah Bernhardt' peony
(*Paeonia*, p. 189) ●

Bigroot geranium
(*Geranium macrorrhizum*, p. 182) ●

'Green Mound' alpine currant
(*Ribes alpinum*, p. 191) ▲

'Alaska' Shasta daisy
(*Chrysanthemum × superbum*, p. 177) ▲

Engelman ivy
(*Parthenocissus quinquefolia* var. *engelmannii*, p. 190) ▲

A cozy corner

This shady retreat is set in a smaller, more intimate planting. The arbor is the same as in the previous design, but here two benches face each other, encouraging conversation. A grass path forms the central axis of a symmetrical planting. Ivy covers the arbor, providing an airy sense of enclosure, reinforced by ranks of shrubs and grasses.

The path to the arbor is flanked from spring to fall with golden yellow daylilies. Inside the arbor, you can enjoy a semicircular garden of daylilies and daisies, backed by fountain-shaped clumps of ornamental grass and silver-blue junipers.

The grass path has a lovely feel and look, but if you are leery about keeping it neatly mowed and edged, substitute crushed rock or wood chips.

Plants & Projects

Ⓐ **Engelman ivy** (use 4 plants)
Small, shiny green, five-pointed leaves of this vine create a delicate covering for the arbor. Grows quickly, and turns bright red in early autumn. See *Parthenocissus quinquefolia* var. *engelmannii*, p. 190.

Ⓑ **'Maney' juniper** (use 6)
An evergreen shrub with blue-green foliage, it adds height and winter color at the back of the planting. Growing about as wide as it is tall, it requires no pruning to form a handsome privacy screen. See *Juniperus chinensis*, p. 186.

Ⓒ **'Anthony Waterer' spirea** (use 8)
The small, fine leaves and rosy pink flowers of this compact deciduous shrub belie its tough nature. Plants will grow natu-

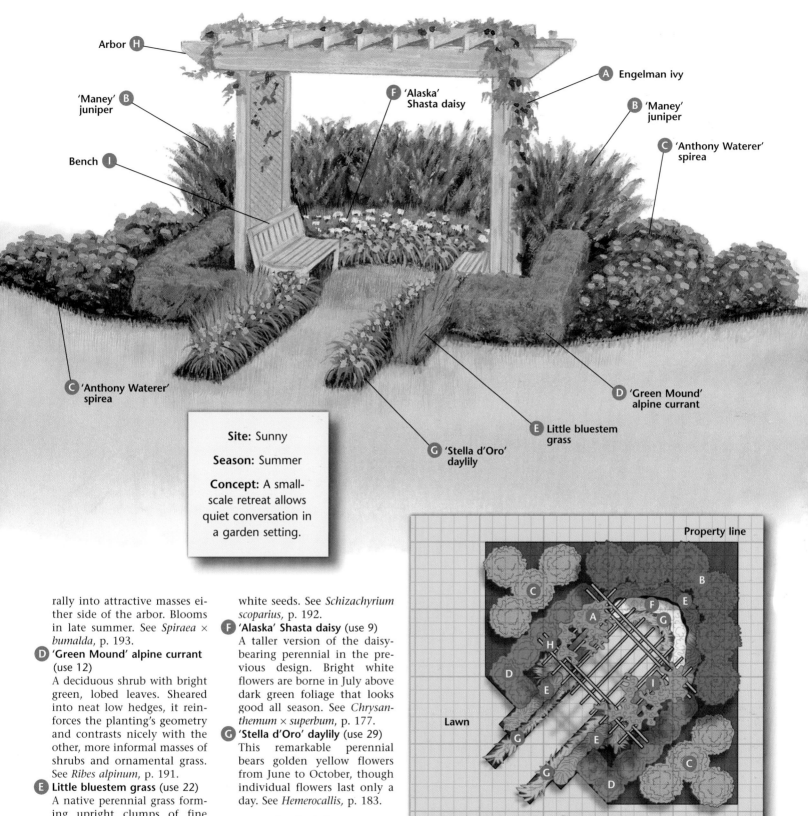

Arbor **H**

'Maney' **B**
juniper

Bench **I**

C 'Anthony Waterer'
spirea

F 'Alaska'
Shasta daisy

A Engelman ivy

B 'Maney'
juniper

C 'Anthony Waterer'
spirea

D 'Green Mound'
alpine currant

E Little bluestem
grass

G 'Stella d'Oro'
daylily

Site: Sunny

Season: Summer

Concept: A small-scale retreat allows quiet conversation in a garden setting.

rally into attractive masses either side of the arbor. Blooms in late summer. See *Spiraea × bumalda*, p. 193.

D **'Green Mound' alpine currant** (use 12)
A deciduous shrub with bright green, lobed leaves. Sheared into neat low hedges, it reinforces the planting's geometry and contrasts nicely with the other, more informal masses of shrubs and ornamental grass. See *Ribes alpinum*, p. 191.

E **Little bluestem grass** (use 22)
A native perennial grass forming upright clumps of fine blue-green leaves. In autumn and winter, the leaves turn a rich cinnamon-brown and are topped by wispy clusters of

white seeds. See *Schizachyrium scoparius*, p. 192.

F **'Alaska' Shasta daisy** (use 9)
A taller version of the daisy-bearing perennial in the previous design. Bright white flowers are borne in July above dark green foliage that looks good all season. See *Chrysanthemum × superbum*, p. 177.

G **'Stella d'Oro' daylily** (use 29)
This remarkable perennial bears golden yellow flowers from June to October, though individual flowers last only a day. See *Hemerocallis*, p. 183.

See p. 57 for the following:

H Arbor

I Bench

Property line

Lawn

1 square = 1 ft.

Create a "Living" Room
A patio garden provides privacy and pleasure

A patio can become a true extension of your living space with the addition of plants to screen views and to create an attractive setting. In this design, plants and a tall louvred fence at one end of the patio form a "wall" of three-dimensional and constantly changing floral motifs. The handsome brick paving accommodates a family barbecue or even a large gathering. Together, plants and patio nicely mingle the "indoors" with the "outdoors."

Scale is particularly important when you're planting near the house. The Japanese tree lilac shades the patio area without overpowering the house. The vine-covered fence and mixed border in front of it function rather like the wall hangings and furniture in a room. Composed of offset rectangles, the patio offers an intimate nook nestled among plants and screened by the fence and a larger area for functions that can spill out onto the lawn.

From early summer through fall the plantings provide a colorful accompaniment to your patio activities. Each season has a special treat—fragrant lilac blossoms in early summer; showy Jackman clematis and purple coneflowers in midsummer; bright asters and aromatic sweet autumn clematis in fall.

Plants & Projects

The patio and fence are sizable projects, but their rewards are large, too. Check local codes before building the fence. Once established, the plants are not demanding. Other than pruning the clematis and roses in late winter or early spring, seasonal cleanup is all that's required.

A Jackman clematis (use 3 plants)
A graceful form, dark green leaves, and striking, rich purple summer flowers make this deciduous vine a favorite. See *Clematis* × *jackmanii*, p. 177.

B Sweet autumn clematis (use 1)
This deciduous vine will quickly cover the fence. Starry white flowers fill the air in August and September with their pleasing fragrance. See *Clematis terniflora*, p. 178.

C Japanese tree lilac (use 1)
The creamy white, fragrant flowers of this small deciduous tree appear in early summer, weeks after regular lilacs bloom. When the flowers are gone, lush green leaves and shiny reddish brown bark provide interest for many months. See *Syringa reticulata*, p. 193.

D 'Green Velvet' boxwood (use 4)
A compact evergreen shrub ideal for making a low, natural hedge to create a patio niche. The shiny leaves complement the flowers and foliage of the nearby roses. See *Buxus*, p. 176.

E 'Bonica' rose (use 1)
Clusters of scentless, soft pink, double flowers cover this carefree shrub rose from June until frost. See *Rosa*, p. 191.

F 'The Fairy' rose (use 2)
This shrub rose's scentless double pink blossoms are borne from early summer to frost on a low, spreading mass of small, shiny leaves. See *Rosa*, p. 191.

G Purple coneflower (use 3)
A native prairie perennial that forms a mound of large green leaves. In late summer, stiff stalks bear large daisylike flowers with deep pink petals surrounding a large orange-brown central "cone." See *Echinacea purpurea*, p. 180.

H 'Purple Dome' New England aster (use 2)
This compact perennial has dark green leaves and blooms for weeks in fall, bearing masses of deep purple flowers, each with a bright yellow eye. See *Aster novae-angliae*, p. 174.

I 'Blue Clips' Carpathian bellflower (use 5)
Bell-shaped blue flowers on slender stalks rising from this perennial's neat mounds of shiny dark green foliage show well against the boxwood. You could substitute or combine with 'White Clips', too. *Campanula carpatica*, p. 177.

J 'Moonbeam' coreopsis (use 2)
Nestled by the house, this durable perennial produces masses of small pale yellow flowers above lacy dark green foliage. Blooms continually from July into September. See *Coreopsis verticillata*, p. 179.

K Louvered fence
Slanting slats of this 6-ft.-tall fence form an effective visual screen, while allowing air to circulate among the plants and people on the patio. See p. 143.

L Patio
The mellow look and feel of brick combine with almost any architectural style. Dressed flagstones or pavers would work well also. See p. 124.

'Green Velvet' **D** boxwood

Site: Sunny

Season: Summer

Concept: Planting provides privacy and a colorful setting for entertaining guests or enjoying the early-morning air on your own.

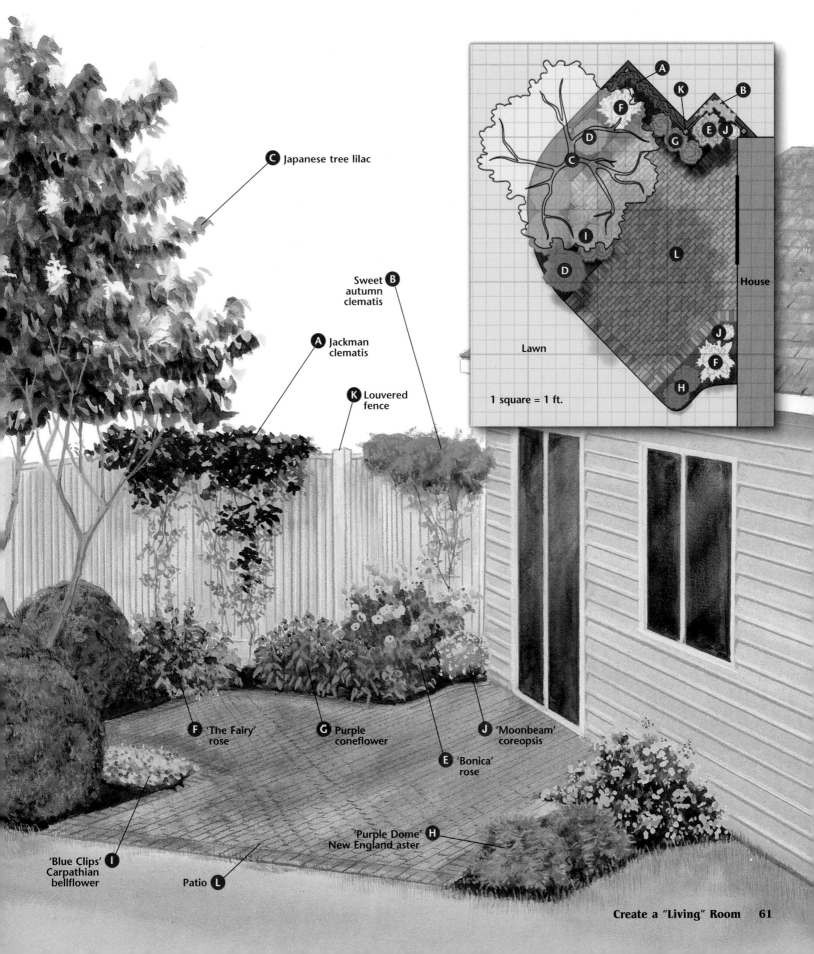

C Japanese tree lilac

B Sweet autumn clematis

A Jackman clematis

K Louvered fence

F 'The Fairy' rose

G Purple coneflower

J 'Moonbeam' coreopsis

E 'Bonica' rose

A | **K** | **B**

F

D

C

G | **E** | **J**

I

D

L

House

J

F

Lawn

H

1 square = 1 ft.

I 'Blue Clips' Carpathian bellflower

Patio **L**

'Purple Dome' New England aster **H**

Plant portraits

Whether you have sun or shade, these plants create a cozy patio niche with attractive flowers and foliage.

● = First design, pp. 60–61
▲ = Second design, pp. 62–63

Pink Japanese anemone
(*Anemone vitifolia* 'Robustissima', p. 173) ▲

Japanese tree lilac
(*Syringa reticulata*, p. 193) ●

'Royal Standard' hosta
(*Hosta*, p. 184) ▲

'Blue Clips' Carpathian bellflower
(*Campanula carpatica*, p. 177) ●

'Sprite' astilbe
(*Astilbe simplicifolia*, p. 174) ▲

Goatsbeard
(*Aruncus dioicus*, p. 174) ▲

A patio in the shade

If your patio is already blessed with a cool canopy of shade, perhaps from a large tree nearby, consider this design. The basic design is the same as on the previous pages, but here we feature a garden of shade-loving shrubs and perennials.

As before, the planting screens and enhances a private niche on the patio. Tall arborvitae block the view from a side yard or neighboring property. Lower-growing shrubs provide a sense of enclosure, while not cutting the patio off from a view of the backyard.

Scented azaleas, a striking rhododendron, and a profusion of small bulbs planted among the hostas highlight the spring. Perennials provide pretty pink and white flowers, as well as handsome foliage, through the summer and into fall.

Plants & Projects

Ⓐ 'Techny' arborvitae
(use 3 plants)
A native evergreen tree that forms a broad cone of fragrant foliage. It extends a wall of the house to make an effective privacy screen and handsome backdrop for the hostas. See *Thuja occidentalis*, p. 194.

Ⓑ 'Olga Mezitt' rhododendron
(use 1)
In spring the shiny dark green leaves of this evergreen shrub set off numerous clusters of clear pink flowers. Foliage turns maroon in winter. See *Rhododendron*, p. 191.

Ⓒ 'White Lights' azalea (use 3)
A hardy deciduous azalea developed in Minnesota, this bears large clusters of fragrant white flowers in late spring. Before bloom, the buds on the bare stems are almost as attrac-

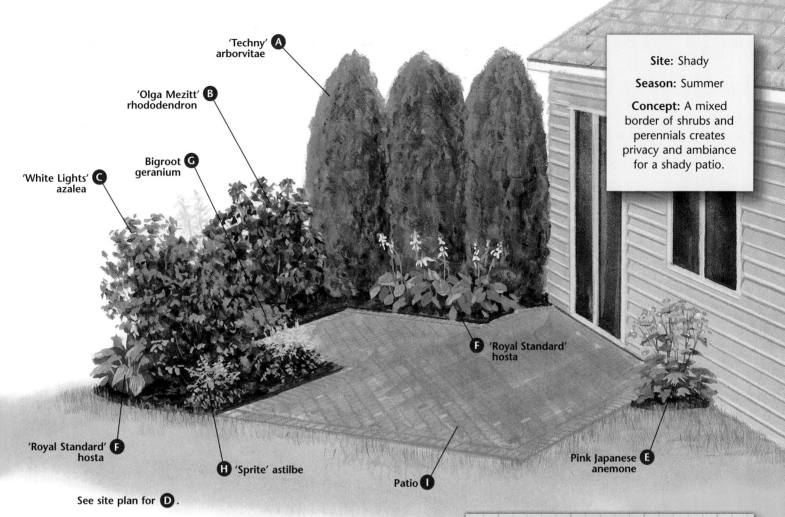

'Techny' **A** arborvitae

'Olga Mezitt' **B** rhododendron

Bigroot **G** geranium

'White Lights' **C** azalea

'Royal Standard' **F** hosta

H 'Sprite' astilbe

Patio **I**

See site plan for **D** .

'Royal Standard' **F** hosta

Pink Japanese **E** anemone

See p. 60 for the following:

Site: Shady

Season: Summer

Concept: A mixed border of shrubs and perennials creates privacy and ambiance for a shady patio.

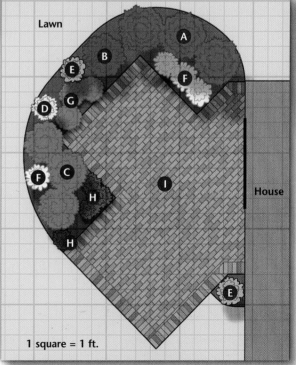

Lawn

House

1 square = 1 ft.

tive as the flowers. See *Rhododendron,* p. 190.

D **Goatsbeard** (use 1)
This robust perennial wildflower forms a clump of lacy leaves that is topped with plumes of creamy flowers in early summer. See *Aruncus dioicus,* p. 174.

E **Pink Japanese anemone** (use 2)
Enjoy carefree color in late summer from this lovely perennial. Tall branching stalks carrying clear pink flowers rise above clumps of dark green, lobed leaves. See *Anemone vitifolia* 'Robustissima', p. 173.

F **'Royal Standard' hosta** (use 4)
This popular perennial offers fragrant white flowers in late summer and fall, to go with its months-long display of attractive glossy green foliage. For additional spring bloom,

you can underplant the hostas (and the astilbes) with small bulbs, such as scillas, snowdrops, and grape hyacinths. See *Hosta,* p. 184.

G **Bigroot geranium** (use 3)
Low mounds of deeply lobed green leaves edge the patio beautifully all season. Bears pink or magenta flowers in June. The leaves are aromatic when touched. See *Geranium macrorrhizum,* p. 182.

H **'Sprite' astilbe** (use 4)
With a form that echoes the much larger goatsbeard, this perennial features finely divided dark green foliage and plumes of tiny pink flowers in mid- to late summer. See *Astilbe simplicifolia,* p. 174.

See p. 60 for the following:

I **Patio**

A Big Splash with a Small Pond
Add an extra dimension to your landscape

A water garden adds a new dimension to a landscape. It can be the eye-catching focal point of the entire property, a center of outdoor entertainment, or a quiet out-of-the-way retreat. A pond can be a hub of activity—a place to garden, watch birds and wildlife, raise ornamental fish, or stage an impromptu paper-boat race. It just as easily affords an opportunity for some therapeutic inactivity; a few minutes contemplating the ripples on the water provides a welcome break in a busy day.

A pond can't be easily moved, so choose your site carefully. Practical considerations are outlined on pp. 126–129 (along with instructions on installation and planting water plants); think about those first. Then consider how the pond and its plantings relate to the surroundings. Before plopping a pond down in the middle of the backyard, imagine how you might integrate it, visually if not physically, with nearby plantings and structures.

The plantings in this design are intended to settle the pond comfortably into an expanse of lawn. From a distance, the shrubs, ornamental grasses, and perennials that frame the pond resemble an island bed. Sitting on the bench near the water's edge, however, you'll find that the plantings provide enclosure, a sense of being on the island, looking at its plants and wildlife.

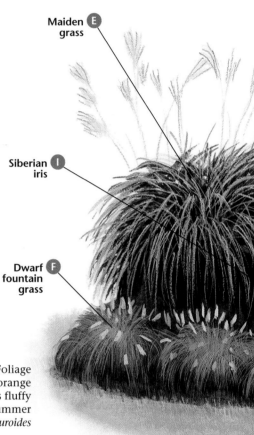

Maiden grass **E**

Siberian iris **I**

Dwarf fountain grass **F**

Plants & Projects

Ponds require regular, though not necessarily time-consuming, attention to keep looking their best, particularly if you add fish. Once established, the plants around the pond will need little more than seasonal cleanup. Cut the red-twig dogwood and dwarf purple willow back in spring to control their size. Cut the grasses back in spring after you've enjoyed their contribution to the winter landscape.

A **'Royal Purple' smoke tree** (use 1 plant)
This large deciduous shrub screens the bench with eye-catching foliage. Leaves are red in spring and dark purple in summer, and then turn gold or orange in fall. Fluffy pink flower plumes are an added treat in summer and fall. See *Cotinus coggygria*, p. 179.

B **'Sibirica' red-twig dogwood** (use 2)
A four-season performer, this deciduous shrub brightens the winter landscape with striking red stems that bear lacy white flowers in spring. Blue or white berries appear in late summer and foliage turns crimson in fall. See *Cornus alba*, p. 179.

C **Dwarf purple willow** (use 1)
Willows and water go together in the Midwest. This deciduous shrub adds a fine texture to the planting with its thin purple twigs and slender blue-gray leaves. See *Salix purpurea* 'Nana', p. 192.

D **'Crimson Pygmy' Japanese barberry** (use 1)
A dense mound of purple foliage, this deciduous shrub makes a fine contrast with the nearby willow. Leaves turn crimson in fall. See *Berberis thunbergii*, p. 175.

E **Maiden grass** (use 3)
Tall, graceful mounds of this perennial grass's narrow, silvery green leaves screen one side of the pond. Sturdy stalks bear fluffy seed heads from late summer through winter. See *Miscanthus sinensis* 'Gracillimus', p. 189.

F **Dwarf fountain grass** (use 4)
The smaller arching clumps of this perennial grass echo those of its larger neighbor. Foliage turns warm shades of orange and tan in autumn. Bears fluffy seed heads from midsummer on. See *Pennisetum alopecuroides* 'Hameln', p. 190.

G **Hay-scented fern** (use 10)
This fern's finely cut fronds release a vanilla-like scent when cut or crushed. Bright green all summer, they turn clear yellow in fall. See Ferns: *Dennstaedtia puntilobula*, p. 181.

H **Japanese iris** (use 6)
Slender erect leaves give this perennial an elegant form, and the magnificent flowers bring rich color to the pond in early to midsummer. See *Iris ensata*, p. 186.

I **Siberian iris** (use 3)
A perennial offering elegant flowers and long, gracefully arching leaves. Blooms early summer. See *Iris sibirica*, p. 186.

J **'Purple Dome' New England aster** (use 3)
Deep purple flowers cover the mounded foliage of this low-growing perennial from mid-August to September. It and the silvery maiden grass are a striking combination. See *Aster novae-angliae*, p. 174.

K **Hardy water lily** (use 1)
Large cuplike blooms nestle on floating green leaves ("lily pads") in midsummer. Comes in shades of white, yellow, and pink; most kinds are fragrant. This and other aquatics grow in pots of heavy soil that are submerged in the pond. See *Nymphaea*, p. 189.

L **Water plants**
You can grow a number of water plants besides water lilies. The three shown here are planted in the pond's shallow end. Arrowhead (*Sagittaria latifolia*) features large green leaves and white summer flowers.

J 'Purple Dome' New England aster

H Japanese iris

M Pond

B 'Sibirica' red-twig dogwood

L Water plants

A 'Royal Purple' smoke tree

C Dwarf purple willow

Hay-scented fern **G**

D 'Crimson Pygmy' Japanese barberry

Path **N**

Hardy water lily **K**

Golden club (*Orontium aquatica*) has shiny leaves and yellow flower spikes in spring. Blue flag iris (*Iris versicolor*) has slender leaves and delicate blue flowers in spring. See Water plants, p. 197.

M Pond

With some energetic helpers, you can dig this pond, install the plastic liner, and lay the flagstone edging in several weekends. See p. 126.

N Path

A gravel path leads to the bench and provides a tidy waterside surface for viewing the planting and pond. Where the path meets the lawn, fieldstones keep gravel from spilling onto the grass. See p. 118.

Site: Sunny

Season: Late summer

Concept: A backyard focal point, the pond nestles among shrubs and perennials and features striking water plants—even fish.

Lawn

1 square = 1 ft.

Garden gem

This little pond provides the pleasures of water gardening for those without the space or energy required to install and maintain a larger pond. Edged with stones of varying sizes and shade-tolerant plants, the pond evokes a woodland scene. Pond and plantings can stand alone in an expanse of lawn, but they will look their best integrated into a larger planting scheme.

Made of a stiff, fiberglass shell, the pond can be installed in a weekend. Here it is shown as a simple reflecting pool, but you can add one or more water plants, a few fish, or even a small pump to create ripples (which birds seem to like). As for a larger pond, consult local or mail-order suppliers to help you choose a combination of plants and fish that will maintain a healthy balance.

Plants & Projects

A **'Olga Mezitt' rhododendron**
(use 3 plants)
These evergreen shrubs form a backdrop along one side of the pool. Clusters of clear pink flowers bloom in early spring; small dark green leaves turn maroon in winter. See *Rhododendron*, p. 191.

B **Marginal wood fern** (use 2)
The lustrous, bright green fronds of this evergreen fern make a graceful ground cover and add to the woodland feel of the planting. See Ferns: *Dryopteris marginalis*, p. 181.

C **Bishop's hat** (use 4)
An elegant perennial with heart-shaped leaves that change color with the seasons, from coppery, to green, to maroon. Bears small pink or white flowers in early spring. See *Epimedium grandiflorum*, p. 180.

D **Dwarf crested iris** (use 3)
A small native perennial with lovely white or blue flowers

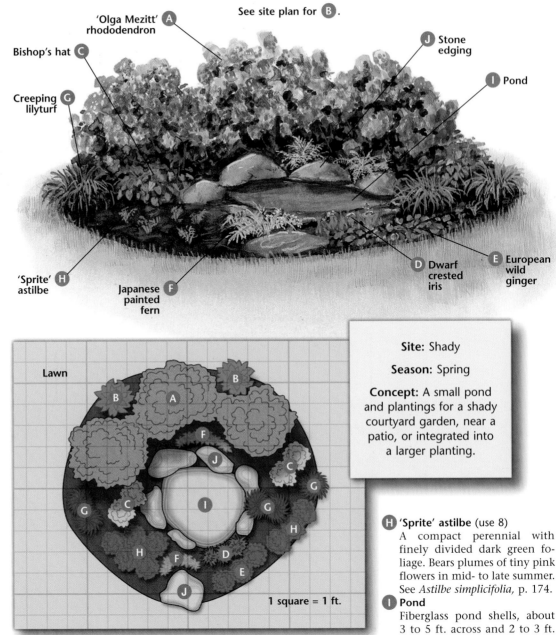

See site plan for **B**.

'Olga Mezitt' **A**
rhododendron

Bishop's hat **C**

Creeping **G**
lilyturf

J Stone
edging

I Pond

H 'Sprite'
astilbe

Japanese **F**
painted
fern

D Dwarf
crested
iris

E European
wild
ginger

1 square = 1 ft.

Site: Shady

Season: Spring

Concept: A small pond and plantings for a shady courtyard garden, near a patio, or integrated into a larger planting.

splashed with a yellow crest. The bladelike blue-green leaves make a fine ground cover. Blooms in early spring. See *Iris cristata*, p. 186.

E **European wild ginger** (use 3)
This perennial ground cover has large, glossy, heart-shaped leaves that create a dense blanket of green at the bed's edge. See *Asarum europaeum*, p. 174.

F **Japanese painted fern** (use 4)
One of the loveliest ferns, with delicate deciduous fronds that

blend green, silver, and maroon hues. The fronds will stand out nicely at the feet of the dark rhododendrons. See Ferns: *Athyrium goeringianum* 'Pictum', p. 181.

G **Creeping lilyturf** (use 6)
This rapidly spreading perennial ground cover makes a grasslike carpet of dark green leaves. Small lavender flower spikes appear in summer but aren't attention-grabbing. See *Liriope spicata*, p. 188.

H **'Sprite' astilbe** (use 8)
A compact perennial with finely divided dark green foliage. Bears plumes of tiny pink flowers in mid- to late summer. See *Astilbe simplicifolia*, p. 174.

I **Pond**
Fiberglass pond shells, about 3 to 5 ft. across and 2 to 3 ft. deep, are available at garden centers in a variety of shapes. (A flexible plastic liner, as shown in the previous design, would also work.) Place smooth beach stones in the bottom to enhance the "woodland" look. See p. 126.

J **Stone edging**
Use stones of similar color but varying sizes to cover the edge of the pond shell and tie the planting into its surroundings. Place larger stones behind the pond to make a pleasing transition to the rhododendrons.

Plant portraits

Whether growing in the water or nearby, these shrubs and perennials will increase your pondside pleasure.

● = First design, pp. 64–65
▲ = Second design, p. 66

Creeping lilyturf
(*Liriope spicata*, p. 188) ▲

European wild ginger
(*Asarum europaeum*, p. 174) ▲

Hardy water lily
(*Nymphaea*, p. 189) ●

Dwarf purple willow
(*Salix purpurea* 'Nana', p. 192) ●

Hay-scented fern
(Ferns: *Dennstaedtia puntilobula*, p. 181) ●

'Royal Purple' smoke tree
(*Cotinus coggygria*, p. 179) ●

Dwarf crested iris
(*Iris cristata*, p. 186) ▲

Garden in the Round

Create a planting with several attractive faces

Plantings in domestic landscapes are usually "attached" to something. Beds and borders hew to property lines, walls, or patios; foundation plantings skirt the house, garage, or deck. Most are meant to be viewed from the front, rather like a wall-mounted sculpture in raised relief.

On the other hand, the planting shown here is only loosely moored to the property line, forming a peninsula jutting into the lawn. It is an excellent option for those who want to squeeze more gardening space from a small lot, add interest to a rectangular one, or divide a large area into smaller "outdoor rooms." Because you can walk around most of the bed, plants can be displayed "in the round," presenting different scenes from several vantage points.

Without a strong connection to a structure or other landscape feature, a bed like this (or its close cousin, the island bed, which floats free of any anchors) requires an active sensitivity to scale. To be successful, the bed must neither dominate its surroundings nor be lost in them. The plants here are large enough to have presence when viewed from a distance, while also providing pleasure on closer inspection.

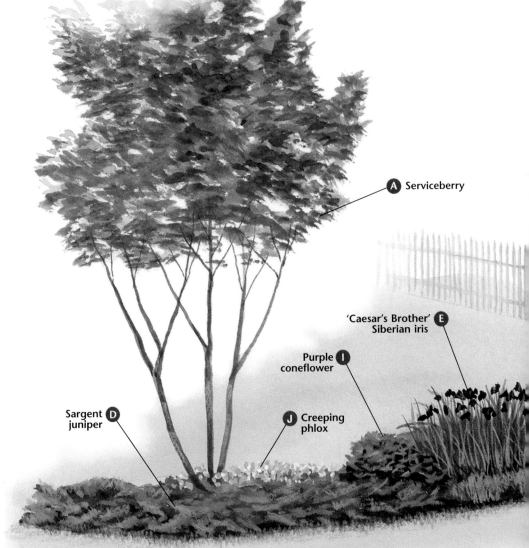

Plants & Projects

A small tree and a selection of shrubs give this bed a four-season presence. Spring (shown here) is the most colorful season, with lots of lovely flowers and fresh new foliage. But summer-flowering perennials and striking fall color provide months of additional enjoyment. In spring and fall, fragrant flowers are an added enticement for a stroll around the planting. Once established, these plants require only routine seasonal maintenance.

Ⓐ Serviceberry (use 1 plant)
This small, multitrunked deciduous tree is attractive year round, offering white flowers in early spring, edible berrylike fruits in summer, brilliant red fall color, and attractive gray bark in winter. See *Amelanchier × grandiflora*, p. 173.

Ⓑ Compact burning bush (use 1)
A deciduous shrub forming a tidy, spherical mound of layered branches. Its green leaves turn coppery from midsummer to fall; they become a striking crimson in October. See *Euonymus alatus* 'Compactus', p. 180.

Ⓒ 'Golden Lights' azalea (use 3)
A deciduous shrub bred for northern gardens, it brightens the bed with large, fragrant yellow flowers in late spring. Its foliage makes a neat, bright green background for the lilies at the edge of the bed. See *Rhododendron*, p. 190.

Ⓓ Sargent juniper (use 3)
A low-growing, spreading evergreen shrub that handsomely rounds out one end of the bed. Foliage looks good in all seasons. See *Juniperus chinensis* var. *sargentii*, p. 186.

Ⓔ 'Caesar's Brother' Siberian iris (use 3)
A perennial noted for its elegant deep purple flowers, which bloom in late spring. The rest of the growing season you'll appreciate its graceful clump of slender upright leaves. See *Iris sibirica*, p. 186.

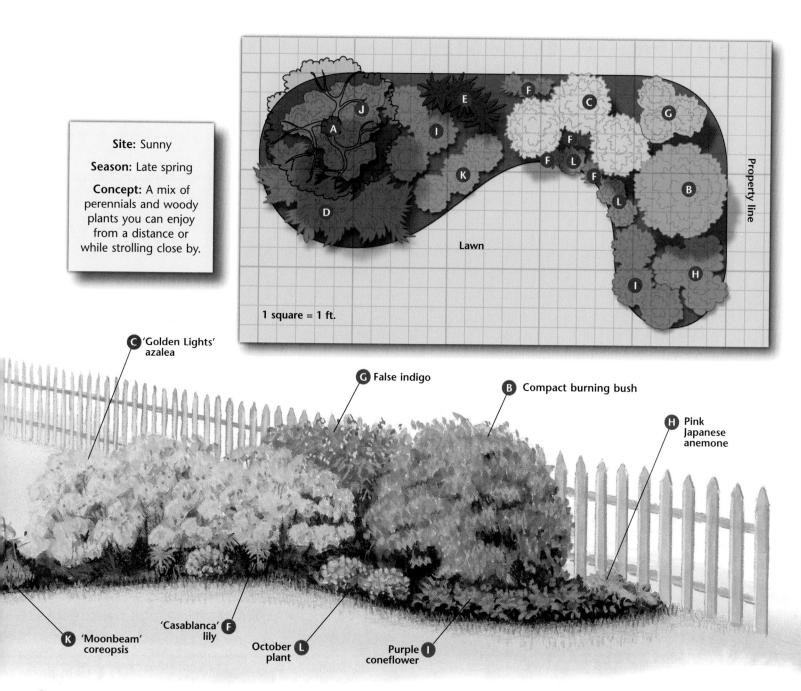

Site: Sunny

Season: Late spring

Concept: A mix of perennials and woody plants you can enjoy from a distance or while strolling close by.

Property line

Lawn

1 square = 1 ft.

C 'Golden Lights' azalea

G False indigo

B Compact burning bush

H Pink Japanese anemone

K 'Moonbeam' coreopsis

F 'Casablanca' lily

L October plant

I Purple coneflower

F **'Casablanca' lily** (use 6)
Displayed on tall stalks, the lovely pure white flowers of this perennial bulb will scent the air around the bed in late summer. See *Lilium*, p. 187.

G **False indigo** (use 3)
In spring, the spikes of indigo blue flowers on this perennial look splendid with the yellow azaleas nearby. Later on, gray-green foliage and gray seed-pods catch the eye. See *Baptisia australis*, p. 175.

H **Pink Japanese anemone** (use 3)
This perennial forms a clump of large, lobed, dark green leaves. In late summer, tall branching stalks display lovely pink flowers. See *Anemone vitifolia* 'Robustissima', p. 173.

I **Purple coneflower** (use 6)
A tough native perennial bearing large daisylike flowers in mid- to late summer. Plant the purple-flowered species next to the serviceberry and place a white-flowered cultivar near the anemones. Let the seed heads ripen to attract birds in the winter. See *Echinacea purpurea*, p. 180.

J **Creeping phlox** (use 24)
The soft green foliage of this little perennial ground cover makes a pool of color beneath the serviceberry. Bears blue or white flowers in spring. See *Phlox stolonifera*, p. 190.

K **'Moonbeam' coreopsis** (use 3)
The tiny pale yellow flowers of this perennial combine well with almost any color, and it blooms from midsummer to early fall. Forms neat mounds of lacy dark green foliage. See *Coreopsis verticillata*, p. 179.

L **October plant** (use 3)
Whorls of succulent blue-gray leaves line the trailing stems of this low-growing perennial. Rosy pink flowers complement the brilliant foliage of the nearby burning bush in fall. See *Sedum sieboldii*, p. 193.

Garden in the Round 69

A woody peninsula

Plantings like this one, devoted entirely to shrubs and trees, have much to offer in the Midwest region. Long after the frost-killed perennial foliage has been cut back to the ground, these plants catch the eye. Deciduous leaves fall to reveal attractive bark and traceries of bare branches, while evergreen shrubs provide rich color as well as form. Embellishing their forms with snow, Nature creates impromptu sculpture gardens.

The other seasons also have much to offer, as the early-summer illustration here shows. Fragrant flowers in spring and summer, pretty fall color, and attractive foliage throughout the growing season round out the year. Once established, this planting will require only a few hours of maintenance a year.

Site: Sunny

Season: Early summer

Concept: An easy-care planting providing something to enjoy in every season.

Plants & Projects

A **Compact cranberrybush viburnum** (use 1 plant)
This deciduous shrub anchors one end of the bed with its dense broad habit, beautiful white flowers in May, and lovely maplelike leaves that turn red in fall. Shiny red fruits that ripen in late summer brighten the winter scene. See *Viburnum trilobum* 'Compactum', p. 195.

B **'Rosy Lights' azalea** (use 3)
A member of the same group of hardy deciduous shrubs that is featured in the previous design, this cultivar bears fragrant flowers that are dark pink with a reddish shading. See *Rhododendron*, p. 190.

C **'Winter Red' winterberry holly** (use 3)
Bunches of bright red berries delight you and birds through the fall and winter months after this upright shrub drops its lustrous dark green leaves. See *Ilex verticillata*, p. 184.

D **'Bonica' rose** (use 1)
Clusters of soft pink double flowers cover this broad deciduous shrub from June until frost. An easy-care rose. Flowers are scentless. See *Rosa*, p. 191.

E **'Little Princess' spirea** (use 3)
This deciduous shrub forms a low mass of fine, dark green leaves. It bears pretty little pink flowers for weeks in early summer and keeps a tidy shape without pruning. See *Spiraea japonica*, p. 193.

See pp. 68–69 for the following:

F **Serviceberry** (use 1)

G **Sargent juniper** (use 3)

H **Creeping phlox** (use 24)

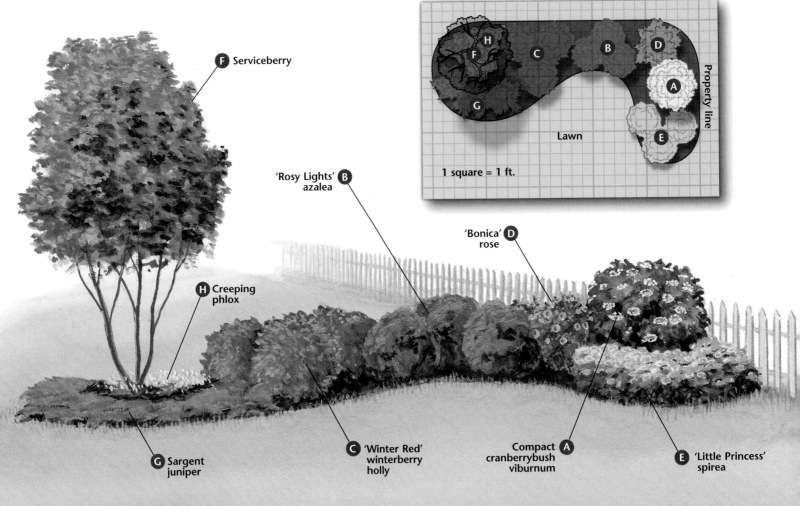

F Serviceberry

H Creeping phlox

'Rosy Lights' **B** azalea

'Bonica' **D** rose

G Sargent juniper

C 'Winter Red' winterberry holly

Compact **A** cranberrybush viburnum

E 'Little Princess' spirea

Property line

Lawn

1 square = 1 ft.

Plant portraits

These plants are attractive viewed close up or at a distance. Whether with form, flowers, or foliage, they perform in every season.

● = First design, pp. 68–69
▲ = Second design, p. 70

False indigo
(*Baptisia australis*, p. 175) ●

'Caesar's Brother' Siberian iris
(*Iris sibirica*, p. 186) ●

Sargent juniper
(*Juniperus chinensis* var. *sargentii*, p. 186) ● ▲

'Bonica' rose
(*Rosa*, p. 191) ▲

Serviceberry
(*Amelanchier* × *grandiflora*, p. 173) ● ▲

A Beginning Border

Flowers and a fence make a traditional design

A mixed border can be one of the most delightful of all gardens. Indeed, that's usually its sole purpose. Unlike many other types of landscape plantings, a traditional border is seldom yoked to any function beyond that of providing as much pleasure as possible. From the first neat mounds of foliage in the spring to the fullness of summer bloom and autumn color, the mix of flowers, foliage, textures, tones, and hues brings enjoyment.

This border is designed for a beginning or busy gardener, using durable plants that are easy to establish and care for. Behind the planting, screening out distraction, is a simple fence. The border is meant to be viewed from the front, so taller plants go at the back. Climbing the fence, a clematis adds a swath of dark green leaves to the backdrop, dappled for weeks in summer with large purple flowers.

Summer, shown here, is the most colorful season, with masses of flowers in shades of purple, blue, yellow, and white set against foliage in a range of greens, with accents of silver. Plant your favorite bulbs among the perennials to add spring color to the clumps of fresh foliage that dot the bed early in the growing season. In fall, fresh purple asters and white boltonia complement the still-blooming blue salvia and yellow coreopsis. The distinctive flat heads of rust-colored sedum flowers provide the perfect autumnal accent.

Plants & Projects

Removing spent flowers and seasonal pruning (cutting stems to the ground) are the main chores in this garden. If you cut back catmint by about one-third after flowering, it will make a return performance. Be sure to use labels to mark where the lilies are planted, so you won't damage them in the fall or spring cleanup. Place a few steppingstones in the bed for easy access to plants near the back. For a larger border, just plant more of each plant to fit the space, or repeat parts of the design.

A Jackman clematis (use 2 plants)
The dark green leaves of this deciduous vine drape gracefully over the fence. Large showy purple flowers last for weeks in summer. Attach twine or heavy string to the fence for the stems to cling to as they climb to the lattice. See *Clematis × jackmanii*, p. 177.

B 'Snowbank' boltonia (use 6)
In autumn, this perennial's small daisylike flowers form clouds of white at the back of the border. Makes a large upright clump of finely cut pale green foliage that looks good all season. See *Boltonia asteroides*, p. 175.

C 'Purple Dome' New England aster (use 3)
A perennial forming attractive mounds of dark green foliage. In early fall, innumerable dark purple flowers with bright yellow "eyes" blanket the plant. See *Aster novae-angliae*, p. 174.

D False indigo (use 2)
A prairie perennial bearing spikes of clear blue flowers in spring. The rest of the growing season its blue-green foliage and sizable gray seedpods make a handsome backdrop for the nearby blazing star and daylilies. See *Baptisia australis*, p. 175.

E 'Kobold' blazing star (use 6)
Another perennial native to the prairies, this bears narrow, showy, magenta flower spikes in July and August above clumps of grassy foliage. The flowers combine beautifully with the yellow daylilies and are great for cutting and drying, and butterflies love them. See *Liatris spicata*, p. 187.

F 'Casablanca' lily (use 6)
In late summer, the regal, pure white flowers of this perennial will scent the entire planting with their rich perfume. Interplant three in each patch of blazing star. See *Lilium*, p. 187.

G 'Goldsturm' black-eyed Susan (use 6)
Large, golden yellow, daisylike flowers with black cones at their centers cover this prairie perennial in late summer. See *Rudbeckia fulgida*, p. 192.

H Daylilies (use 9)
Combining early- and late-blooming cultivars of this perennial gives an extended show of lovely lilylike flowers on attractive grasslike foliage. We show the white-flowered 'Ice Carnival', fragrant pale yellow 'Hyperion', and golden 'Stella d'Oro', which blooms from early summer until frost. See *Hemerocallis*, p. 183.

I 'Autumn Joy' sedum (use 6)
The flat-topped flower clusters and fleshy gray-green leaves of this perennial provide months of interest at the front of the border. Flowers start out creamy white in August, maturing through shades of pink to a rich rust-colored seed head that can stand through the winter. See *Sedum*, p. 193.

J 'East Friesland' salvia (use 6)
This reliable perennial's spikes of blue-purple flowers will bloom from early summer until frost if you keep removing spent blooms. The flowers are lovely companions for white lilies and gold daylilies. See *Salvia superba*, p. 192.

Fence **M**

'Snowbank' **B**
boltonia

'East Friesland' **J**
salvia

A Jackman clematis

C 'Purple Dome' New England aster

D False indigo

B 'Snowbank' boltonia

G 'Goldsturm' black-eyed Susan

H 'Hyperion' daylilies

I 'Autumn Joy' sedum

K 'Blue Wonder' catmint

H 'Ice Carnival' daylilies

L 'Moonbeam' coreopsis

F 'Casablanca' lily

E 'Kobold' blazing star

H 'Stella d'Oro' daylilies

Site: Sunny

Season: Summer

Concept: A simple fence and colorful easy-care perennials make this border ideal for novice and experienced gardeners alike.

K **'Blue Wonder' catmint** (use 3) This fine front-of-the-border perennial bears loose spikes of violet-blue flowers that rise above soft mounds of silvery foliage in June and repeat through the season. See *Nepeta × faassenii*, p. 189.

L **'Moonbeam' coreopsis** (use 5) This perennial's finely cut foliage contrasts well with nearby plants. Bears numerous small lemon yellow flowers from July into September. See *Coreopsis verticillata*, p. 179.

M **Fence** Combining open lattice and narrow slats, this fence provides privacy and a backdrop for the planting. See p. 144.

Lawn

1 square = 1 ft.

Mixing it up

In a mixed border, shrubs and small trees join perennials, seasonal bulbs, and even annuals. Because of the all-season physical presence of woody plants, mixed borders are sometimes called upon to perform functional tasks, serving, for example, as screens or barriers.

Like the previous design, however, this one is intended primarily to be beautiful. Evergreen and deciduous shrubs and ornamental grasses give this border a distinctly different character and extend its appeal throughout the growing season as well as through the winter.

Clematis, daylilies, butterfly weed, boltonia, and asters provide ample flowers in summer and fall to complement the forms, colors, and textures of the shrubs and grasses. A liberal interplanting of bulbs will brighten the border in spring.

Seasonal cleanup is about all that's required to maintain the border once the plants are established. Cut the switchgrass to the ground in spring so you can enjoy its tawny leaves and seed heads in winter.

Plants & Projects

Ⓐ Golden clematis (use 2 plants)
Yellow flowers cover this deciduous vine throughout the summer. Interesting feathery seed heads cling on the plant into winter. Fix twine or string to the lower portion of the fence for the stems to climb. See *Clematis tangutica*, p. 178.

Ⓑ 'Pathfinder' juniper (use 1)
This small evergreen tree anchors one corner of the planting with its upright, pyramidal form and blue-gray foliage. See *Juniperus scopulorum*, p. 186.

Ⓒ 'Blue Star' juniper (use 2)
Placed diagonally across the

Golden clematis Ⓐ 'Purple Dome' New England aster Ⓙ Fence Ⓚ Switchgrass Ⓔ Ⓒ 'Blue Star' juniper Ⓘ 'Snowbank' boltonia Ⓗ Butterfly weed

1 square = 1 ft.

Lawn

bed from its upright cousin, this low, spreading evergreen has sparkly rich blue foliage. An ideal shrub for the front of the border. See *Juniperus squamata*, p. 186.

Ⓓ 'Crimson Pygmy' Japanese barberry (use 1)
A deciduous shrub with a dense, rounded, naturally tidy form. Striking foliage is purple in summer and crimson in fall. See *Berberis thunbergii*, p. 175.

Ⓔ Switchgrass (use 3)
The narrow leaves of this native grass form a graceful, upright clump that is a lovely background for the shorter perennials and shrubs. Leaves change from bright green to gold to tan. In late summer a pinkish cloud of flower panicles floats above the leaves. The cultivar 'Hanse Hermes', with red fall color, is shown here. See *Panicum virgatum*, p. 189.

Ⓕ Blue oat grass (use 3)
This perennial grass forms a rounded clump of blue-gray leaves at the front of the border. Foliage may hold its color through the winter. See *Helictotrichon sempervirens*, p. 182.

Ⓖ 'Hyperion' daylily (use 3)
A perennial that produces a fresh batch of sweet-scented yellow flowers daily in midsummer. The grassy foliage is a nice contrast to the neighbor-

B 'Pathfinder' juniper

G 'Hyperion' daylily

D 'Crimson Pygmy' Japanese barberry

F Blue oat grass

Site: Sunny

Season: Early fall

Concept: Adding woody plants and grasses creates a distinctively different but equally attractive border.

ing shrub and tree. See *Hemerocallis*, p. 183.

H Butterfly weed (use 5)
Butterflies flock to the clusters of bright orange flowers on this native perennial in early summer. Large pods bursting with silky seeds follow the flowers in autumn. See *Asclepias tuberosa*, p. 174.

See pp. 72–73 for the following:

I 'Snowbank' boltonia (use 3)

J 'Purple Dome' New England aster (use 3)

K Fence

Plant portraits

Whether you are a beginning gardener or an old hand, you'll appreciate the masses of bloom these plants provide, with so little care.

● = First design, pp. 72–73
▲ = Second design, pp. 74–75

Jackman clematis
(*Clematis* × *jackmanii*, p. 177) ●

'Purple Dome' New England aster
(*Aster novae-angliae*, p. 174) ● ▲

'Hyperion' daylily
(*Hemerocallis*, p. 183) ● ▲

Butterfly weed
(*Asclepias tuberosa*, p. 174) ▲

'Snowbank' boltonia
(*Boltonia asteroides*, p. 175) ● ▲

Back to Nature

Create a wooded retreat in your backyard

The open spaces and squared-up property lines in many new developments (and some old neighborhoods as well) can make a homeowner long for the seclusion of a wooded landscape. It may come as a surprise that you can create just such a retreat on a property of even modest size. With a relatively small number of carefully placed trees and shrubs, you can have your own backyard nature park.

Trees and shrubs take time to reach the sizable proportions we associate with a woodland. The plants in this design were chosen in part because they make an attractive setting in their early years, too. Here we show the young planting a few years after installation. On the following pages you'll see the planting as it appears at maturity.

Creeping ground covers and patches of bright spring bulbs make a colorful carpet in the area around and between the trees and shrubs. Prairie wildflowers and grasses fill the two central islands when the planting is young. Years later, when the red maple tree provides more shade, you can replace the prairie plants with some woodland wildflowers.

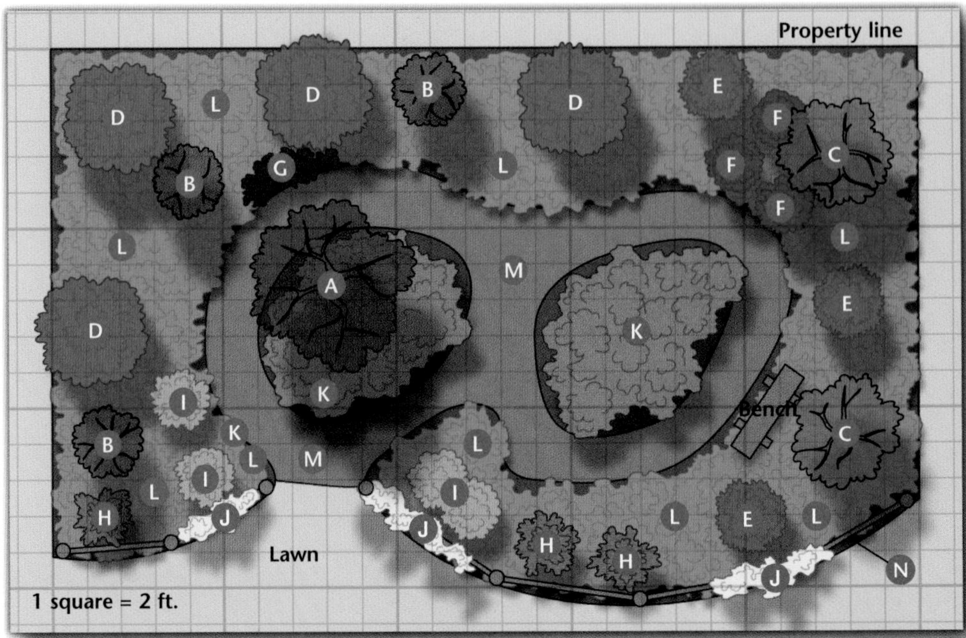

Property line

1 square = 2 ft.

Lawn

Bench

Site: Sunny

Season: Fall

Concept: Trees, shrubs, and wildflowers create a small nature park across the back of a lot. Shown here just a few years after planting.

American holly **D**

Black chokeberry **G**

Red maple **A**

Serviceberry **B**

'Frau Dagmar Hartop' rose **H**

Compact cranberrybush viburnum **I**

Sweet autumn clematis **J**

Wildflowers and grasses **K**

Plants & Projects

Prepare the soil throughout the entire area with a rototiller. Then plant, mulching the entire area immediately to control weeds and to keep the soil moist. Add more mulch every year or two in spring.

A **Red maple** (use 1 plant)
A fast-growing deciduous tree with blazing fall color and red flower clusters in early spring. See *Acer rubrum*, p. 172.

B **Serviceberry** (use 3)
This small deciduous tree offers white flowers in early spring, edible berrylike fruits, brilliant fall color, and attractive gray bark in winter. See *Amelanchier × grandiflora*, p. 173.

C **Washington hawthorn** (use 2)
Another small deciduous tree whose dark green leaves sometimes turn red in fall. White, early June flowers give rise to red fall fruits. See *Crataegus phaenopyrum*, p. 180.

D **American holly** (use 4)
A native evergreen tree with glossy green leaves. Plant a male cultivar with three female seedlings to ensure berries. See *Ilex opaca*, p. 184.

E **Linden viburnum** (use 3)
A large deciduous shrub with clusters of white May flowers, dark green leaves that turn red-orange in fall, and pretty berries that persist into winter. See *Viburnum dilatatum*, p. 195.

F **Winterberry holly** (use 3)
Planted with one male, female cultivars of this native evergreen shrub produce bushels of bright red berries that attract birds in fall and winter. See *Ilex verticillata*, p. 184.

G **Black chokeberry** (use 2)
A deciduous shrub with white flowers in spring, shiny dark green leaves that blaze scarlet in autumn, and dark berries. See *Aronia melanocarpa*, p. 173.

H **'Frau Dagmar Hartop' rose** (use 3)
A large deciduous shrub that bears single pink, fragrant flowers all summer followed by large red hips. See *Rosa*, p. 191.

I **Compact cranberrybush viburnum** (use 4)
A deciduous shrub with white flowers in late spring, shiny red fruits, and red autumn foliage. See *Viburnum trilobum* 'Compactum', p. 195.

J **Sweet autumn clematis** (use 3)
Climbing on the fence, this deciduous vine offers small light green leaves and starry white, fragrant flowers in autumn. See *Clematis terniflora*, p. 178.

K **Wildflowers and grasses**
Sun-loving native plants will add color and attract butterflies to the two central islands. You can try seeding the area, or you can simply buy a few dozen small plants of false indigo (*Baptisia australis*, p. 175), purple coneflower (*Echinacea purpurea*, p. 180), blazing star (*Liatris spicata*, p. 187), bee balm (*Monarda*, p. 189), black-eyed Susan (*Rudbeckia fulgida*, p. 192), New England aster (*Aster novae-angliae*, p. 174), and little bluestem grass (*Schizachyrium scoparius*, p. 192). Space the plants 2 to 3 ft. apart.

L **Ground covers and bulbs**
Fill the area around and between the trees and shrubs with low-growing, fast-spreading ground covers such as goutweed (*Aegopodium podagraria* 'Variegatum', p. 172), carpet bugle (*Ajuga reptans*, p. 172), lily-of-the-valley (*Convallaria majalis*, p. 179), and sweet woodruff (*Galium odoratum*, p. 181). Space ground-cover seedlings about 1 ft. apart. For spring color, plant clusters of small bulbs such as grape hyacinth, squill, and dwarf daffodils. (See Bulbs, p. 176.)

M **Path**
Wood chips make a soft, quiet surface suited to this natural space. See p. 118.

N **Fence**
Buy a simple rail fence at your home or garden center; set it just inside the edge of the planting beds so you don't have to mow lawn beneath it.

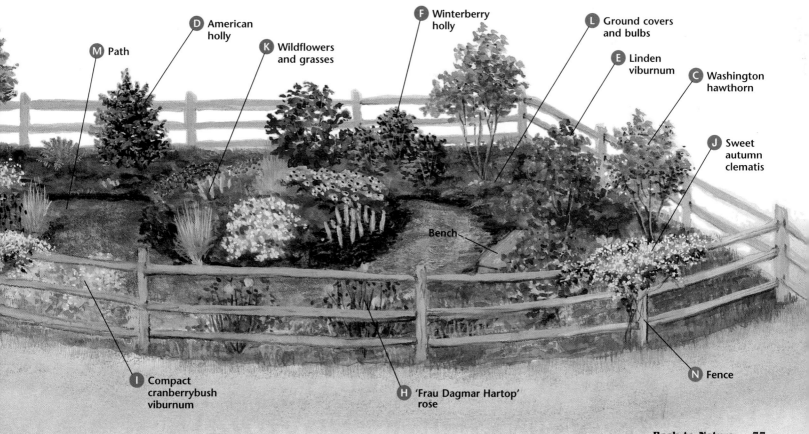

D American holly
M Path
K Wildflowers and grasses
F Winterberry holly
L Ground covers and bulbs
E Linden viburnum
C Washington hawthorn
J Sweet autumn clematis
I Compact cranberrybush viburnum
Bench
H 'Frau Dagmar Hartop' rose
N Fence

The mature woodland

Change and growth are the rule among living things, but when plants are small, it's not easy to imagine what they'll look like in 12 or 15 years. So we've done it for you.

The bare, sunny lot has been transformed into the oasis of dappled shade you envisioned. The maple, about 25 feet tall now, forms a wide canopy over the island beds. The trees and shrubs planted near the property line have filled out to form a handsome backdrop and effective privacy screen. Along the fence, roses and viburnums rise to shoulder height, creating a cozy sense of enclosure within the planting, while not blocking the view from the house and lawn.

Shade-tolerant woodland wildflowers now grace the island beds, replacing the sun-loving prairie plants. Try bleeding heart (*Dicentra spectabilis*, p. 180), foamflower (*Tiarella cordifolia*, p. 195), wild ginger (*Asarum*, p. 174), sweet violet (*Viola odorata*, p. 197), and a selection of ferns (p. 181). Springtime, shown here, is awash with bulbs, basking in the sunlight streaming through the branches and emerging leaves of the deciduous trees and shrubs.

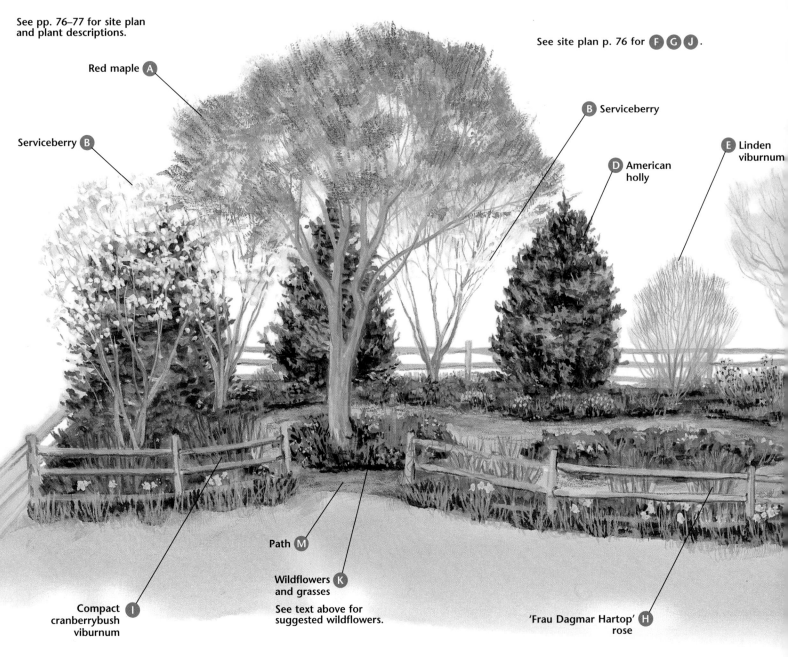

See pp. 76–77 for site plan and plant descriptions.

See site plan p. 76 for F G J.

Red maple A

Serviceberry B

B Serviceberry

E Linden viburnum

D American holly

Path M

Wildflowers K and grasses

See text above for suggested wildflowers.

Compact I cranberrybush viburnum

'Frau Dagmar Hartop' H rose

C Washington hawthorn

N Fence

L Ground covers and bulbs

Plant portraits

A nature park calls for trees and shrubs with a relaxed, informal look. Most of these are native plants, and many offer fruits to entice birds and other wildlife.

Compact cranberrybush viburnum
(*Viburnum trilobum* 'Compactum', p. 195)

Red maple
(*Acer rubrum*, p. 172)

American holly
(*Ilex opaca*, p. 184)

Winterberry holly
(*Ilex verticillata*, p. 184)

Linden viburnum
(*Viburnum dilatatum*, p. 195)

Washington hawthorn
(*Crataegus phaenopyrum*, p. 180)

Make a No-Mow Slope

A terraced planting transforms a steep site

Site: Sunny

Season: Summer

Concept: Retaining walls and low-care plantings create a multilevel stroll-through garden.

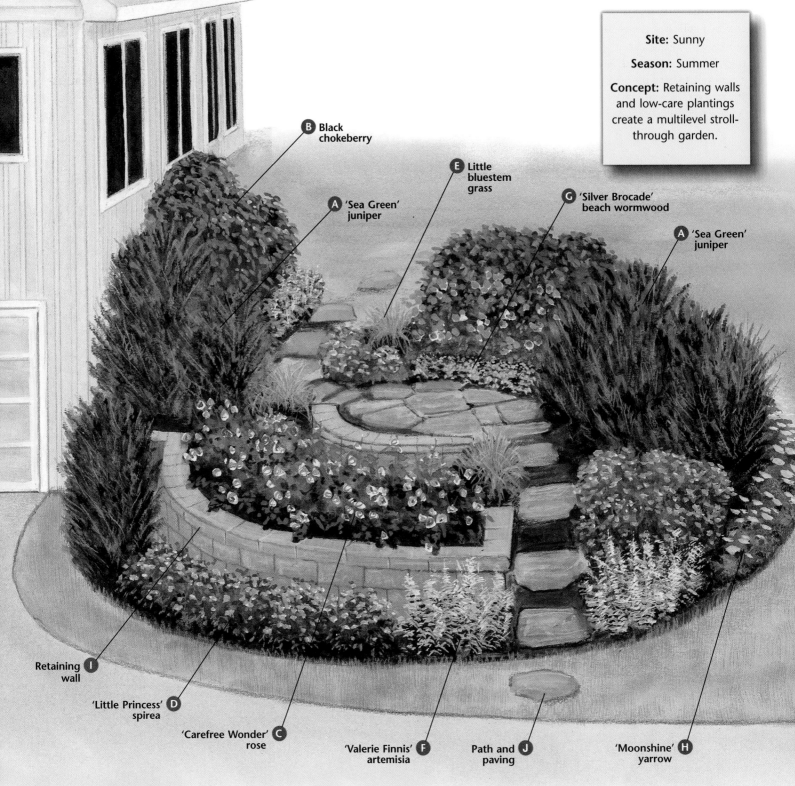

B Black chokeberry

A 'Sea Green' juniper

E Little bluestem grass

G 'Silver Brocade' beach wormwood

A 'Sea Green' juniper

I Retaining wall

D 'Little Princess' spirea

C 'Carefree Wonder' rose

F 'Valerie Finnis' artemisia

J Path and paving

H 'Moonshine' yarrow

Loved by children with sleds, steep slopes can be a landscape headache for adults. They're a chore to mow, and they can present problems of erosion and maintenance if you try to establish other ground covers or plantings. One solution to this dilemma is shown here—tame the slope with low retaining walls, and plant the resulting flat (or flatter) beds with interesting low-care shrubs and perennials.

Steep slopes near the house are common on properties with walk-out basements or lower-level garages. Here, two low retaining walls create three terraces that mirror the curve of the driveway. Near the house, the design can tie into existing foundation plantings or establish a style for a new foundation planting. Away from the house, the plants make a pleasing transition between the terraced and sloped portions of the site and the flatter, more open areas of lawn that border it.

The design is attractive whether viewed from above or below. Seen from the sidewalk, it frames the house and directs attention to the front entrance. It also screens the semiprivate area of drive and garage from the more public entrance.

Shrubs in a variety of sizes, shapes, textures, and colors make the planting attractive year round. During the growing season, some of the brightest colors in the garden are provided by perennials. Steppingstones lead to an area of flagstone pavers at the center of the planting. Partially screened from the street by shrubs, this is an ideal spot for a small table and chairs where you might have coffee in the morning or enjoy a pleasant drink after a day's work.

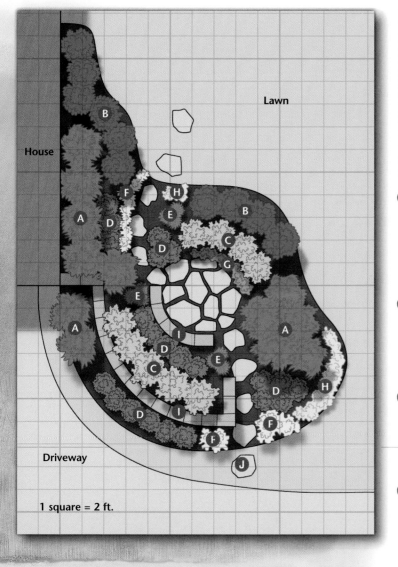

Lawn

House

Driveway

1 square = 2 ft.

Plants & Projects

Reshaping the slope, building the retaining walls, and preparing the planting beds is a big job. But once it is done and the plants are established, this design will provide years of enjoyment with a minimum of maintenance. If you'd like extra flowers, plant small bulbs (crocus, squill, grape hyacinth, small daffodils) in clumps of six or more, scattered among the shrubs.

A 'Sea Green' juniper (use 12 plants)
A broad evergreen shrub with arching branches of dark green fine-textured foliage that add color to the slope through all four seasons. See *Juniperus chinensis*, p. 186.

B Black chokeberry (use 10)
This deciduous shrub bears small white flowers in May. Dark berries follow in late summer. Shiny dark green leaves turn scarlet in fall. See *Aronia melanocarpa*, p. 173.

C 'Carefree Wonder' rose (use 9)
A deciduous shrub bearing fragrant double pink-and-white flowers all summer. Easily pruned to make informal low hedges by the upper wall and lawn. See *Rosa*, p. 191.

D 'Little Princess' spirea (use 22)
Forming small mounds of fine leaves and deep pink flowers, this deciduous shrub thrives in the dry heat near the concrete driveway and keeps blooming throughout June and July. See *Spiraea japonica*, p. 193.

E Little bluestem grass (use 9)
Clumps of this native perennial grass accent the area around the flagstone paving year round. Slender leaves turn from dark blue-green in summer to a muted reddish purple in autumn, fading to light tan by spring. See *Schizachyrium scoparius*, p. 192.

F 'Valerie Finnis' artemisia (use 15)
Patches of this perennial's striking silvery white foliage draw the eye to the steppingstone path (even in the evening). See *Artemisia ludoviciana*, p. 174.

G 'Silver Brocade' beach wormwood (use 7)
The large, coarse, silver-gray leaves of this mat-forming perennial ground cover make an attractive edging all season long for the flagstone paving. See *Artemisia stelleriana*, p. 174.

H 'Moonshine' yarrow (use 12)
Flat heads of lemon yellow flowers and gray-green ferny foliage of this perennial stand out against the darker green junipers and chokeberry. See *Achillea*, p. 172.

I Retaining wall
After you've reshaped the slope, you can build the two retaining walls in a few weekends using a precast concrete wall system. See p. 130.

J Path and paving
Flagstones in a variety of shapes lend an informal air to the steppingstone path and small paved area. See p. 118.

Design for a shady slope

Once again, the challenge is to make a steep slope attractive and easy to maintain. But now the slope is shaded (perhaps by the house or a large tree).

Here, a single wall creates a flat area next to the drive and a more gently sloping area on top. The wall declines in height as the slope lessens; the plantings in front of it, next to the drive, are similarly graduated.

With its dramatic sweeping curve, the planting provides a bold setting for the house and backdrop for the lawn. Tree-form hydrangeas make a striking focal point. Lower-growing shrubs spill down the hill. Perennials edge the lawn with colorful foliage and flowers.

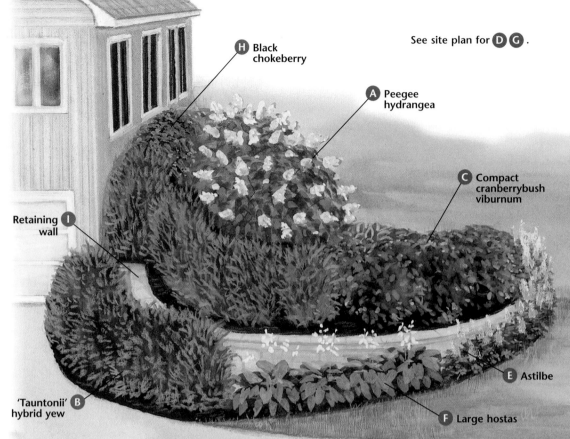

See site plan for **D** **G** .

H Black chokeberry

A Peegee hydrangea

C Compact cranberrybush viburnum

Retaining **I** wall

E Astilbe

'Tauntonii' **B** hybrid yew

F Large hostas

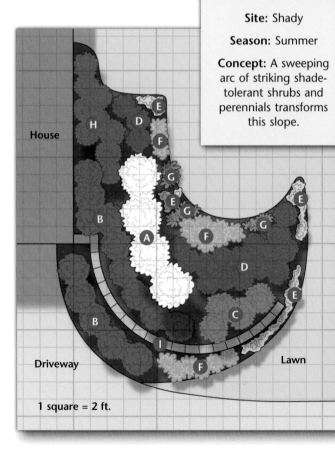

Site: Shady

Season: Summer

Concept: A sweeping arc of striking shade-tolerant shrubs and perennials transforms this slope.

House

Driveway

Lawn

1 square = 2 ft.

Plants & Projects

A **Peegee hydrangea**
(use 4 plants)
Trained and pruned here to grow as a small tree, this deciduous shrub bears showy flowers that turn from white to pink to tan as midsummer turns to fall. See *Hydrangea paniculata* 'Grandiflora', p. 184.

B **'Tauntonii' hybrid yew** (use 14)
This spreading evergreen shrub makes informal hedges that look good all year. See *Taxus × media*, p. 193.

C **Compact cranberrybush viburnum** (use 4)
A native shrub with four-season interest. Lacy white flowers bloom in May; the maplelike leaves are green in summer, red in fall. Shiny red berries appear in fall and last through the winter. See *Viburnum trilobum* 'Compactum', p. 195.

D **Dwarf bush honeysuckle**
(use 18)
This deciduous shrub forms a thicket of dark green foliage that sometimes shows bright fall colors. Bears small yellow flowers in summer. See *Diervilla lonicera*, p. 180.

E **Astilbe** (use 32)
In early summer, this perennial bears plumes of tiny flowers on mounds of dark, deeply cut foliage. Choose a pink- or white-flowered cultivar. See *Astilbe × arendsii*, p. 174.

F **Large hostas** (use 17)
These perennials add subtle color and texture from spring until frost. Try 'Royal Standard', with glossy green foliage and fragrant white flowers; 'Aureo-marginata', with gold-edged leaves and lilac-colored flowers; and 'Honeybells', with pale green leaves and fragrant purple flowers. See *Hosta*, p. 184.

G **'Ginko Craig' hosta** (use 27)
Makes smaller clumps than its nearby cousins. Lance-shaped leaves are edged with white. See *Hosta*, p. 184.

See p. 81 for the following:

H Black chokeberry (use 9)

I Retaining wall

Plant portraits

In sun or shade, these distinctive shrubs and perennials will add character to a terraced slope.

● = First design, pp. 80–81
▲ = Second design, p. 82

Peegee hydrangea
(*Hydrangea paniculata* 'Grandiflora', p. 184) ▲

'Silver Brocade' beach wormwood
(*Artemisia stelleriana*, p. 174) ●

'Tauntonii' hybrid yew
(*Taxus × media*, p. 193) ▲

Black chokeberry
(*Aronia melanocarpa*, p. 173) ● ▲

Dwarf bush honeysuckle
(*Diervilla lonicera*, p. 180) ▲

'Carefree Wonder' rose
(*Rosa*, p. 191) ●

Astilbe
(*Astilbe × arendsii*, p. 174) ▲

Under the Old Shade Tree
Create a cozy garden in a cool spot

This planting is designed to help homeowners blessed with a large shade tree make the most of their good fortune. A bench is provided, of course. What better spot to rest on a hot summer day? But why stop there? The tree's high, wide canopy affords an ideal setting for a planting of understory shrubs and perennials. The result is a woodland garden that warrants a visit any day of the year.

The planting roughly coincides with the pool of shade cast by the tree. We've shown a handsome red oak here; like hickory and ash, this tree doesn't compete as tenaciously with understory plants as do some maples. A row of yews creates a shallow niche for the bench. You can orient the planting so the yews screen the bench from the view of neighbors or passersby. A colorful azalea lends additional height in a handsome selection of woodland ground covers.

The planting has something to offer in every season. Spring, shown here, is awash with flowers. Drifts of small white blossoms carpet the ground and play off the dark green foliage of the yews. Striking trusses of fragrant white azalea flowers scent the air near the bench. In summer, foliage in a range of greens predominates, accented by white astilbe flowers and elegant lilies, whose sweet scent adds to the appeal of a visit to the bench.

Foliage carries the planting through fall, when white Japanese anemone flowers join the maroon leaves of bishop's hat and the red and yellow oak leaves in a colorful display. In winter, snow covers the dormant perennial ground covers and sets off the rich foliage of the yews.

Plants & Projects

For best results, thin the tree canopy, if necessary, to produce dappled rather than deep shade. Also remove limbs to a height of 8 ft. or more to provide headroom. Although the oak we've shown here has deeper roots than some shade trees, it still competes for moisture with nearby plants. Judicious supplemental watering and moisture-conserving mulch will help get plants started and improve their performance. (For more on planting under a shade tree, see pp. 116, 150, and 157.)

A **'Tauntonii' hybrid yew**
(use 3 plants)
These compact evergreen shrubs will fill out to form a solid mass behind the bench. They do well in heat and hold their color through the winter. See *Taxus × media*, p. 193.

B **'Everlow' hybrid yew** (use 2)
A wide-spreading, low-growing shrub with graceful, arching evergreen branches. Provides structure, backdrop, and contrast for the planting's perennial ground covers. See *Taxus × media*, p. 193.

C **'White Lights' azalea** (use 1)
Developed specially for northern climates, this deciduous shrub bears clusters of lovely, scented white flowers in late spring and attractive foliage through the growing season. See *Rhododendron*, p. 190.

D **'Sissinghurst White' lungwort** (use 18)
A perennial ground cover that has large leaves dappled with white spots. Clusters of small white flowers last for weeks in early spring. See *Pulmonaria saccharata*, p. 190.

E **Bishop's hat** (use 19)
The heart-shaped leaves of this perennial ground cover change from copper to green to maroon during the growing season. Bears tiny pink or white flowers in early spring. See *Epimedium grandiflorum*, p. 180.

F **Sweet woodruff** (use 16)
This perennial ground cover will spread quickly to form a bright green patch opposite the bench. Sprinkled with numerous tiny white flowers in May. See *Galium odoratum*, p. 181.

G **Foamflower** (use 33)
Another quick-spreading, low-growing perennial ground cover. In spring, little white flowers rise on short stalks above the dense mat of maple-like leaves. Foliage stays green through the winter. See *Tiarella cordifolia*, p. 195.

H **White bleeding heart** (use 3)
A woodland perennial forming mounds of lacy foliage. In May and June, tiny heart-shaped white flowers dangle from curving stalks. See *Dicentra spectabilis* 'Alba', p. 180.

I **White astilbe** (use 15)
The deeply divided leaves of this perennial contrast nicely with nearby foliage. Bears striking plumes of tiny white flowers in early summer. See *Astilbe × arendsii*, p. 174.

J **'Casablanca' lily** (use 12)
In late summer, tall leafy stalks of this perennial rise from among the anemones and bear clusters of large sweet-scented flowers. See *Lilium*, p. 187.

K **White Japanese anemone** (use 18)
This perennial enlivens the fall with white daisylike flowers borne on tall stalks above handsome mounds of large dark green leaves. See *Anemone japonica* 'Alba', p. 173.

L **Bench**
A comfortable bench is an ideal spot for enjoying the sights and smells of the planting.

M **Steppingstones**
A row of large, precast pavers (or flagstones) provides passage to the bench. See p. 118.

'Tauntonii' hybrid yew **A**

Sweet **F** woodruff

M Steppingstone

Foamflower **G**

Plant lilies **J** among the Japanese anemones **K**.

Lawn

1 square = 1 ft.

Site: Shady

Season: Spring

Concept: Woodland understory plants make an oasis beneath a mature shade tree.

H White bleeding heart

C 'White Lights' azalea

L Bench

B 'Everlow' hybrid yew

G Foamflower

Bishop's hat **E**

I White astilbe

B 'Everlow' hybrid yew

D 'Sissinghurst White' lungwort

See site plan for **J** **K** .

Plant portraits

These shade-loving perennials help create a soothing setting beneath a stately shade tree.

● = First design, pp. 84–85
▲ = Second design, pp. 86–87

White Japanese anemone
(*Anemone japonica* 'Alba', p. 173) ●

Bishop's hat
(*Epimedium grandiflorum*, p. 180) ●

Creeping phlox
(*Phlox stolonifera*, p. 190) ▲

'Francee' hosta
(*Hosta*, p. 184) ▲

'Sissinghurst White' lungwort
(*Pulmonaria saccharata*, p. 190) ●

Hosta haven

Spread beneath a venerable maple, this little garden showcases hostas. Few types of plants look as attractive or grow as well in shade as hostas do. And few offer the same variety. Leaves may be slender or broad, smooth or puckered, large as a serving platter or small as a teacup. Colors include light greens, dark greens, blue-greens, and yellow-greens; leaves may be edged, striped, or dappled with white, gold, or other greens.

These perennials also offer flowers in mid- to late summer. In some cultivars, the trumpet-shaped blossoms of lavender, purple, or white rival the leaves for interest—particularly when the flowers are scented.

Completing the planting is an edging of creeping phlox, a carefree ground cover that makes an attractive transition to the lawn. Three half-barrels planted with impatiens add additional color to the shade.

Plants & Projects

Ⓐ 'Francee' hosta (use 6 plants) This hosta forms a medium-size clump of heart-shaped dark green leaves with white edges. Bears lavender flowers. See *Hosta*, p. 184.

Ⓑ Gold-margined hosta (use 8) Large heart-shaped green leaves sport a wide edge that is gold in spring and turns creamy in summer. The flowers are lilac-colored. See *Hosta fortunei* 'Aureo-marginata', p. 184.

Ⓒ 'Gold Standard' hosta (use 10) These heart-shaped leaves change with the season, from pale green with dark green edges in spring to gold with light green edges in summer. The flowers are lavender. See *Hosta*, p. 184.

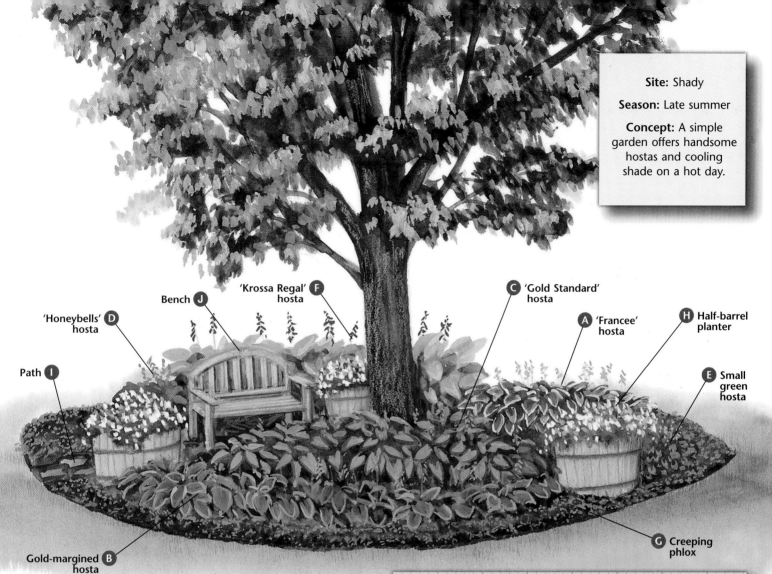

Site: Shady

Season: Late summer

Concept: A simple garden offers handsome hostas and cooling shade on a hot day.

'Krossa Regal' **F** hosta

Bench **J**

'Honeybells' **D** hosta

Path **I**

C 'Gold Standard' hosta

A 'Francee' hosta

H Half-barrel planter

E Small green hosta

G Creeping phlox

Gold-margined **B** hosta

D **'Honeybells' hosta** (use 7)
Robust and fast-growing, this large hosta has oblong pale green leaves. Its flowers are lilac-colored and scented. See *Hosta*, p. 184.

E **Small green hosta** (use 15)
The slender green leaves of this hosta form a low patch and contrast prettily with the larger-leaved cultivars nearby. See *Hosta lancifolia*, p. 184.

F **'Krossa Regal' hosta** (use 9)
Arching powder blue leaves form a tall erect clump. Lilac-colored flowers are borne well above the foliage on stiff stalks. See *Hosta,* p. 184.

G **Creeping phlox** (use 75)
The low, soft green foliage of this quickly spreading peren-

nial ground cover frames the hostas. Bears fragrant blue or white flowers in spring. See *Phlox stolonifera*, p. 190.

H **Half-barrel planters**
(use 6 plants per barrel)
Planted with shade-tolerant annuals, the barrels brighten the planting all summer long. Shown here are white annual impatiens; brightly colored impatiens are also available.

I **Path**
Flagstones of random shapes and sizes lead to the bench. You could pave a larger area in front of the bench to accommodate a table. See p. 118.

See p. 84 for the following:

J **Bench**

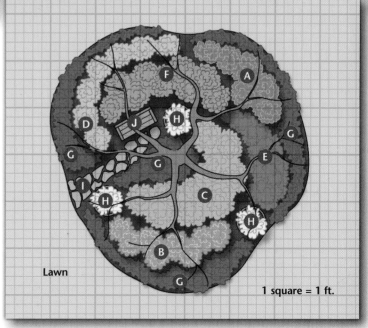

Lawn

1 square = 1 ft.

A Pleasant Passage

Reclaim a narrow side yard for a shade garden

Many residential lots include a slim strip of land between the house and a property line. Usually overlooked by everyone except children and dogs racing between the front yard and the back, this often shady corridor can become a valued addition to the landscape. In the design shown here, a selection of shrubs bordering a comfortable flagstone path makes a garden that invites adults, and even children, to linger as they stroll from one part of the property to another.

The wall of the house and a tall, opaque fence on the property line shade the space most of the day and give it a closed-in feeling, like a long empty hallway or a narrow room. The path and plantings create a cozy passage, and, like the furnishings of a room, they make a small space seem bigger than it is. A rose-covered arch flanked by tall, narrow junipers marks one entrance, while a pair of junipers alone frame the entrance at the other end. In between, evergreen and deciduous shrubs, vines, and ground covers delight the eye in all seasons with a mixture of foliage textures and colors, as well as weeks of flowers and bright berries. Lily-of-the-valley lines the path, and in spring its sweet-scented flowers perfume the entire passageway. In fall, the starry flowers of the sweet autumn clematis covering the fence perform the same service.

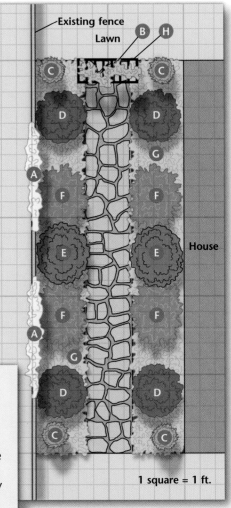

Site: Shady

Season: Early fall

Concept: Plants with colorful foliage of varying textures make an enticing stroll garden in a frequently neglected area.

1 square = 1 ft.

Plants & Projects

Flowers brighten the shade for many weeks of the growing season, but foliage is this planting's main attraction. To keep the foliage looking its best, keep pruning shears handy and snip off damaged or diseased growth as soon as you see it. In spring or fall, prune to control the size and shape of the clematis, rose, and Japanese holly. Every few years, cut the weigela to the ground; the new growth will look better than ever.

A Sweet autumn clematis
(use 2 plants)
This vigorous deciduous vine will cover the fence with small light green leaves on twining stems. In autumn the sweet fragrance of its starry white flowers wafts over the path. Attach lengths of polypropylene cord horizontally to the fence at 1-ft. intervals for the vines to climb on. See *Clematis terniflora*, p. 178.

B 'Zéphirine Drouhin' rose
(use 1)
An unusually shade-tolerant rose, ideal for a trellis in a partially shaded spot. Long, nearly thornless canes carry fragrant pink blooms from early summer to frost. See *Rosa*, p. 191.

C 'Skyrocket' juniper (use 4)
The blue-green foliage of these tall and very narrow evergreen shrubs handsomely frames the entrances at each end of the planting. See *Juniperus scopulorum*, p. 186.

D 'Hetzii' Japanese holly (use 4)
A compact evergreen shrub whose dense mass of small dark green leaves contrasts in form and texture with the nearby junipers. See *Ilex crenata*, p. 184.

E Compact cranberrybush viburnum (use 2)
A four-season performer, this deciduous shrub anchors the center of the planting with beautiful white flowers in May, lovely maplelike leaves that turn red in fall, and shiny red fruits that last through winter. See *Viburnum trilobum* 'Compactum', p. 195.

F Variegated weigela (use 4)
With cream-colored edges, the leaves of this deciduous shrub add a subtle touch to the passageway. Bears light pink flowers in early summer. See *Weigela florida*, p. 197.

G Lily-of-the-valley (use 100)
A perennial ground cover that forms a carpet of upright leaves. In spring, tiny white, bell-shaped, fragrant flowers dangle from slender stalks. Leaves turn a rich golden yellow mingled with green in fall. See *Convallaria majalis*, p. 179.

H Arched trellis
Well-made free-standing arched trellises of wrought iron, wire, or wood are available at most garden centers or through mail-order catalogs. Buy one wide enough to accommodate people walking side by side or pushing wheelbarrows.

I Flagstone path
Irregular flagstones set in a random pattern make a pleasantly informal path. Unobtrusive wooden edging contains the sand filling gaps between the flags. See p. 118.

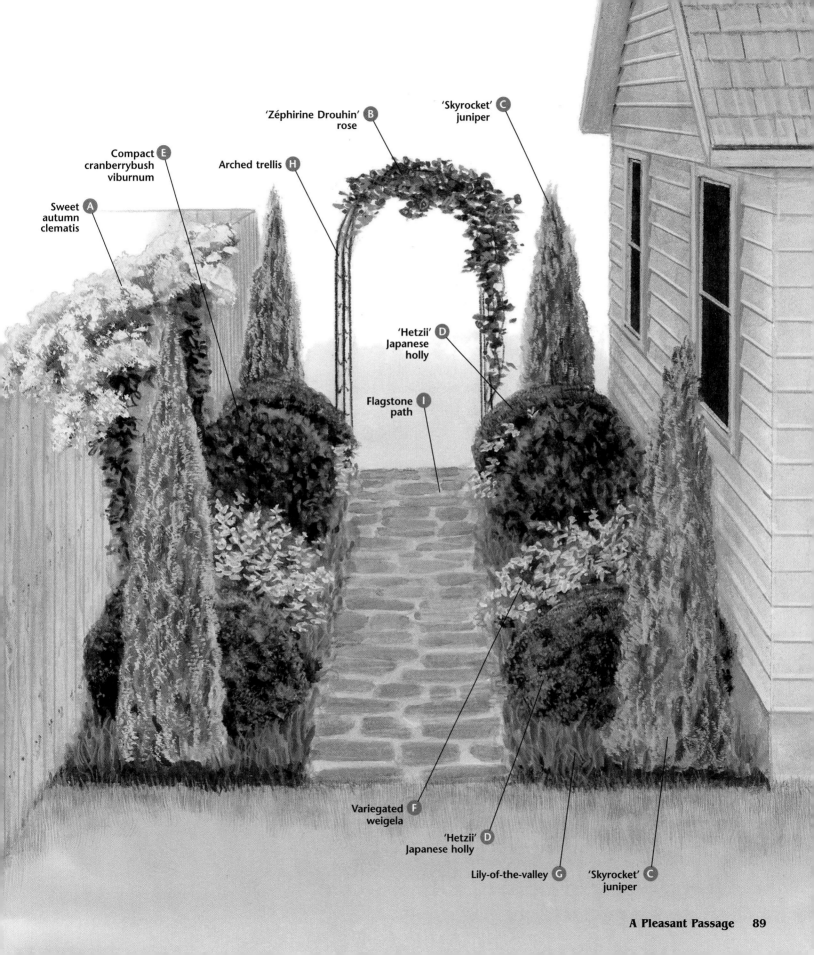

Sweet autumn clematis **A**

Compact cranberrybush viburnum **E**

'Zéphirine Drouhin' rose **B**

Arched trellis **H**

'Skyrocket' juniper **C**

'Hetzii' Japanese holly **D**

Flagstone path **I**

Variegated weigela **F**

'Hetzii' Japanese holly **D**

Lily-of-the-valley **G**

'Skyrocket' juniper **C**

Plant portraits

Understated plants for an overlooked spot; the subtle attractions of these plants will make your little side-yard stroll garden a favorite.

● = First design, pp. 88–89
▲ = Second design, pp. 90–91

'Hetzii' Japanese holly
(*Ilex crenata*, p. 184) ●

Toad lily
(*Tricyrtis hirta* 'Miyazaki', p. 195) ▲

Mountain laurel
(*Kalmia latifolia* 'Ostbo Red', p. 186) ▲

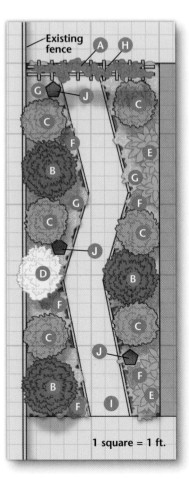

Dwarf Hinoki cypress
(*Chamaecyparis obtusa* 'Nana Gracilis', p. 177) ▲

Ostrich fern
(Ferns: *Matteuccia struthiopteris*, p. 181) ▲

Variegated weigela
(*Weigela florida* 'Variegata', p. 197) ●

Simpler pleasures

This side yard is narrow, but without a tall fence it is more open than the site on the previous pages. This design, inspired by the refined simplicity of Japanese gardens, provides privacy without screening out the surroundings entirely.

A tidy gravel path zigzags past groupings of dwarf Hinoki cypress, mountain laurels, chokeberries, and ferns, each offering a fine display of foliage color and texture as well as flowers in spring and early summer. Ruby red clematis flowers cover the wide, but shallow, entry arbor for months in summer.

Existing fence

1 square = 1 ft.

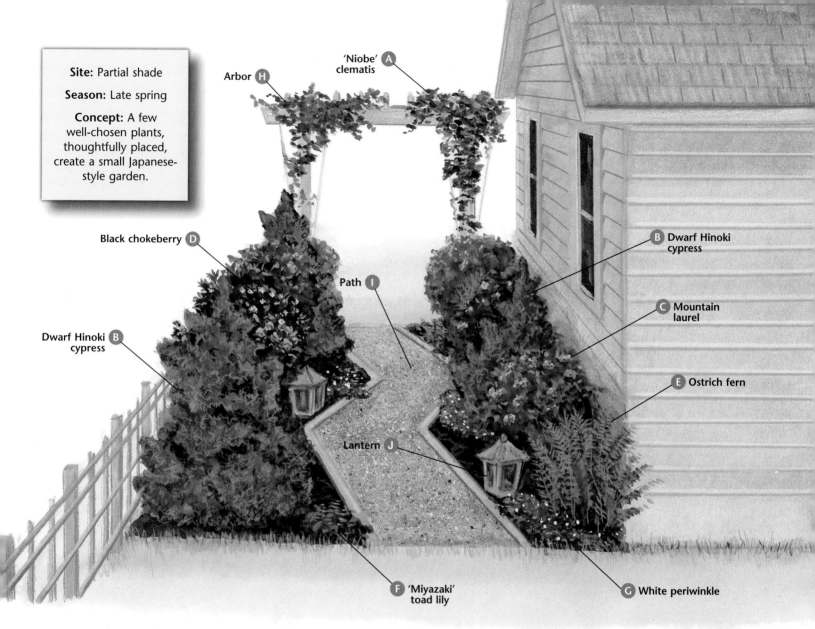

Site: Partial shade

Season: Late spring

Concept: A few well-chosen plants, thoughtfully placed, create a small Japanese-style garden.

'Niobe' clematis Ⓐ

Arbor Ⓗ

Black chokeberry Ⓓ

Dwarf Hinoki cypress Ⓑ

Path Ⓘ

Ⓑ Dwarf Hinoki cypress

Ⓒ Mountain laurel

Ⓔ Ostrich fern

Lantern Ⓙ

Ⓖ White periwinkle

Ⓕ 'Miyazaki' toad lily

Plants & Projects

Ⓐ 'Niobe' clematis (use 2 plants)
This graceful deciduous vine shows its ruby red flowers against a backdrop of dark green leaves for months in summer and early fall. Add coarse rope or cord to the arbor to help the vine climb. See *Clematis*, p. 177.

Ⓑ Dwarf Hinoki cypress (use 3)
Distinctive sprays of dense, shiny evergreen foliage give an interesting texture to this slow-growing pyramidal evergreen tree. See *Chamaecyparis obtusa* 'Nana Gracilis', p. 177.

Ⓒ Mountain laurel (use 6)
These lovely broad-leaved ever-

green shrubs bloom in late spring with clusters of small cup-shaped flowers. 'Ostbo Red', which is shown here, has striking dark red buds opening to deep pink flowers. See *Kalmia latifolia*, p. 186.

Ⓓ Black chokeberry (use 1)
This deciduous shrub offers clusters of white flowers in spring and dark blue berries in late summer. The shiny dark green leaves turn scarlet in fall. See *Aronia melanocarpa*, p. 173.

Ⓔ Ostrich fern (use 8)
A tall, upright fern whose clumps of deciduous bright green fronds make a lush dis-

play between the nearby mountain laurels. See Ferns: *Matteuccia struthiopteris*, p. 181.

Ⓕ 'Miyazaki' toad lily (use 5)
A perennial woodland wildflower forming clumps of arching stems and lance-shaped leaves. Bears orchidlike white flowers for weeks in fall. If it is unavailable, use 5 Japanese anemones instead. See *Tricyrtis hirta*, p. 195.

Ⓖ White periwinkle (use 100)
Planted between the shrubs and next to the path, this durable evergreen ground cover has shiny dark green leaves dotted in late spring with

white flowers. See *Vinca minor* 'Alba', p. 197.

Ⓗ Arbor
This shallow arbor marks the entrance to the planting. Can be built easily in an afternoon. See p. 145.

Ⓘ Path
Made of gravel or crushed rock, this is a durable path. When neatly raked, it reinforces the Japanese "feel" of the design. See p. 118.

Ⓙ Lanterns
Two or three small Japanese-style lanterns or similar ornaments add interest to a stroll along the path.

Down to Earth

Harmonize your deck with its surroundings

A second-story deck is a perfect spot for enjoying your garden and yard. Too often, however, the view of the deck from the yard is less pleasing. Perched atop skinny posts, towering over a patch of lawn, an elevated deck frequently looks out of place, like an ungainly visitor uncomfortable in its surroundings.

In the design shown here, attractive landscaping brings the deck, house, and yard into balance. Combined with a simple homemade lattice skirting attached to the posts, plants form a broad pedestal of visual support for the deck. Decreasing in height from the deck to the yard, the planting makes it easier for our eyes to move between the levels.

The planting is as pretty as it is functional. Anchoring one side, at the corners of house and deck, are a lilac and a viburnum, whose scented flowers sweeten the springtime air. On the other side, tall ornamental grasses sway and rustle in the breeze, their clouds of pinkish flowers greeting viewers looking down from the deck. On the lattice (and the deck railing if you wish), fragrant roses bloom from early summer, joined in late August by scented clematis flowers.

Completing the planting, perennials provide bursts of summer color and low-growing junipers form a rough-textured "throw rug" at the base of deck and house, tying the taller elements of the design together. Grass paths lead to the enclosed area beneath the deck. Cover the ground there with crushed stone and use the space to store garden tools or bicycles.

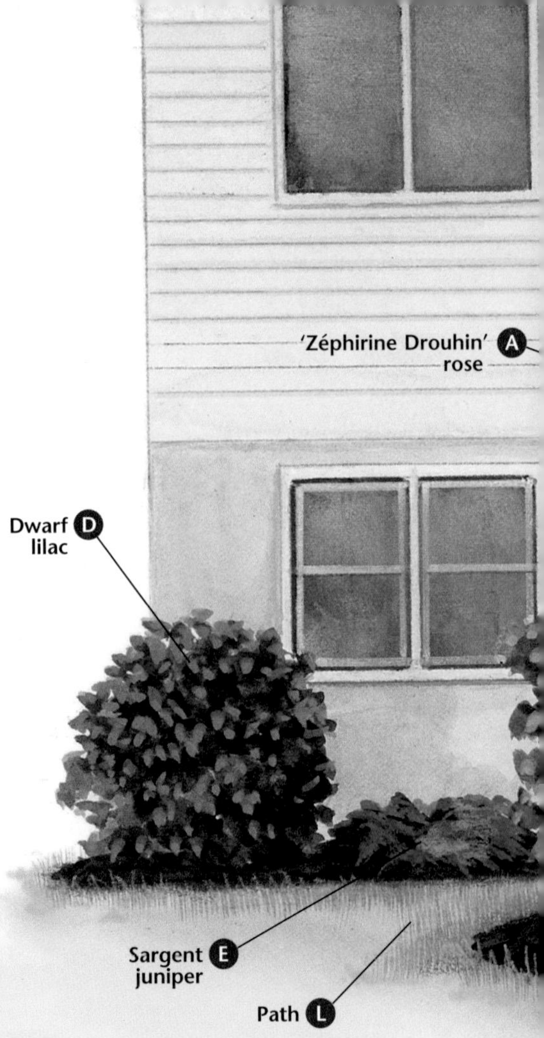

Site: Sunny

Season: Summer

Concept: A pleasing mix of shrubs, perennials, and grasses leads the eye comfortably from ground to deck.

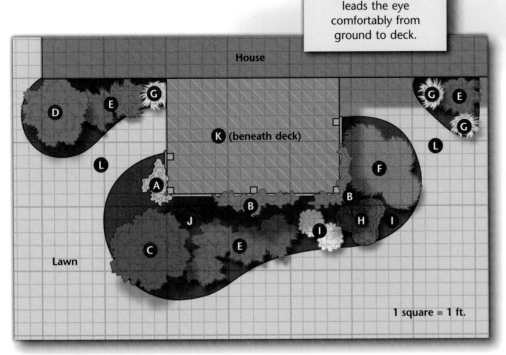

'Zéphirine Drouhin' rose **A**

Dwarf lilac **D**

Sargent juniper **E**

Path **L**

House

K (beneath deck)

Lawn

1 square = 1 ft.

Plants & Projects

The shrubs, rose, and clematis will take a few years to fill out, during which time you can fill in the open spaces with low-growing annuals. (See p. 154 for more on this maturing process.) Once established, the planting requires only seasonal pruning and cleanup.

A **'Zéphirine Drouhin' rose**
(use 1 plant)
This deciduous climber covers its portion of the lattice with long, nearly thornless canes; shiny green leaves; and fragrant rose-pink flowers that bloom from early summer to frost. See *Rosa*, p. 191.

B **Sweet autumn clematis** (use 2)
This twining deciduous vine will clothe the lattice and deck railing with its small light green leaves. Starry white flowers fill the air with their sweet scent in August and September. See *Clematis terniflora*, p. 178.

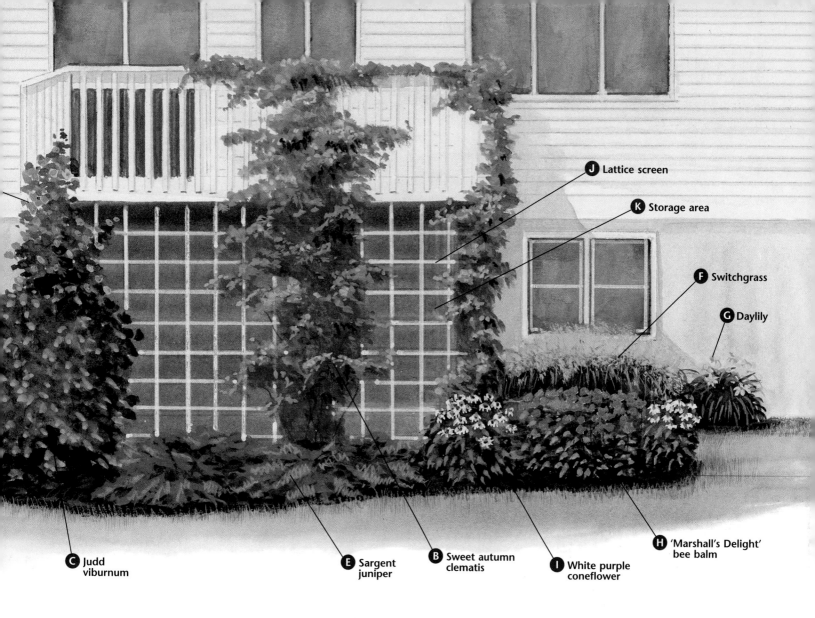

J Lattice screen

K Storage area

F Switchgrass

G Daylily

C Judd viburnum

E Sargent juniper

B Sweet autumn clematis

I White purple coneflower

H 'Marshall's Delight' bee balm

C Judd viburnum (use 1)
This large deciduous shrub helps broaden the visual base of the deck. Its dark green leaves are an ideal backdrop to the spicy-scented white flowers that appear in May. See *Viburnum × juddii*, p. 195.

D Dwarf lilac (use 1)
Forming a bushy clump at the corner of the house, this deciduous shrub bears fragrant lilac flowers in May and offers purple fall foliage. See *Syringa meyeri* 'Palibin', p. 193.

E Sargent juniper (use 7)
This low-growing, spreading evergreen shrub provides year-round color and texture to the planting. See *Juniperus chinensis* var. *sargentii*, p. 186.

F Switchgrass (use 4)
A native perennial grass that forms graceful upright clumps of narrow leaves topped in late summer by a pinkish cloud of flowers.

Foliage turns from bright green in summer to gold in autumn and tan in winter. See *Panicum virgatum*, p. 189.

G Daylily (use 3)
Choose from this dependable perennial's nearly limitless variety of flower colors. All have long, grasslike leaves that are attractive after the flowers have finished. Shown here is 'Hyperion', which bears scented pale yellow flowers in July. See *Hemerocallis*, p. 183.

H 'Marshall's Delight' bee balm (use 3)
This perennial forms clumps of mintlike foliage topped in July and August with big, globe-shaped, pink flowers that may attract hummingbirds and butterflies to the deck area. See *Monarda*, p. 189.

I White purple coneflower (use 3)
Use a white-flowered cultivar of this native prairie perennial. Flowers are carried on

sturdy stalks above large clumps of coarse green leaves. Blooms in July and August; dry seed heads provide winter interest and food for birds. See *Echinacea purpurea*, p. 180.

J Lattice screen
Easy to make and attach to the deck posts, this lattice dresses up the deck and provides support for the clematis vines and rose canes. Stain to match your house, or let the natural wood weather. See p. 146.

K Storage area
For a durable tidy surface, cover the ground beneath the deck with 2 in. of crushed stone. Use a wooden edging to keep the stone out of the surrounding beds.

L Path
Access to the storage area can be a strip of lawn, as shown here. Install a crushed-stone surface (see p. 118) if traffic is too heavy for a grass path.

Plant portraits

Combining flowers, foliage, and form, these plants help integrate a tall deck with its surroundings.

● = First design, pp. 92–93
▲ = Second design, pp. 94–95

Sweet autumn clematis
(*Clematis terniflora*, p. 178) ●

Arrowwood viburnum
(*Viburnum dentatum*, p. 195) ▲

'Zéphirine Drouhin' rose
(*Rosa*, p. 191) ●

Marginal wood fern
(Ferns: *Dryopteris marginalis*, p. 181) ▲

Switchgrass
(*Panicum virgatum*, p. 189) ●

White purple coneflower
(*Echinacea purpurea*, p. 180) ●

Skirting a shady deck

Like the design on the previous pages, this one integrates the deck with its surroundings but does so in a shady environment. This design looks similar to the previous one, but its shade-tolerant plants reflect the altered conditions.

The color scheme is white and green, with just a dash of pink. Spring and early summer is white, with viburnums, hydrangea, and goatsbeard providing the flowers and some lovely fragrances. Astilbes provide the pink in midsummer, followed by white hostas, whose sweet scent cheers late summer's dog days. Deciduous and evergreen foliage in a range of greens is on view all year.

Plants & Projects

A **Dutchman's pipe** (use 1 plant) This vigorous deciduous vine will soon cover the trellis with large heart-shaped leaves. It bears pipe-shaped flowers in early summer. See *Aristolochia durior,* p. 173.

B **Arrowwood viburnum** (use 1) A carefree shrub with white flowers in June and blue berries in fall. The glossy deciduous leaves turn rich maroon in fall. See *Viburnum dentatum*, p. 195.

C **Compact Korean spice viburnum** (use 1) This deciduous shrub nicely complements its larger-size "cousin" by the deck. It bears clusters of spicy-scented white flowers in midspring and attractive leaves through summer and fall. See *Viburnum carlesii* 'Compactum', p. 195.

D **'Annabelle' hydrangea** (use 1) A deciduous shrub with large leaves and much larger clusters

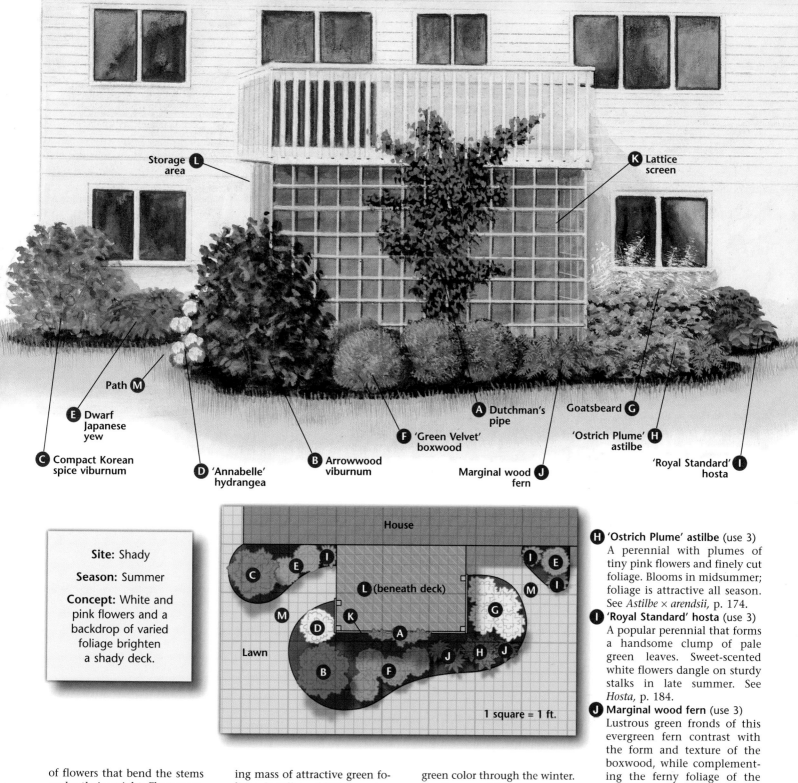

Storage area **L**

K Lattice screen

Path **M**

E Dwarf Japanese yew

C Compact Korean spice viburnum

D 'Annabelle' hydrangea

B Arrowwood viburnum

F 'Green Velvet' boxwood

A Dutchman's pipe

Goatsbeard **G**

'Ostrich Plume' **H** astilbe

Marginal wood **J** fern

'Royal Standard' **I** hosta

Site: Shady

Season: Summer

Concept: White and pink flowers and a backdrop of varied foliage brighten a shady deck.

House

C

E **I**

L (beneath deck)

M

D **K**

A

B

F

J **H** **J**

I **E**

M

G

Lawn

1 square = 1 ft.

---

of flowers that bend the stems under their weight. Flowers are white in early summer, changing to green in summer and then to beige by autumn. See *Hydrangea arborescens*, p. 184.

E Dwarf Japanese yew (use 3)
This slow-growing evergreen shrub forms a compact spread-ing mass of attractive green foliage. It will need little pruning to keep it within bounds. See *Taxus cuspidata* 'Nana', p. 193.

F 'Green Velvet' boxwood (use 4)
An elegant evergreen shrub with a naturally rounded form. The tiny leaves hold their rich green color through the winter. See *Buxus*, p. 176.

G Goatsbeard (use 4)
Large, airy plumes made up of many small creamy flowers rise above this perennial's lacy green foliage in June. A striking sight from the ground or deck. See *Aruncus dioicus*, p. 174.

H 'Ostrich Plume' astilbe (use 3)
A perennial with plumes of tiny pink flowers and finely cut foliage. Blooms in midsummer; foliage is attractive all season. See *Astilbe × arendsii*, p. 174.

I 'Royal Standard' hosta (use 3)
A popular perennial that forms a handsome clump of pale green leaves. Sweet-scented white flowers dangle on sturdy stalks in late summer. See *Hosta*, p. 184.

J Marginal wood fern (use 3)
Lustrous green fronds of this evergreen fern contrast with the form and texture of the boxwood, while complementing the ferny foliage of the astilbe. See Ferns: *Dryopteris marginalis*, p. 181.

See p. 93 for the following:

K Lattice screen

L Storage area

M Path

A Woodland Link
Create a shrub border for nearby woods

The woodlands of the Midwest are treasured by all who live in the region. Subdivisions, both new and old, incorporate woodland areas, with homes bordering landscapes of stately trees and large shrubs. And in some older neighborhoods, mature trees on adjacent lots create almost the same woodland feeling.

The planting shown here integrates a domestic landscape with a woodland at its edge. It makes a pleasant transition between the open area of lawn and the woods beyond. The design takes inspiration from the buffer zone of small trees and shrubs nature provides at the sunny edge of a wood, and it should have the same attraction to wildlife (and to the people who enjoy them) as its natural counterpart does.

Shrubs of various sizes mingle in the planting, larger ones toward the back, imitating natural layered growth. A small tree anchors one corner, its height echoing the taller trees in the woods behind. A path winds through the planting, and a bench offers a spot to enjoy the surroundings.

Whether viewed up close or from across the yard, the planting is appealing all year. Golden rhododendron flowers glow among bright red dogwood stems and the light greens of emerging leaves in the spring. Spireas and potentilla follow in summer with masses of pink, crimson, and yellow flowers. In fall, foliage in red, gold, and maroon catches the eye. In winter, a tracery of bare stems becomes an impromptu sculpture garden when the first snow falls.

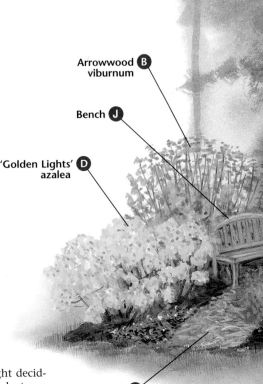

Arrowwood viburnum **B**

Bench **J**

'Golden Lights' azalea **D**

Path **K**

Plants & Projects

Dig and improve the soil throughout the entire area (except under the path) before planting. These plants will need little care after the first year or so. A deep mulch of shredded leaves and wood chips and regular watering the first summer will speed establishment. Cut back the dogwoods every few years to promote growth of bright red twigs, and trim any dead or damaged stems off the other shrubs.

A **Witch hazel** (use 1 plant)
Unusual, sweet-scented, spidery yellow flowers appear on this small multitrunked deciduous tree in late fall when the then-golden leaves are falling. See *Hamamelis virginiana*, p. 182.

B **Arrowwood viburnum** (use 1)
A deciduous shrub with erect, arrow-straight stems bearing white flowers in June that stand out against glossy dark green leaves. In fall, blue berries appear and the leaves turn maroon. See *Viburnum dentatum*, p. 195.

C **Red-twig dogwood** (use 5)
This deciduous shrub's vigorous stems are bright scarlet in winter. Creamy white flowers in May are followed by berries that attract birds in fall. Dark green summer foliage turns crimson in autumn. See *Cornus sericea*, p. 179.

D **'Golden Lights' azalea** (use 6)
In late spring, this hardy deciduous shrub's large clusters of fragrant yellow flowers reward a stroll along the path. Foliage is attractive the rest of the season. See *Rhododendron*, p. 190.

E **'Anthony Waterer' spirea** (use 3)
A compact deciduous shrub, slightly wider than tall, whose form contrasts nicely with that of the upright dogwoods behind. Small dark green leaves are covered by dark pink flowers in midsummer. See *Spiraea* × *bumalda*, p. 193.

F **Winterberry holly** (use 3)
Bunches of bright red berries shine through the fall and into winter after this upright deciduous shrub drops its lustrous dark green leaves. The bench is a fine perch for watching the robins and cedar waxwings the berries attract. Plant two female cultivars and one male to ensure a crop of berries. See *Ilex verticillata*, p. 184.

G **'Primrose Beauty' potentilla** (use 5)
This fast-growing deciduous shrub is a beauty, with its airy texture, light green leaves, and creamy yellow flowers that bloom all summer and complement the golden foliage of the nearby spirea. See *Potentilla fruticosa*, p. 190.

H **'Goldflame' spirea** (use 5)
Similar in size and form to its "cousin" across the path, this deciduous shrub has eye-catching foliage that changes from gold to chartreuse to orange-red through the growing season. Bears crimson flowers on and off all summer. See *Spiraea* × *bumalda*, p. 193.

I **Ground covers** (use 1 per square foot)
Carpet the open spaces in the planting with low-growing perennials. Periwinkle (see *Vinca minor*, p. 197) forms a mat of evergreen leaves dotted in late spring with lavender-blue flowers. Plant sweet violet (see *Viola odorata*, p. 197) near the bench to enjoy the fragrant purple flowers in spring. Use sweet woodruff (see *Galium odoratum*, p. 181), with its fine-textured foliage and tiny white spring flowers, near the path.

J **Bench**
Nestled among shrubs, a bench provides a comfortable spot to enjoy the planting.

K **Path**
A deep carpet of wood chips makes an ideal woodland path. See p. 118.

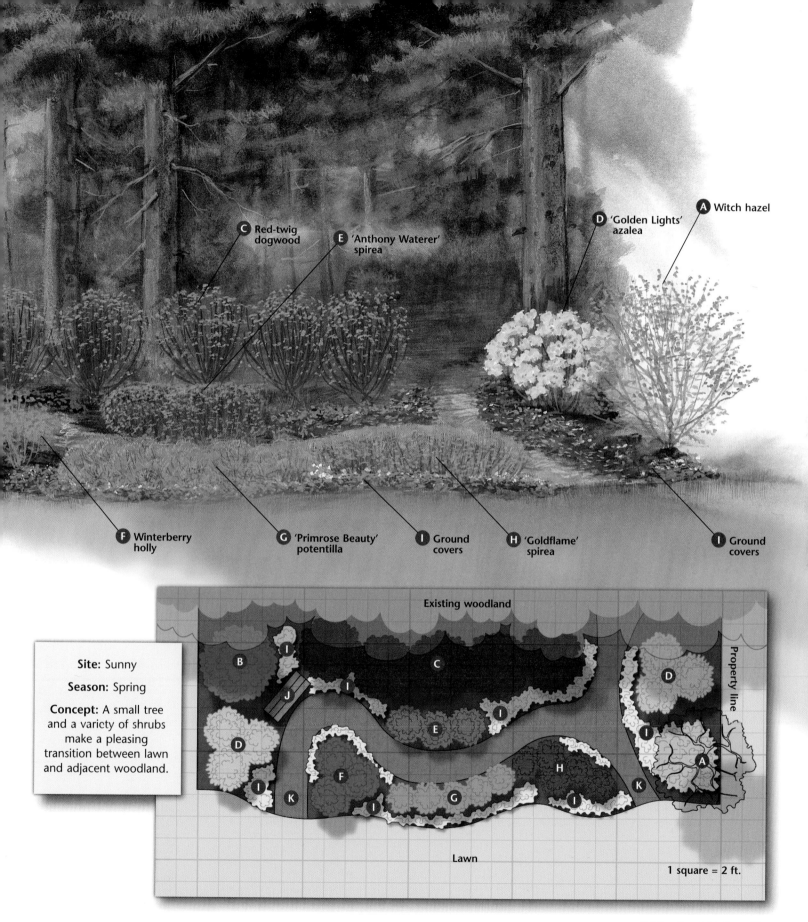

C Red-twig dogwood

E 'Anthony Waterer' spirea

D 'Golden Lights' azalea

A Witch hazel

F Winterberry holly

G 'Primrose Beauty' potentilla

I Ground covers

H 'Goldflame' spirea

I Ground covers

Existing woodland

Property line

Site: Sunny

Season: Spring

Concept: A small tree and a variety of shrubs make a pleasing transition between lawn and adjacent woodland.

Lawn

1 square = 2 ft.

Evergreens for shade

An evergreen border is ideal for the shadier conditions at the edge of a deciduous woodland. Mature oaks and other large trees create a greater shade canopy than erect pines, and their bare winter limbs contrast pleasantly with the snow-sculpted forms of evergreens at their feet.

The layout of the planting bed is similar to that of the previous design, including the same meandering path for up-close enjoyment. These trees and shrubs provide a pleasing range of forms and textures, and a subtle display of greens throughout the year. Striking red azalea flowers, the gold foliage of the arborvitae, and a sprinkling of white flowers on the ground covers accent the spring scene. The planting is a cool, green haven in the summer and fall. In winter (shown here), this will be the most colorful part of the landscape.

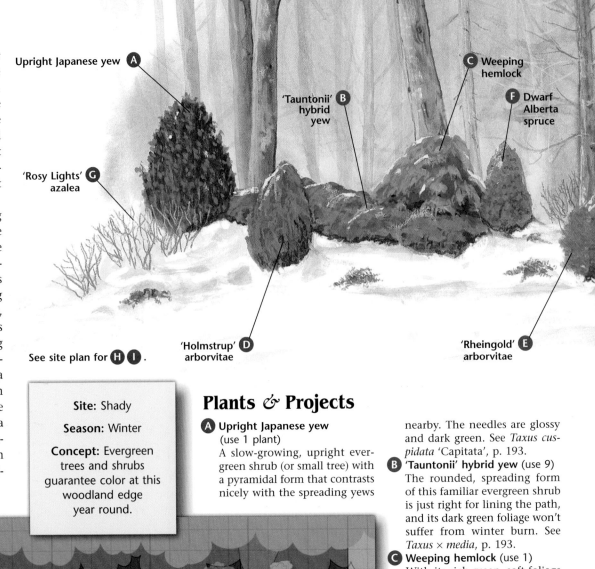

Upright Japanese yew **A**

'Rosy Lights' azalea **G**

See site plan for **H** **I** .

C Weeping hemlock

'Tauntonii' hybrid yew **B**

F Dwarf Alberta spruce

'Holmstrup' arborvitae **D**

'Rheingold' **E** arborvitae

Site: Shady

Season: Winter

Concept: Evergreen trees and shrubs guarantee color at this woodland edge year round.

Plants & Projects

A **Upright Japanese yew**
(use 1 plant)
A slow-growing, upright evergreen shrub (or small tree) with a pyramidal form that contrasts nicely with the spreading yews nearby. The needles are glossy and dark green. See *Taxus cuspidata* 'Capitata', p. 193.

B **'Tauntonii' hybrid yew** (use 9)
The rounded, spreading form of this familiar evergreen shrub is just right for lining the path, and its dark green foliage won't suffer from winter burn. See *Taxus × media*, p. 193.

C **Weeping hemlock** (use 1)
With its rich green, soft foliage and interesting mounded form, this evergreen tree makes a good centerpiece for the planting. See *Tsuga canadensis* var. *sargentii*, p. 195.

D **'Holmstrup' arborvitae** (use 1)
This small evergreen tree marks a sharp bend in the path with rich green foliage and a compact, conical shape. See *Thuja occidentalis*, p. 194.

E **'Rheingold' arborvitae** (use 2)
The rounded profile of this bushy evergreen mirrors the path's gentler bend. Soft-textured foliage is golden yellow in summer, bronze in winter. See *Thuja occidentalis*, p. 194.

Existing woodland

Property line

Lawn

1 square = 2 ft.

E 'Rheingold'
arborvitae

B 'Tauntonii'
hybrid yew

Plant portraits

This selection of trees, shrubs, and ground covers will enhance any woodland setting.

● = First design, pp. 96–97
▲ = Second design, pp. 98–99

Witch hazel
(*Hamamelis virginiana*, p. 182) ●

Goutweed
(*Aegopodium podagraria* 'Variegatum', p. 172) ▲

Sweet violet
(*Viola odorata*, p. 197) ●

F **Dwarf Alberta spruce** (use 1)
The very neat, symmetrical shape and pale green foliage of this small evergreen tree are a striking contrast to the weeping hemlock. See *Picea glauca* 'Conica', p. 190.

G **'Rosy Lights' azalea** (use 6)
The fragrant rosy red flowers of this hardy deciduous shrub add color to the planting in spring. See *Rhododendron*, p. 190.

H **Ground covers**
(use 1 per square foot)
Plant ground covers between shrubs and near the path. Goutweed (see *Aegopodium podagraria* 'Variegatum', p. 172) has green-and-white foliage and bears white flowers in early summer. Marginal wood fern (see Ferns: *Dryopteris marginalis*, p. 181) has evergreen fronds. Plant lily-of-the-valley (see *Convallaria majalis*, p. 179) by the path for its fragrant white spring flowers.

See p. 96 for the following:

I **Path**

Weeping hemlock
(*Tsuga canadensis* var. *sargentii*, p. 195) ▲

Red-twig dogwood
(*Cornus sericea*, p. 179) ●

Upright Japanese yew
(*Taxus cuspidata* 'Capitata', p. 193) ▲

Gateway Garden

Striking structure and plantings make a handsome entry

Entrances are an important part of any landscape. They can welcome visitors onto your property; highlight a special feature, such as a rose garden; or mark passage between two areas with different character or function.

The design shown here can serve in any of these situations. A low board fence and massed shrubs and perennials create a friendly, attractive barrier that can signal the confines of the front yard or contain the family dog. Draped with vines, the gabled latticework arbor is an evocative, welcoming entryway.

There are flowers from early summer to frost, set off by the colorful foliage of evergreen and deciduous shrubs. The design is subtly, almost playfully, symmetrical. Only by viewing from each side of the fence can you "discover" the symmetry.

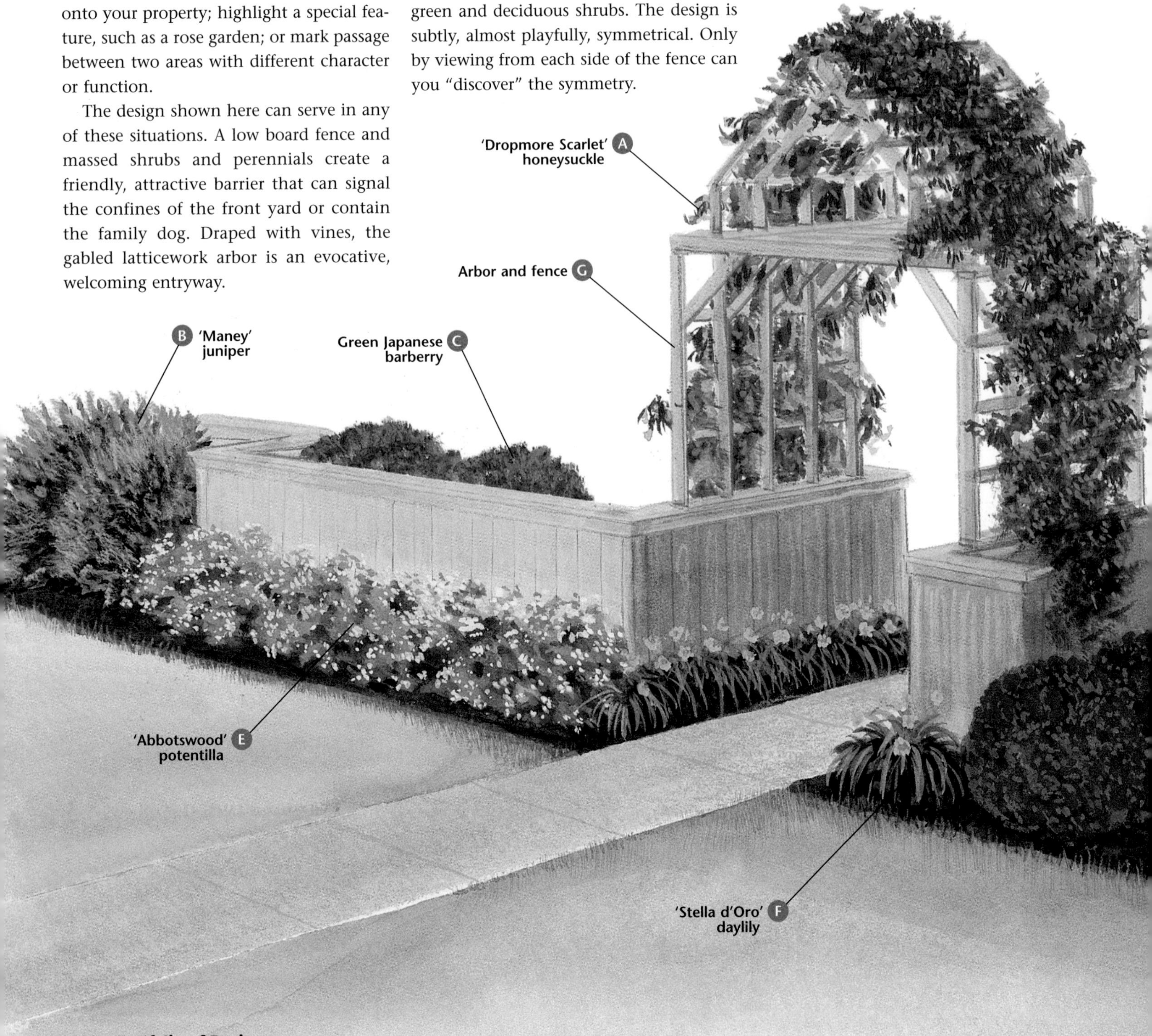

'Dropmore Scarlet' honeysuckle **A**

Arbor and fence **G**

B 'Maney' juniper

Green Japanese barberry **C**

'Abbotswood' potentilla **E**

'Stella d'Oro' daylily **F**

Plants & Projects

This design requires a number of weekends of concentrated work to install. Once established, however, the plants are not demanding. In addition to routine seasonal cleanup, you'll just need to trim the junipers and the green Japanese barberry to maintain their height and shape.

(A) 'Dropmore Scarlet' honeysuckle (use 4 plants)
Red-orange flowers (hummingbird favorites) cover this deciduous vine from June until frost. A vigorous plant, it should clamber over most of the latticework in two to three years. See *Lonicera × brownii*, p. 188.

(B) 'Maney' juniper (use 4)
These evergreen shrubs add silvery blue winter color at the ends of the planting. Trim them to the height of the fence, but give them a "natural" rather than a sheared, geometric look. See *Juniperus chinensis*, p. 186.

(C) Green Japanese barberry (use 3)
A reliable deciduous shrub with small green leaves that turn bright red in autumn. Red berries decorate the thorny stems in winter. Keep the plants trimmed to neat mounds. See *Berberis thunbergii*, p. 175.

(D) 'Crimson Pygmy' Japanese barberry (use 18)
A smaller, naturally rounded version of the previous shrub whose leaves are purple in summer and crimson in fall. See *Berberis thunbergii*, p. 175.

(E) 'Abbotswood' potentilla (use 12)
These compact deciduous shrubs require little trimming to form a tidy "natural" hedge. Snow-white flowers stand out against the dark green leaves for much of the summer. See *Potentilla fruticosa*, p. 190.

(F) 'Stella d'Oro' daylily (use 20)
This durable, carefree perennial bears golden yellow flowers from June to October. Its grassy foliage makes a neat edging. See *Hemerocallis*, p. 183.

(G) Arbor and fence
Imaginatively assembled from simple elements, this arbor and board fence are well suited to a relatively large site. See p. 146.

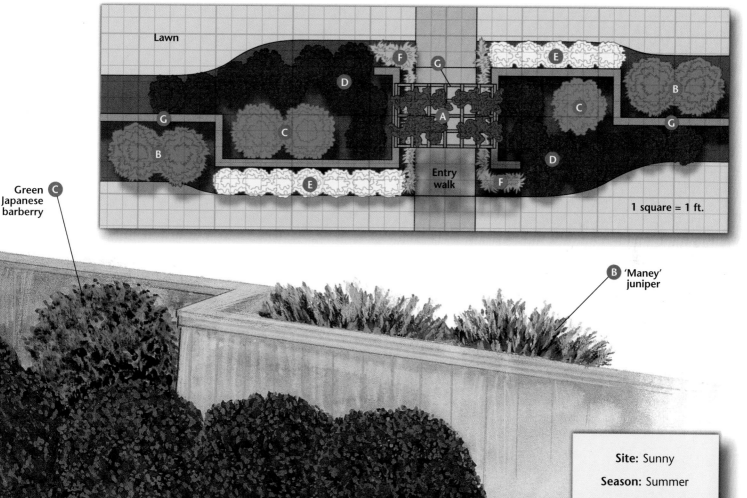

Green Japanese barberry **C**

'Crimson Pygmy' **D** Japanese barberry

B 'Maney' juniper

Site: Sunny

Season: Summer

Concept: Flowers, foliage, and a distinctive arbor and fence make an enticing entryway.

Arbor oasis

Not every situation calls for a fenced enclosure. In this simpler design, a rose-covered arbor is flanked by two mixed plantings of shrubs and perennials. The result is an entrance with the feel of an oasis or island.

Anchored by the large evergreen junipers, long-blooming plants brighten the entry for much of the summer. Fragrant double pink roses encourage lingering beneath the arbor, while pale yellow yarrow, bright gold daylilies, and pink spireas all invite a stroll around the planting beds.

Site: Sunny

Season: Summer

Concept: A rose-bedecked entry arbor is the centerpiece of this island garden.

Plants & Projects

Ⓐ 'William Baffin' climbing rose (use 4 plants)
Starting in early summer and repeating into fall, this climbing rose produces fragrant, double, clear pink flowers on canes that grow 8 to 10 ft. tall. Keep tying them to the arbor to train them up and over it. See *Rosa*, p. 191.

Ⓑ 'Little Princess' spirea (use 17)
The fine-textured deep green foliage, pink flowers, and compact form of this low-growing deciduous shrub create a lovely informal hedge that outlines much of the planting. Blooms in June and July. See *Spiraea japonica*, p. 193.

Ⓒ 'Sea Green' juniper (use 3)
This broad evergreen shrub has arching branches of dark green foliage that add mass to the planting and provide color through the winter. See *Juniperus chinensis*, p. 186.

Ⓓ 'Moonshine' yarrow (use 11)
Flat heads of tightly clustered tiny yellow flowers stand on stiff stems above aromatic gray-green foliage. A contrast in texture and color to the nearby junipers. See *Achillea*, p. 172.

See p. 101 for the following:

Ⓔ 'Stella d'Oro' daylily (use 34)

Ⓕ Arbor

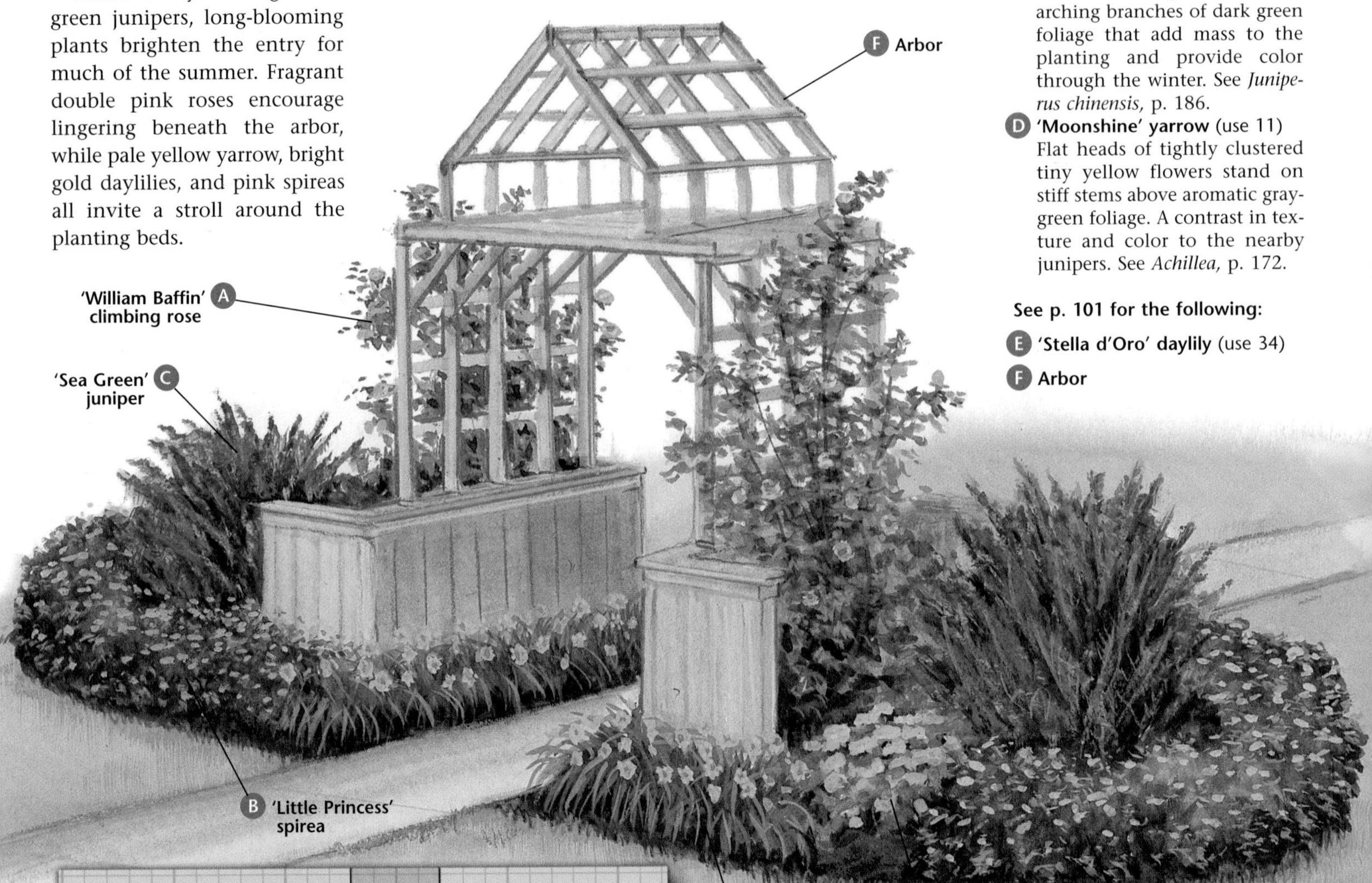

Ⓕ Arbor

'William Baffin' Ⓐ climbing rose

'Sea Green' Ⓒ juniper

Ⓑ 'Little Princess' spirea

Ⓔ 'Stella d'Oro' daylily

Ⓓ 'Moonshine' yarrow

Ⓑ 'Little Princess' spirea

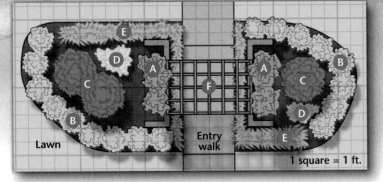

Lawn

Entry walk

1 square = 1 ft.

Plant portraits

Clambering over its lattice frame or spread at its feet, these plants bring an entry arch to life.

● = First design, pp. 100–101
▲ = Second design, p. 102

Green Japanese barberry
(*Berberis thunbergii*, p. 175) ●

'Abbotswood' potentilla
(*Potentilla fruticosa*, p. 190) ●

'Stella d'Oro' daylily
(*Hemerocallis*, p. 183) ● ▲

'Maney' juniper
(*Juniperus chinensis*, p. 186) ●

'William Baffin' climbing rose
(*Rosa*, p. 191) ▲

'Little Princess' spirea
(*Spiraea japonica*, p. 193) ▲

A Pleasing Postal Planting

Provide a perennial setting for the daily mail

For some, the lowly mailbox may seem a surprising candidate for landscaping. But posted like a sentry by the driveway entrance, the mailbox is highly visible to visitors and passersby. And it is one of the few places on your property that you visit nearly every day. A simple, handsome planting like the one shown here pleases the passing public and rewards your daily postal journey, as well as that of your friendly letter carrier.

Plantings around mailboxes too often suffer from timidity—too few plants in too little space. This design makes a bold display, covering a good-size area with color for many months. The long-blooming perennials here are all well suited to the hot, sunny, and often dry conditions that prevail by most streetside mailboxes.

Summer, shown here, is abloom from beginning to end, as both the catmint and salvia will produce flowers from June into fall. The feather reed grass and sedum are at their most striking in late summer and fall. The sedum flowers mature to a rich russet color that beautifully complements the tawny foliage of the feather reed grass. In winter, when the perennials are covered with snow, the graceful dried leaves and seed heads of the grass continue to enhance the daily mail run.

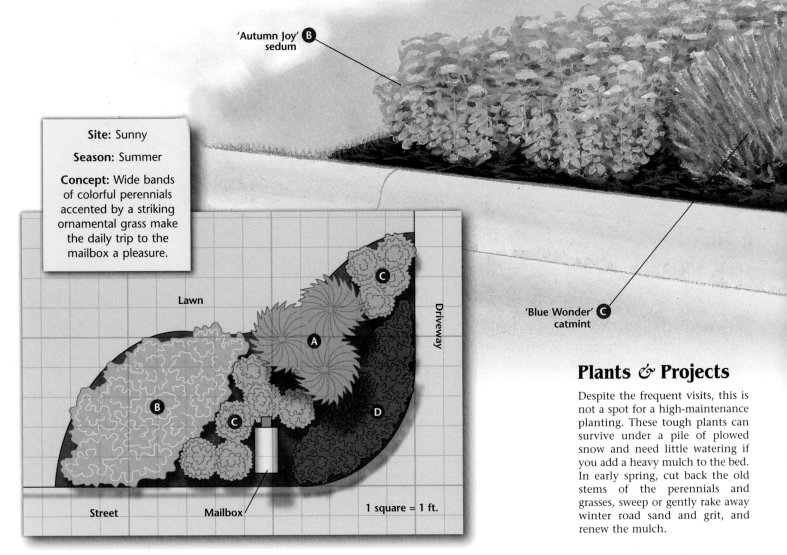

Site: Sunny

Season: Summer

Concept: Wide bands of colorful perennials accented by a striking ornamental grass make the daily trip to the mailbox a pleasure.

'Autumn Joy' sedum B

'Blue Wonder' catmint C

Lawn

Driveway

A

B

C

D

Street

Mailbox

1 square = 1 ft.

Plants & Projects

Despite the frequent visits, this is not a spot for a high-maintenance planting. These tough plants can survive under a pile of plowed snow and need little watering if you add a heavy mulch to the bed. In early spring, cut back the old stems of the perennials and grasses, sweep or gently rake away winter road sand and grit, and renew the mulch.

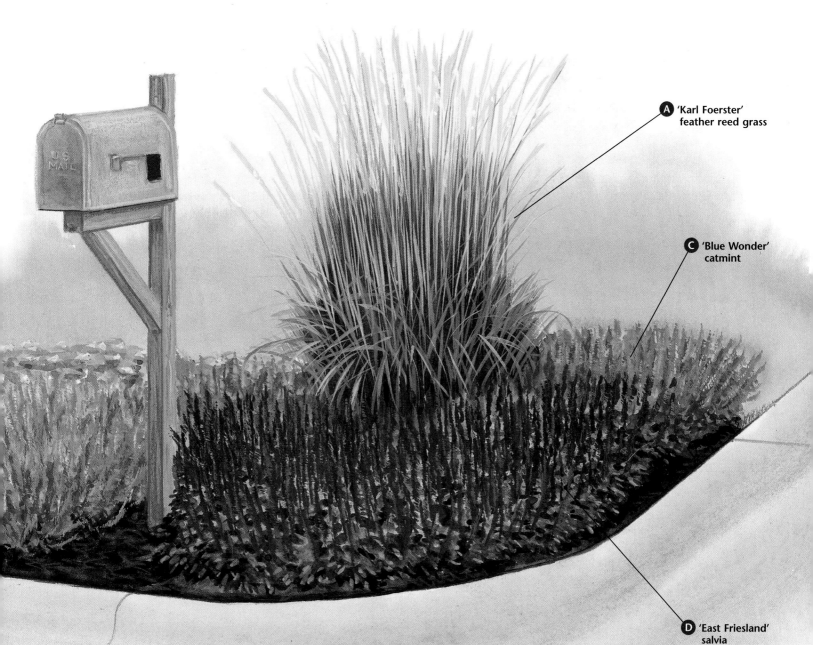

A 'Karl Foerster' feather reed grass

C 'Blue Wonder' catmint

 D 'East Friesland' salvia

A 'Karl Foerster' feather reed grass (use 3 plants)
A perennial grass forming upright clumps of graceful foliage. Thin stalks topped by narrow spikes of tiny flowers rise high above the foliage in midsummer. Leaves and flowers turn from green to beige or tan as they mature and dry, and they make a fine winter display that stands up well under light snow cover. See *Calamagrostis × acutiflora,* p. 176.

B 'Autumn Joy' sedum (use 12)
This perennial's thick, fleshy, gray-green leaves contrast with the slender grass and loose spikes of catmint. Flat-topped flower clusters put on a long show of color, maturing from white in late summer through pink to russet red in the autumn. See *Sedum,* p. 193.

C 'Blue Wonder' catmint (use 10)
Spikes of small violet-blue flowers appear above the handsome silvery gray foliage of this perennial in June. Will bloom through the summer if old flowers are sheared off. See *Nepeta × faassenii,* p. 189.

D 'East Friesland' salvia (use 9)
For masses of color at the curbside, this is a choice perennial. Forms a continuous patch of dark green foliage that sets off the distinctive slender spikes of blue-purple flowers. Flowers will keep coming from June until frost if you remove spent blooms from time to time. See *Salvia superba,* p. 192.

Leaf play

Foliage can be as eye-catching as flowers, as this postal planting shows. Silvery artemisia, sparkly blue junipers, and spirea foliage that changes throughout the seasons are a match for plantings boasting more flowers. Even in winter, when the artemisia has been cut to the ground, the spirea's rusty twigs and the unchanging blue of the juniper are a pleasing sight.

As in the previous design, these plants all tolerate the sometimes stressful conditions often found near the street and require little care beyond seasonal cleanup.

C 'Valerie Finnis' artemisia

'Goldflame' spirea **B**

A 'Blue Star' juniper

Site: Sunny

Season: Late summer

Concept: Foliage offers all the appeal of colorful flowers in this easy-care planting.

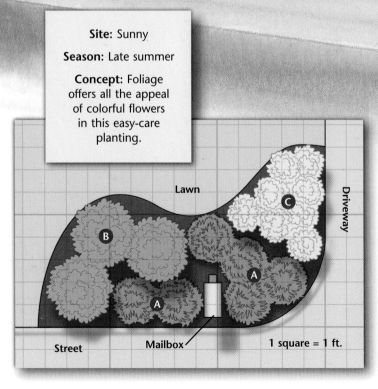

Lawn

Driveway

C

B

A

A

Street

Mailbox

1 square = 1 ft.

Plants & Projects

A **'Blue Star' juniper**
(use 6 plants)
The rich blue needles and irregular, mounded form of this low-growing evergreen shrub look great along the curb winter and summer. See *Juniperus squamata*, p. 186.

B **'Goldflame' spirea** (use 3)
This durable deciduous shrub is a colorful partner for the blue juniper throughout the growing season. Leaves are gold in spring, turning chartreuse in summer and orange-red in fall. Almost as a bonus, it bears crimson flowers through much of the summer. See *Spiraea × bumalda*, p. 193.

C **'Valerie Finnis' artemisia**
(use 8)
This perennial forms a striking silvery white patch of foliage next to the driveway. It nicely complements the blue juniper foliage and changing colors of the spirea leaves. See *Artemisia ludoviciana*, p. 174.

Plant portraits

Send a cheerful message with this selection of rugged, colorful plants.

● = First design, pp. 104–105
▲ = Second design, p. 106

'Valerie Finnis' artemisia
(*Artemisia ludoviciana*, p. 174) ▲

'Blue Star' juniper
(*Juniperus squamata*, p. 186) ▲

'Autumn Joy' sedum
(*Sedum*, p. 193) ●

'Karl Foerster' feather reed grass
(*Calamagrostis × acutiflora*, p. 176) ●

'East Friesland' salvia
(*Salvia superba*, p. 192) ●

'Goldflame' spirea
(*Spiraea × bumalda*, p. 193) ▲

Elegant Symmetry
Add a formal touch to your backyard

Formal landscaping often lends dignity to the public areas around a home (see p. 28). Formality can also be rewarding in a more private setting. There, the groomed plants, geometric lines, and symmetrical layout of a formal garden can help to organize the surrounding landscape, provide an elegant area for entertaining, or simply be enjoyed for their own sake.

In the design shown here, square and rectangular shapes are layered and juxtaposed within the confines of a large circle.

An edging and paths of brick create four identical quadrants. In each, handsome woody shrubs form a gently curving backdrop to square beds of colorful perennials grouped around a majestic fountain of ornamental grass. Foliage is the backbone of this planting, but trusses of pink rhododendrons grace the paths in spring, while in late summer (shown here) lilies reward a stroller with their delicious fragrance.

Formal gardens like this one look self-contained on paper, neatly packaged within

rigid boundaries. But even more than other types of landscaping, actual formal gardens work well only when carefully correlated with other elements in the landscape, such as the house, patio, and major plantings. Transitions, both physical and visual, between formal and more casual areas are particularly important. An expanse of lawn, changes of level that separate one area from another, or plantings that screen sight lines can all help formal and informal elements coexist comfortably.

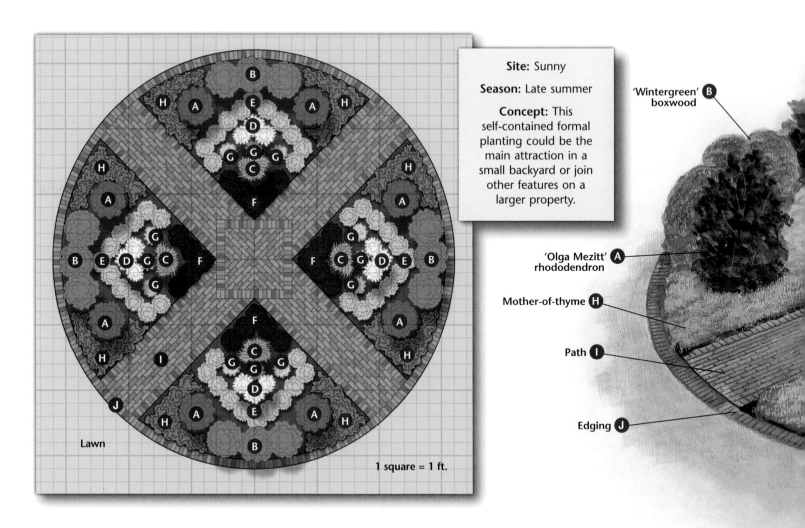

Site: Sunny

Season: Late summer

Concept: This self-contained formal planting could be the main attraction in a small backyard or join other features on a larger property.

'Wintergreen' **B** boxwood

'Olga Mezitt' **A** rhododendron

Mother-of-thyme **H**

Path **I**

Edging **J**

Lawn

1 square = 1 ft.

Plants & Projects

Laying out and installing the edging and paths requires care, patience, and elbow grease. Once established in well-prepared soil, the plants will require little maintenance beyond seasonal pruning and cleanup.

A **'Olga Mezitt' rhododendron**
(use 8 plants)
This compact broad-leaved evergreen shrub bears clear pink flowers in spring. Shiny foliage is maroon in winter and dark green the rest of the year. See *Rhododendron*, p. 191.

B **'Wintergreen' boxwood**
(use 12)
Unsheared, this evergreen shrub forms a loose, but tidy, hedge in each quadrant. The mass of small green leaves holds its color through the winter. See *Buxus*, p. 176.

C **Maiden grass** (use 4)
A perennial grass with long arching leaves. Tall stalks carry tiny pink flowers and fluffy seed heads that make a lovely show in winter. See *Miscanthus sinensis* 'Gracillimus', p. 189.

D **'Casablanca' lily** (use 12)
Tall leafy stalks bear large clear white flowers that waft a sweet scent over the planting in late summer. See *Lilium*, p. 187.

E **Rue** (use 44)
This attractive perennial herb forms mounds of ferny blue-gray foliage. In midsummer, it bears clusters of small yellow flowers. The compact form of the cultivar 'Jackman's Blue', which doesn't flower, works well in this design. See *Ruta graveolens*, p. 192.

F **'Palace Purple' heuchera**
(use 20)
Tidy mounds of this perennial's striking purple leaves add season-long color next to the paths. Small white flowers appear in summer. See *Heuchera micrantha*, p. 183.

G **'White Clips' Carpathian bellflower** (use 12)
The cuplike white flowers of this little perennial add sparkle to the garden all summer long. Its small spreading mounds of delicate, glossy green leaves are pretty as well. See *Campanula carpatica*, p. 177.

H **Mother-of-thyme**
(use about 60)
Fill spaces around the shrubs with this perennial ground cover. Spreads to form a dense carpet of wiry stems and tiny fragrant leaves. Bears tiny flowers in midsummer. See *Thymus serpyllum*, p. 195.

I **Paths**
We've shown brick here, but precast pavers, or crushed stone with brick edging, might better suit your site, your budget, or your do-it-yourself confidence. See p. 118.

J **Edging**
Bricks laid on edge establish the perimeter of the design and function as a mowing strip, too. See p. 150.

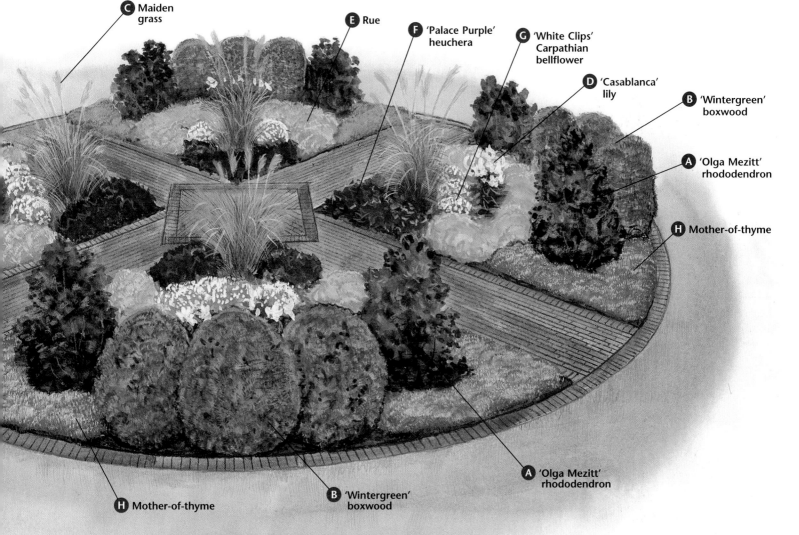

C Maiden grass

E Rue

F 'Palace Purple' heuchera

G 'White Clips' Carpathian bellflower

D 'Casablanca' lily

B 'Wintergreen' boxwood

A 'Olga Mezitt' rhododendron

H Mother-of-thyme

H Mother-of-thyme

B 'Wintergreen' boxwood

A 'Olga Mezitt' rhododendron

Fragrant formality

This design provides a lovely spot for an intimate lunch or a restful hour with a favorite book. And to enhance the experience, the surrounding plants have been chosen for their fragrance as well as for their handsome flowers and foliage.

The basic layout remains the same as in the previous design, but now there are two pairs of mirror-image quadrants, each with a more relaxed arrangement of plants. An abundance of flowers blooms from early spring through summer. And in winter, the deciduous and evergreen shrubs are a pleasing sight from the house.

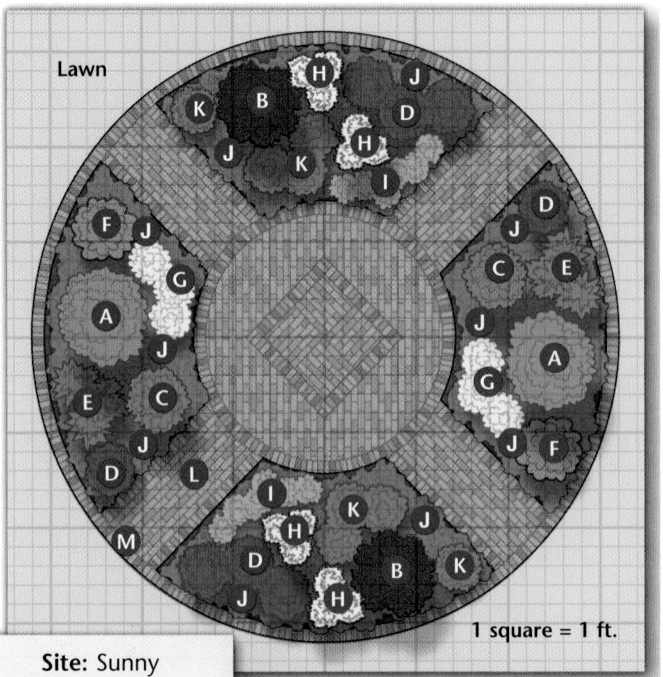

Lawn

1 square = 1 ft.

Site: Sunny

Season: Summer

Concept: A formal setting for informal get-togethers or relaxation amidst beautiful fragrant flowers.

Plants & Projects

A **Compact Korean spice viburnum** (use 2 plants)
This deciduous shrub with a neat rounded form anchors two quadrants. In May, pink buds produce white flowers with a spicy scent. Foliage is a good backdrop through summer and fall. See *Viburnum carlesii* 'Compactum', p. 195.

B **'Othello' shrub rose** (use 2)
The focal point of the other quadrant design, this deciduous shrub displays large, fragrant, double crimson flowers against dark green foliage. Will bloom all summer. Other shrub roses will work equally well here. See *Rosa*, p. 191.

C **'Rosy Lights' azalea** (use 2)
This hardy deciduous azalea brightens the patio in spring with large, scented, dark pink flowers. Before bloom, the buds on the bare stems are almost as fine as the flowers; after, the foliage looks good all season. See *Rhododendron*, p. 190.

See site plan for **E**.

Compact **A** Korean spice viburnum

'Rosy Lights' **C** azalea

Rue **K**

B 'Othello' shrub rose

H 'Stargazer' hybrid lily

H 'Casablanca' hybrid lily

C 'Rosy Lights' azalea

I 'Blue Clips' Carpathian bellflower

G 'Miss Lingard' phlox

'Marshall's Delight' **F** bee balm

Path **L**

Edging **M**

Periwinkle **J**

'Green Velvet' **D** boxwood

H 'Casablanca' hybrid lily

B 'Othello' shrub rose

J Periwinkle

K Rue

D 'Green Velvet' boxwood (use 8)

Marking the entrances to the garden, this elegant broad-leaved evergreen shrub needs no pruning to maintain its compact, rounded form. The tiny leaves hold their good green color through the winter. See *Buxus,* p. 176.

E 'Caesar's Brother' Siberian iris (use 6)

This perennial's graceful, blue-purple flowers add brilliant color to the garden in June. After flowering, the erect grassy leaves provide a nice contrast to the rounded shrubs. See *Iris sibirica,* p. 186.

F 'Marshall's Delight' bee balm (use 2)

Big, moplike, pink flowers float above this perennial's loose clumps of erect stems and green leaves in July and August. The flowers complement the white phlox nearby. See *Monarda,* p. 189.

G 'Miss Lingard' phlox (use 6)

A popular perennial that bears long stems of pure white fragrant flowers in midsummer. The dark green foliage is highly resistant to the mildew that plagues other phlox. See *Phlox carolina,* p. 190.

H Hybrid lilies (use 12)

Perennials that bloom in August. Mix the dark crimson-pink flowers of 'Stargazer' with the fragrant white flowers of 'Casablanca'. See *Lilium,* p. 187.

I 'Blue Clips' Carpathian bellflower (use 12)

Summer-long bloom from this blue-flowered cultivar of the perennial that is used in the previous design. See *Campanula carpatica,* p. 177.

J Periwinkle (use about 60)

This perennial ground cover's shiny dark green leaves form an evergreen edging along the paths and carpet open spaces between the plants. Bears blue flowers in spring. See *Vinca minor,* p. 197.

See p. 109 for the following:

K Rue (use 8)

L Paths

M Edging

Plant portraits

These plants add scented flowers and foliage and tidy forms to a formal design.

● = First design, pp. 108–109
▲ = Second design, pp. 110–111

'Casablanca' lily
(*Lilium,* p. 187) ● ▲

Periwinkle
(*Vinca minor,* p. 197) ▲

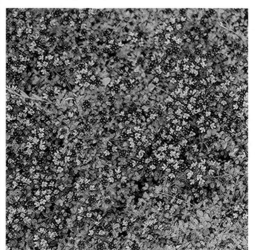

Mother-of-thyme
(*Thymus serpyllum,* p. 195) ●

Rue
(*Ruta graveolens,* p. 192) ● ▲

Maiden grass
(*Miscanthus sinensis* 'Gracillimus', p. 189) ●

Guide to Installation

In this section, we introduce the hard but rewarding work of landscaping. Here you'll find information on all the tasks you need to install any of the designs in this book, organized in the order in which you'd most likely tackle them. Clearly written text and numerous illustrations help you learn how to plan the job; clear the site; construct paths, patios, ponds, fences, arbors, and trellises; prepare the planting beds; and install and maintain the plantings. Roll up your sleeves and dig in. In just a few weekends, you can create a landscape feature that will provide years of enjoyment.

Organizing Your Project

If your gardening experience is limited to mowing the lawn, pruning the bushes, and growing some flowers and vegetables, the thought of starting from scratch and installing a whole new landscape feature might be intimidating. But in fact, adding one of the designs in this book to your property is completely within reach, if you approach it the right way. The key is to divide the project into a series of steps and take them one at a time. This is how professional landscapers work. It's efficient and orderly, and it makes even big jobs seem manageable.

On this and the facing page, we'll explain how to think your way through a landscaping project and anticipate the various steps. Subsequent topics in this section describe how to do each part of the job. Detailed instructions and illustrations cover all the techniques you'll need to install any design from start to finish.

The step-by-step approach

Choose a design and adapt it to your site. The designs in this book address parts of the home landscape. In the most attractive and effective home landscapes, all the various parts work together. Don't be afraid to change the shape of beds; alter the number, kinds, and positions of plants; or revise paths and structures to bring them into harmony with their surroundings.

To see the relationships with your existing landscape, you can draw the design on a scaled plan of your property. Or you can work on the site itself, placing wooden stakes, pots, tricycles, or whatever is handy to represent plants and structures. With a little imagination, either method will allow you to visualize basic relationships.

Lay out the design on site. Once you've decided what you want to do, you'll need to lay out the paths and structures and outline the beds. Some people are comfortable laying out a design "freehand," pacing off distances and relying on their eye to judge sizes and relative positions. Others prefer to transfer the grid from the plan full size onto the site in order to place elements

Digging postholes

Amending soil

precisely. (Garden lime, a grainy white powder available at nurseries, can be used like chalk on a blackboard to "draw" a grid or outlines of planting beds.)

Clear the site. (See pp. 116–117.) Sometimes you may need to work around existing features—a nice big tree, a building or fence, a sidewalk—but it's usually easiest to start a new landscaping project if you clear as much as possible down to ground level. That means removing unwanted structures or pavement and killing, cutting down, or uprooting all the plants. Needless to say, this can generate a lot of debris, and you'll need to figure out how to dispose of it all. Still, it's often worth the trouble to make a fresh start.

Build the "hardscape." (See pp. 118–147.) "Hardscape" means anything you build as part of a landscape—a fence, trellis, arbor, retaining wall, walkway, edging, outdoor lighting, or whatever. If you're going to do any building, do it first, and finish the construction before you start any planting. That way you won't have to worry about stepping on any of the plants, and they won't be in the way as you work.

Prepare the soil. (See pp. 148–151.) On most properties, it's uncommon to find soil that's as good as it should be for growing plants. Typically, the soil around a house is shallow, compacted, and infertile. It may be rocky or contain buried debris. Some plants tolerate such poor conditions, but they don't thrive. To grow healthy, attractive plants, you need to improve the quality of the soil throughout the entire area that you're planning to plant.

Do the planting and add mulch. (See pp. 152–157.) Putting plants in the ground usually goes quite quickly and gives instant gratification. Spreading mulch over the soil makes the area look neat and "finished" even while the plants are still small.

Maintain the planting. (See pp. 157–169.) Most plantings need regular watering and occasional weeding for the first year or two. After that, depending on the design you've chosen, you'll need to do some routine maintenance—pruning, shaping, cutting back, and cleaning up—to keep the plants looking their best. This may take as little as a few hours a year or as much as an hour or two every week throughout the growing season.

Planting

Setting flagstones

Clearing the Site

The site you've chosen for a landscaping project may or may not have any man-made objects (fences, old pavement, trash, etc.) to be removed, but it will almost certainly be covered with plants.

Before you start cutting plants down, try to find someone—a friend or neighbor who enjoys gardening—to identify them for you. As you walk around together, make a sketch that shows which plants are where, and attach labels to the plants, too. Determine if there are any desirable plants worth saving—mature shade trees that you should work around, shapely shrubs that aren't too big to dig up and relocate or give away, worthwhile perennials and ground covers that you could divide and replant, healthy sod that you could lay elsewhere. Likewise, decide which plants have to go—diseased or crooked trees, straggly or overgrown shrubs, weedy brush, invasive ground covers, tattered lawn.

You can clear small areas yourself, bundling the brush for pickup and tossing soft-stemmed plants on the compost pile, but if you have lots of woody brush or any trees to remove, you might want to hire someone else to do the job. A crew armed with power tools can turn a thicket into a pile of wood chips in just a few hours. Have them pull out the roots and grind the stumps, too. Save the chips; they're good for surfacing paths, or you can use them as mulch.

Working around a tree

If there are any large, healthy trees on your site, be careful as you work around them. It's okay to prune off some of a tree's limbs, as shown on the facing page, but respect its trunk and its roots. Try never to cut or wound the bark on the trunk (don't nail things to a tree), as that exposes the tree to disease organisms. Don't pile soil or mulch against the trunk, since that keeps the bark wet and can cause it to rot.

Killing perennial weeds

Some common weeds that sprout back from perennial roots or runners are bedstraw, bindweed, blackberry and other briers, ground ivy, poison ivy, quackgrass, and sorrel. Garden plants that can become weedy include ajuga, artemisia, bee balm, bishop's weed, Japanese bamboo, lily-of-the-valley, loosestrife, mint, sundrops, and tansy. Once they get established, perennial weeds are hard to eliminate. You can't just cut off the tops, because they keep sprouting back. You need to dig the weeds out, smother them with mulch, or kill them with an herbicide. Regardless of the method, it's better to eradicate weeds before rather than after you plant a bed.

Digging. In many cases, you can do a pretty good job of removing a perennial weed if you dig carefully where the stems enter the ground, find the roots, and follow them as far as possible through the soil, pulling out every bit of root that you find. Some plant roots go deeper than you can dig, and most plants will sprout back from the small bits that you miss, but these leftover sprouts are easy to pull.

Smothering. This technique is easier than digging, particularly for eradicating large infestations, but much slower. First mow or cut the tops of the weeds as close to the ground as possible ❶. Then cover the area with thick sections of newspaper, overlapped like shingles ❷, or flattened-out cardboard boxes. Top with a layer of

Smothering weeds

❶ Smothering kills weeds by depriving them of light. Cut the tops off close to the ground.

❷ Cover with thick newspaper or cardboard.

❸ Top with several inches of mulch. Wait a few months to be sure weeds are dead; then till rotted newspaper and mulch into the soil.

Moving turf

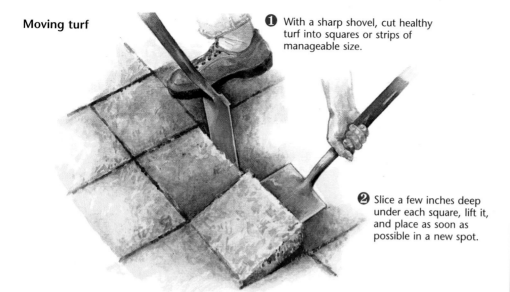

❶ With a sharp shovel, cut healthy turf into squares or strips of manageable size.

❷ Slice a few inches deep under each square, lift it, and place as soon as possible in a new spot.

mulch, such as straw, grass clippings, tree leaves, wood chips, or other organic material spread several inches deep ❸.

Smothering works by excluding light, which stops photosynthesis. If any shoots reach up through the covering and produce green leaves, pull them out immediately. Wait a few months, until you're sure the weeds are dead, before you dig into the smothered area and plant there.

Spraying. Herbicides are easy, fast, and effective weed killers when chosen and applied with care. Look for those that break down quickly into more benign substances, and make sure the weed you're trying to kill is listed on the product label. Apply all herbicides exactly as directed by the manufacturer. After spraying, you usually need to wait from one to four weeks for the weed to die completely, and some weeds need to be sprayed a second or third time before they give up. Some weeds just "melt away" when they die, but if there are tough or woody stems and roots, you'll need to dig them up and discard them.

Replacing turf

If the area where you're planning to add a landscape feature is currently part of the lawn, you have a fairly easy task ahead — easier than clearing brush or killing weeds,

anyway. How to proceed depends on the condition of the turf and on what you want to put in its place. If the turf is healthy, you can "recycle" it to replace, repair, or extend the lawn on other parts of your property.

The drawing above shows a technique for removing relatively small areas of strong healthy turf for replanting elsewhere. First, with a sharp shovel, cut turf into squares or strips about 1 to 2 ft. square (these small pieces are easy to lift) ❶. Then slice a few inches deep under each square and lift the squares, roots and all, like brownies from a pan ❷. Quickly transplant the squares to a previously prepared site; water them well until the roots are established. You can rent a sod-cutting machine for larger areas you wish to recycle.

If you don't need the turf anywhere else, or if it's straggly or weedy, leave it in place and kill the grass. One way to kill grass is to cover it with a tarp or a sheet of black plastic for about four weeks during the heat of summer. A single application of herbicide kills some grasses, but you may need to spray vigorous turf twice. After you've killed the grass, dig or till the bed, shredding the turf, roots and all, and mixing it into the soil. This is hard work if the soil is dry but less so if the ground has been softened by a recent rain or watering.

Removing large limbs

If there are large trees on your property now, you may want to remove some of the lower limbs so you can walk and see underneath them and so more light can reach plantings you're planning beneath them. Major pruning of large trees is a job for a professional arborist, but you can remove limbs smaller than 4 in. in diameter and less than 10 ft. above the ground yourself with a simple bow saw or pole saw.

Use the three-step procedure shown below to remove large limbs safely and without harming the tree. First, saw partway through the bottom of the limb, approximately 1 ft. out from the trunk ❶. This keeps the bark from tearing down the trunk when the limb falls. Then make a corresponding cut down through the top of the limb ❷ — be prepared to get out of the way when the limb drops. Finally, remove the stub ❸. Undercut it slightly or hold it as you finish the cut, so it doesn't fall away and peel bark off the trunk. Note that the cut is not flush with the trunk but is just outside the thick area at the limb's base, called the branch collar. Leaving the branch collar helps the wound heal quickly and naturally. Wound dressing is considered unnecessary today.

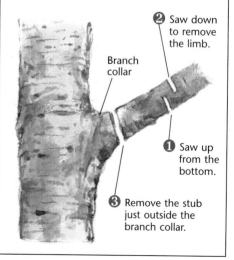

❷ Saw down to remove the limb.

Branch collar

❶ Saw up from the bottom.

❸ Remove the stub just outside the branch collar.

Making Paths and Walkways

Every landscape needs paths and walkways if for no other reason than to keep your feet dry as you move from one place to another. A path can also divide and define the spaces in the landscape, orchestrate the way the landscape is viewed, and even be a key element enhancing its beauty.

Whether it is a graceful curving garden path or a utilitarian slab leading to the garage, a walk has two main functional requirements: durability and safety. It should hold up through seasonal changes. It should provide a well-drained surface that is easy to walk on and to maintain.

A path's function helps determine its surface and its character. In general, heavily trafficked walkways leading to a door, garage, or shed need hard, smooth (but not slick) surfaces and should take you where you want to go fairly directly. A path to a backyard play area could be a strip of soft wood bark, easy on the knees of impatient children. A relaxed stroll in the garden might require only a hopscotch collection of flat stones meandering from one prized plant to another.

Before laying out a walk or path, spend some time observing existing traffic patterns. If your path makes use of a route people already take (particularly children), they'll be more likely to stay on the path and off the lawn or flowers. Avoid areas that are slow to drain. When determining path width, consider whether the path must accommodate rototillers and wheelbarrows or two strollers walking abreast, or just provide steppingstone access for maintaining the plants.

Dry-laid paths

You can make a path simply by laying bricks or spreading wood chips on top of bare earth. While quick and easy, this method has serious drawbacks. Laid on the surface, with no edging to contain them, loose materials are soon scattered, and solid materials are easily jostled out of place. If the earth base doesn't drain very well, the path will be a swamp or sheet of ice after a rainstorm or snowmelt. And in winter, repeated expansion and contraction of the soil will heave bricks or flagstones out of alignment, making the path unsightly and potentially dangerous.

The method we recommend—laying surface material on an excavated sand-and-gravel base—minimizes these problems. The sand and gravel improve drainage and provide a cushion against the freeze-thaw movement of the soil. Excavation can place the path surface at ground level, where the surrounding soil or an installed edging can contain loose materials and prevent solid materials from shifting.

All styles, from a "natural" wood-bark path to a formal cut-stone entry walk, and all the materials discussed here can be laid on an excavated base of gravel and sand.

Drainage

Few things are worse than a path dotted with puddles or icy patches. To prevent these from forming, the soil around and beneath the path should drain well. The path's location and construction should ensure that rainwater does not collect on the surface. Drainage also affects frost heaving. In cold-winter areas, the soil expands and contracts as the water in it freezes and

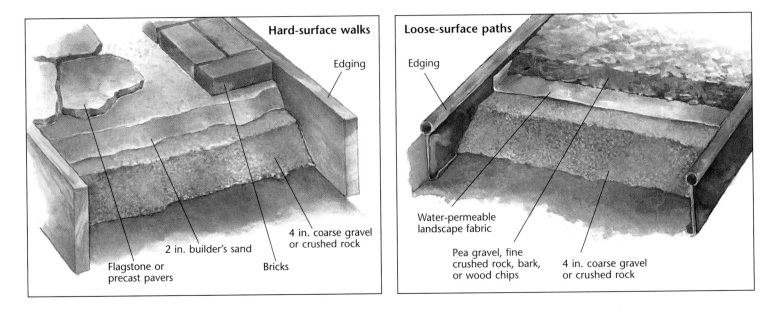

Hard-surface walks

Edging

Flagstone or precast pavers

2 in. builder's sand

Bricks

4 in. coarse gravel or crushed rock

Loose-surface paths

Edging

Water-permeable landscape fabric

Pea gravel, fine crushed rock, bark, or wood chips

4 in. coarse gravel or crushed rock

Choosing a surface

Walkways and paths can be made of either hard or soft material. Your choice of material will depend on the walkway's function, your budget, and your personal preferences.

Soft materials, including bark, wood chips, pine needles, and loose gravel, are best for informal and low-traffic areas. Inexpensive and simple to install, they settle, scatter, or decompose and must be replenished or replaced every few years.

Hard materials, such as brick, flagstone, and concrete pavers, are more expensive and time-consuming to install, but they are permanent, requiring only occasional maintenance. (Compacted crushed stone can also make a hard-surface walk.) Durable and handsome, they're ideal for high-traffic, "high-profile" areas.

Bark, wood chips, and pine needles

Perfect for a "natural" look or a quick temporary path, these loose materials can be laid directly on the soil or, if drainage is poor, on a gravel bed. Bagged materials from a nursery or garden center will be cleaner, more uniform, and considerably more expensive than bulk supplies bought by the cubic yard. Check with local tree services to find the best prices on bulk material.

Gravel and crushed rock

Loose rounded gravel gives a bit underfoot, creating a "soft" but somewhat messy path. The angular facets of crushed stone eventually compact into a "hard" and tidier path that can, if the surrounding soil is firm enough, be laid without an edging. Gravel and stone type and color vary from area to area within a region. Buy these materials by the ton or cubic yard.

Concrete pavers

Precast concrete pavers are versatile, readily available, and often the least expensive hard-surface material. They come in a range of colors and shapes, including interlocking patterns. Precast edgings are also available. Most home and garden centers carry a variety of precast pavers, which are sold by the piece.

Precast pavers

Brick

Widely available in a range of sizes, colors, and textures, brick complements many design styles, both formal and informal. When carefully laid on a well-prepared sand-and-gravel base, brick provides an even, safe, and long-lasting surface. Buy paving brick instead of the softer "facing" brick, which may break up after a few freeze-thaw cycles. (If you buy used brick, pick the densest and hardest.) Avoid brick with glazed faces; the glaze traps moisture and salts, which eventually damage the brick.

Running bond

Two-brick basket weave

Herringbone

Diagonal herringbone

Flagstone

"Flagstone" is a generic term for stratified stone that can be split to form pavers. Limestone, sandstone, and bluestone are common paving materials. The surfaces of marble and slate are usually too smooth to make safe paving because they are slippery when wet. Cut into squares or rectangles, flagstone can be laid as individual stepping-stones or in interesting patterns. Flags with irregular outlines present other patterning opportunities. Flagstones come in a range of colors, textures, and sizes. Flags for walks should be at least 2 in. thick; thinner stones fracture easily. Purchased by weight, surface area, or pallet load, flagstones are usually the most expensive paving choice.

Cut flagstone

Cut and irregular flagstone

Irregular flagstone

Edgings

All walk surfaces need to be contained in some fashion along their edges. Where soil is firm or tightly knit by turf, neatly cut walls of the excavation can serve as edging. An installed edging often provides more effective containment, particularly if the walk surface is above grade. It also prevents damage to bricks or stones on the edges of paths. Walkway edgings are commonly made of 1- or 2-in.-thick lumber, thicker landscaping timbers, brick, or stone.

Wood edging

Wood should be rot-resistant redwood, cedar, or cypress or pressure-treated for ground-contact use. If you're working in loose soils, fix a deep wooden edging to support stakes with double-headed nails. When the path is laid, pull the nails, and fill and tamp behind the edging. Then drive the stakes below grade. In firmer soils, or if the edging material is not wide enough, install it on top of the gravel base. Position the top of the edging at the height of the path. Dimension lumber 1 in. thick is pliable enough to bend around gradual curves.

Treated dimensional lumber with support stakes

Landscape timbers with crossties laid on gravel base

Brick and stone edging

In firm soil, a row of bricks laid on edge and perpendicular to the length of the path adds stability. For a more substantial edging, stand bricks on end on the excavated soil surface, add the gravel base, and tamp earth around the base of the bricks on the outside of the excavation. Stone edgings laid on end can be set in the same way. "End-up" brick or stone edgings are easy to install on curved walks.

Bricks on edge, laid on gravel base

Bricks on end, laid on soil

---

thaws. As the soil moves, so do path and walkway materials laid on it. The effect is minimal on loose materials such as wood chips or gravel, but frost heaving can shift brick and stone significantly out of line.

Before you locate a path, observe runoff and drainage on your property during and after heavy rains. Avoid routing a path through areas where water courses, collects, or is slow to drain.

While both loose and hard paving can sometimes be successfully laid directly on well-drained soil, laying surface materials on a base of gravel and sand will help improve drainage and minimize frost heaving. In most situations, a 4-in. gravel bed topped with 2 in. of sand will be sufficient. Water moves through these materials quickly, and they "cushion" the surface materials from the expansion and contraction of the underlying soil. Very poorly drained soils may require more gravel, an additional layer of coarse rock beneath the gravel, or even drain tiles. If you suspect your site has serious drainage problems, consult a specialist for advice.

Finally, keep water from pooling on a walk by making its surface higher in the center than at the edges. The center of a 4-ft.-wide walk should be at least $1/2$ in. higher than its edges. If you're using a drag board to level the sand base, curve its lower edge to create this "crown." Otherwise, crown the surface by eye.

Preparing the base

Having decided on location and materials, you can get down to business. The initial steps of layout and base preparation are much the same for all surface materials.

Layout

Lay out straight sections with stakes and string. You can plot curves with stakes and "fair" the curve with a garden hose, or you can outline the curve with the hose alone, marking it with lime or sand ❶.

Preparing the base

❶ Lay out the path with stakes, string, garden hose, and lime.

❷ Dig out path between layout string and lime lines.

❸ Install the edging.

❹ Rake out gravel base.

Lay out free-form curved sections with garden hose and mark with lime.

Mark straight sections with 1x2 stakes and string.

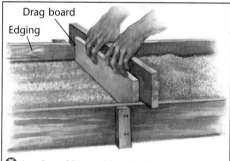

Drag board

Edging

❺ Level sand base with a drag board.

Excavation

The excavation depth depends on how much sand-and-gravel base your soil's drainage calls for, the thickness of the surface material, and its position above or below grade ❷. Mark the depth on a stake or stick and use this to check depth as you dig. Walking surfaces are most comfortable if they are reasonably level across their width. Check the bottom of the excavation with a level as you dig. If the walk cuts across a slope, you'll need to remove soil from the high side and use it to fill the low side to produce a level surface. If you've added soil or if the subsoil is loose, compact it by tamping.

Edging installion

Some edgings can be installed immediately after excavation; others are placed on top of the gravel portion of the base ❸. (See the sidebar "Edgings" on the facing page.) If the soil's drainage permits, you can lay soft materials now on the excavated, tamped, and edged soil base. To control

weeds, and to keep bark, chips, or pine needles from mixing with the subsoil, you can spread water-permeable landscape fabric over the excavated soil base.

Laying the base

Now add gravel (if required), rake it level, and compact it ❹. Use gravel up to 1 in. in diameter or $1/4$- to $3/4$-in. crushed stone, which drains and compacts well. You can rent a hand tamper (a heavy metal plate on the end of a pole) or a machine compactor if you have a large area to compact.

If you're making a loose-gravel or crushed-stone walk, add the surface material on top of the base gravel. (See "Loose materials" below.) For walks of brick, stone, or pavers, add a 2-in. layer of builder's sand, not the finer sand masons use for mixing mortar.

Rake the sand smooth with the back of a level-head rake. You can level the sand with a wooden drag board, also called a screed ❺. Nail together two 1x4s or notch a 1x6 to place the lower edge at the desired

height of the sand, and run the board along the path edging. To settle the sand, dampen it thoroughly with a hose set on fine spray. Fill any low spots, rake or drag the surface level, then dampen it again.

Laying the surface

Whether you're laying a loose or hard material, take time to plan your work. Provide access for delivery trucks, and have material deposited as close to the worksite as possible.

Loose materials

Install water-permeable landscape fabric over the gravel base to prevent gravel from mixing with the surface material. Spread bark or wood chips 2 to 4 in. deep. For a pine-needle surface, spread 2 in. of needles on top of several inches of bark or chips. Spread loose pea gravel about 2 in. deep. For a harder, more uniform surface, add $1/2$ in. of fine crushed stone on top of the gravel. You can let traffic compact crushed-rock surfaces, or compact them by hand or with a machine.

Bricks and precast pavers

Take time to figure out the pattern and spacing of the bricks or pavers by laying them out on the lawn or driveway, rather than disturbing your carefully prepared sand base. When you're satisfied, begin in a corner, laying the bricks or pavers gently on the sand so the base remains even ❶. Lay full bricks first; then cut bricks to fit as needed at the edges. To produce uniform joints, space bricks with a piece of wood cut to the joint width. You can also maintain alignment with a straightedge or with a string stretched across the path between nails or stakes. Move the string as the work proceeds.

As you complete a row or section, bed the bricks or pavers into the sand base with several firm raps of a rubber mallet or a hammer on a scrap 2x4. Check with a level or straightedge to make sure the surface is even ❷. (You'll have to do this by feel or eye across the width of a crowned path.) Lift low bricks or pavers carefully and fill beneath them with sand; then reset them. Don't stand on the walk until you've filled the joints.

When you've finished a section, sweep fine, dry mason's sand into the joints, working across the surface of the path in all directions ❸. Wet thoroughly with a fine spray and let dry; then sweep in more sand if necessary. If you want a "living" walk, sweep a loam-sand mixture into the joints and plant small, tough, ground-hugging plants, such as thyme, in them.

Rare is the brick walk that can be laid without cutting something to fit. To cut brick, mark the line of the cut with a dark

Loose materials

Cover gravel base with water-permeable landscape fabric and add 2 to 4 in. of bark or wood chips.

❶ Begin laying in a corner.

Bricks and precast pavers

To turn square corners, align the edging board with a carpenter's square.

❷ Check the surface with a level or straightedge. Fill under low bricks; tamp down high ones. Use a plank to distribute your weight if you must work on the path.

❸ Sweep fine, dry sand into the joints to fix the bricks or pavers in place.

Cutting bricks

Wear safety glasses.

Scored line

Brickset chisel

pencil all around the brick. With the brick resting firmly on sand or soil, score the entire line by rapping a wide mason's chisel called a "brickset" with a heavy wooden mallet or a soft-headed steel hammer as shown on the facing page. Place the brickset in the scored line across one face and give it a sharp blow with the hammer to cut the brick.

If you have a lot of bricks to cut, or if you want greater accuracy, consider renting a masonry saw. Whether you work by hand or machine, always wear safety glasses.

Flagstones

Install cut stones of uniform thickness as described for bricks and pavers. Working out patterns beforehand is particularly important—stones are too heavy to move around more than necessary. To produce a level surface with cut or irregular stones of varying thickness, you'll need to add or remove sand for each stone. Set the stone carefully on sand; then move it back and forth to work it into place ❶. Lay a level or straightedge over three or four stones to check the surface's evenness ❷. When a section is complete, fill the joints with sand or with sand and loam as described for bricks and pavers.

You can cut flagstone with a technique similar to that used for bricks. Score the line of the cut on the top surface with a brickset and hammer. Prop the stone on a piece of scrap wood, positioning the line of cut slightly beyond the edge of the wood. Securing the bottom edge of the stone with your foot, place the brickset on the scored line and strike sharply to make the cut.

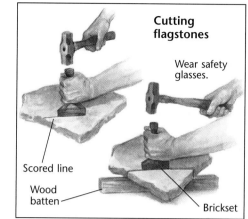

Cutting flagstones

Wear safety glasses.

Scored line

Wood batten

Brickset

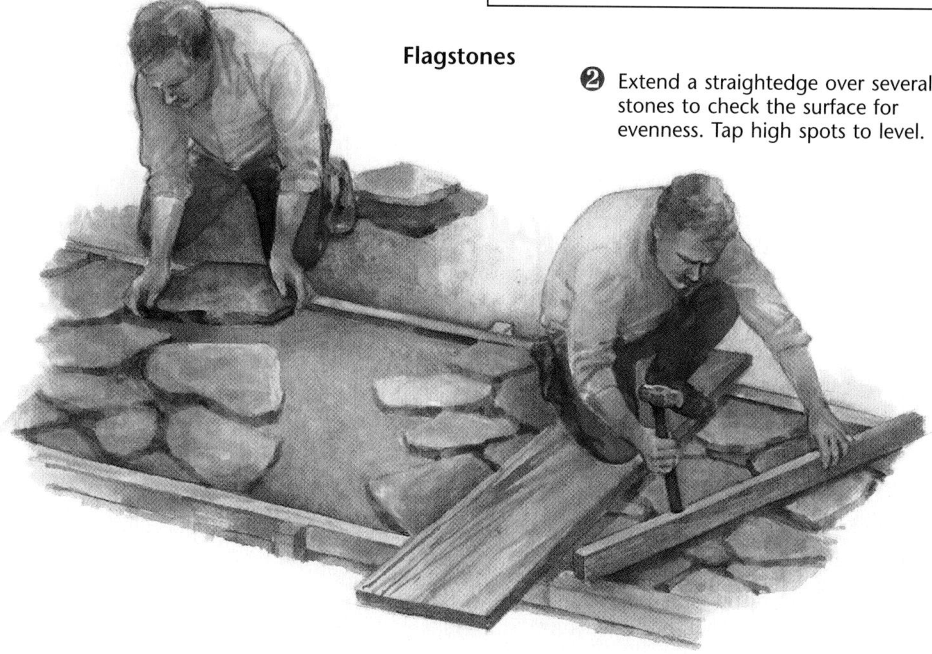

❶ Set flagstones in place carefully to avoid disturbing the sand base.

❷ Extend a straightedge over several stones to check the surface for evenness. Tap high spots to level.

Flagstones

Steppingstones

A steppingstone walk set in turf creates a charming effect and is very simple to lay. You can use cut or irregular flagstones or fieldstone, which is irregular in thickness as well as in outline. Arrange the stones on the turf; then set them one by one. Cut into the turf around the stone with a sharp flat shovel or trowel, and remove the stone; then dig out the sod with the shovel. Placing stones at or below grade will keep them away from mower blades. Fill low spots beneath the stone with earth or sand so the stone doesn't move when stepped on.

Cut around steppingstone with shovel or trowel.

Remove sod and soil.

Set in place, filling with sand or soil to bed stone firmly.

Laying a Patio

You can make a simple patio using the same techniques and materials we have discussed for paths. To ensure good drainage, an even surface, and durability, lay hard surfaces such as brick, flagstone, and pavers on a well-prepared base of gravel, sand, and compacted soil. (Crushed-rock and gravel surfaces likewise benefit from a sound base.) Make sure the surface drains away from any adjacent structure (house or garage); a drop-off of ¼ in. per foot is usu-ally adequate. If the patio isn't near a struc-ture, make it higher in the center to avoid puddles.

Establish the outline of the patio as described for paths; then excavate the area roughly to accommodate 4 in. of gravel, 2 in. of sand, and the thickness of the paving surface. (Check with a local nursery or landscape contractor to find out if local conditions require alterations in the type or amounts of base material.) Now grade the rough excavation to provide drainage, using a simple 4-ft. grid of wooden stakes as shown in the drawings.

Drive the first row of stakes next to the house (or in the center of a freestanding patio), leveling them with a 4-ft. builder's level or a smaller level resting on a straight 2x4. The tops of these stakes should be at the height of the top of the sand base (fin-ish grade of the patio less the thickness of the surface material) ❶. Working from this row of stakes, establish another row about 4 to 5 ft. from the first. Make the tops of these stakes 1 in. lower than those of the first row, using a level and spacer

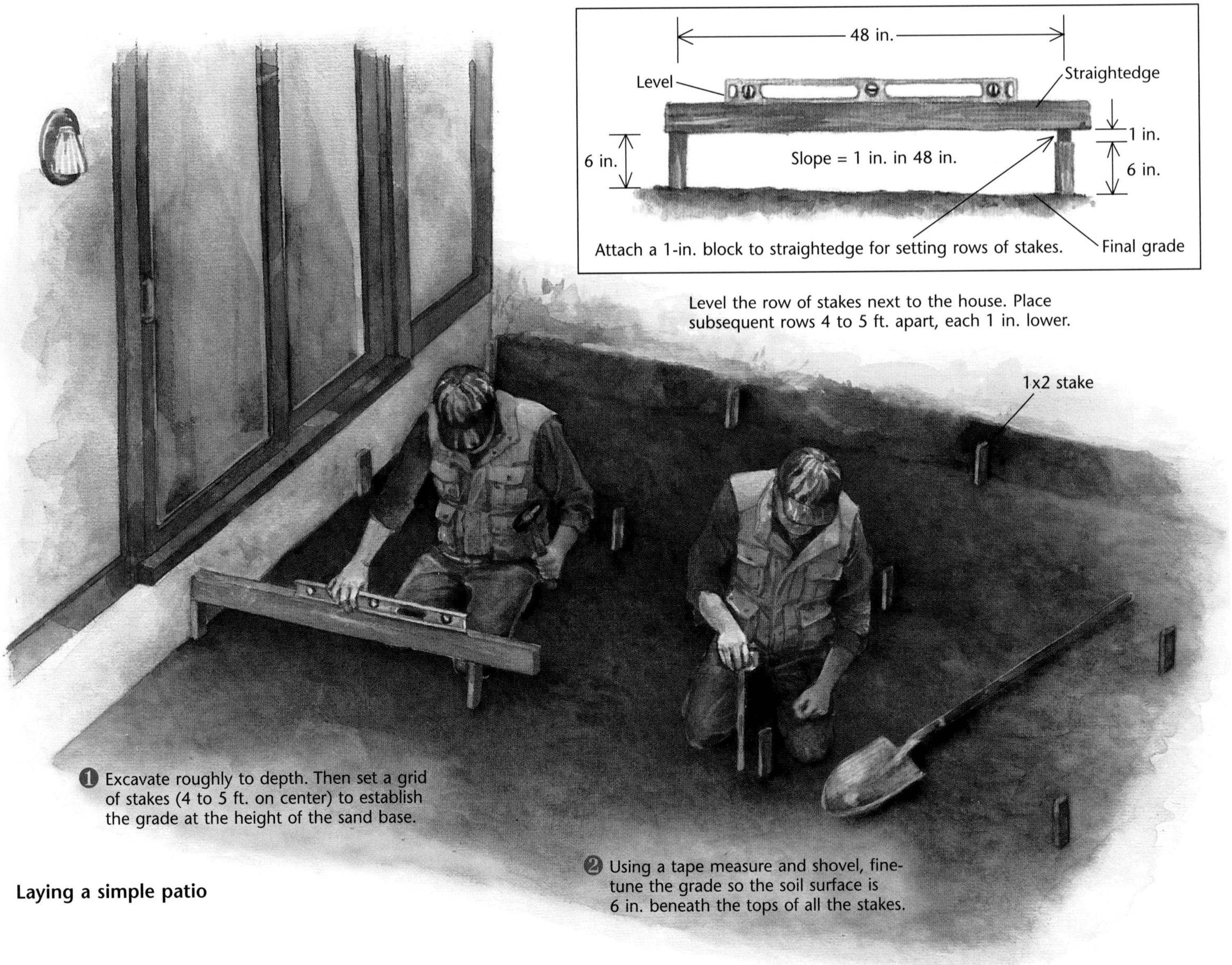

48 in.

Level · Straightedge

6 in.

Slope = 1 in. in 48 in.

1 in.

6 in.

Attach a 1-in. block to straightedge for setting rows of stakes. · Final grade

Level the row of stakes next to the house. Place subsequent rows 4 to 5 ft. apart, each 1 in. lower.

1x2 stake

❶ Excavate roughly to depth. Then set a grid of stakes (4 to 5 ft. on center) to establish the grade at the height of the sand base.

Laying a simple patio

❷ Using a tape measure and shovel, fine-tune the grade so the soil surface is 6 in. beneath the tops of all the stakes.

block, as shown on the facing page. Continue adding rows of stakes, each 1 in. lower than the previous row, until the entire area is staked. Then, with a tape measure or ruler and a shovel, fine-tune the grading by removing or adding soil until the excavated surface is 6 in. (the thickness of the gravel-sand base) below the tops of all the stakes ❷.

When installing the sand-and-gravel base, you'll want to maintain the drainage grade you've just established and produce an even surface for the paving material. If you have a good eye or a very small patio, you can do this by sight. Otherwise, you can use the stakes to install a series of 1x3 or 1x4 "leveling boards," as shown in the drawing below. (Before adding gravel, you may want to cover the soil with water-permeable landscape fabric to keep perennial weeds from growing; just cut slits to accommodate the stakes.)

Add a few inches of gravel ❸. Then set leveling boards along each row of stakes, with the boards' top edges even with the top of the stakes ❹. Drive additional stakes to sandwich the boards in place (don't use nails). Distribute the remaining inch or so of gravel and compact it by hand or machine, then the 2 in. of sand. Dragging a straight 2x4 across two adjacent rows of leveling boards will produce a precise grade and an even surface ❺. Wet the sand and fill low spots that settle.

You can install the patio surface as previously described for paths, removing the leveling boards as the bricks or pavers reach them ❻. Disturbing the sand surface as little as possible, slide the boards out from between the stakes and drive the stakes an inch or so beneath the level of the sand. Cover the stakes and fill the gaps left by the boards with sand, tamped down carefully; then continue laying the surface. Finally, sweep fine sand into the joints.

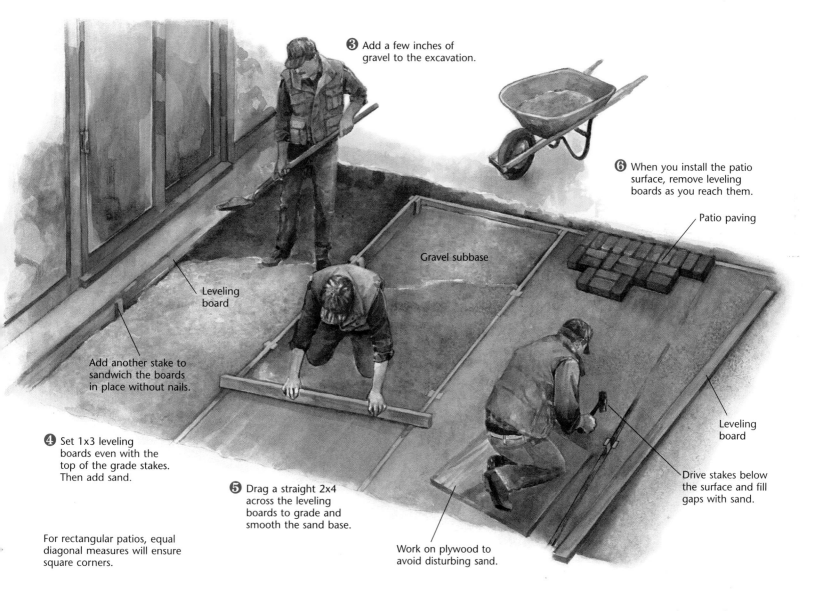

❸ Add a few inches of gravel to the excavation.

❻ When you install the patio surface, remove leveling boards as you reach them.

Patio paving

Gravel subbase

Leveling board

Add another stake to sandwich the boards in place without nails.

❹ Set 1x3 leveling boards even with the top of the grade stakes. Then add sand.

❺ Drag a straight 2x4 across the leveling boards to grade and smooth the sand base.

For rectangular patios, equal diagonal measures will ensure square corners.

Work on plywood to avoid disturbing sand.

Leveling board

Drive stakes below the surface and fill gaps with sand.

Installing a Pond

It wasn't so long ago that a garden pond like the one in this book required yards of concrete, an expert mason, and deep pockets. Today's strong, lightweight, and long-lasting synthetic liners and rigid fiberglass shells have put garden pools in reach of every homeowner. Installation does require some hard labor, but little expertise: just dig a hole, spread the liner or seat the shell, install edging, and plant. We'll discuss installation of a linered pond in the main text; see below for installing a smaller, fiberglass pool.

Liner notes

More and more nurseries and garden centers are carrying flexible pond liners; you can also buy them from mail-order suppliers specializing in water gardens. Synthetic rubber liners are longer lasting but more expensive than PVC liners. (Both are much cheaper than rigid fiberglass shells.) Buy only liners specifically made for garden ponds—don't use ordinary plastic sheeting. Many people feel that black liners look best; blue liners tend to make the pond look like a swimming pool.

Before you dig

First, make sure you comply with any rules your town may have about water features. Then keep the following ideas in mind when locating your pond. Avoid trees whose shade keeps sun-loving water plants from thriving; whose roots make digging a chore; and whose flowers, leaves, and seeds clog the water, making it unsightly and inhospitable to plants or fish. Avoid the low spot on your property; otherwise your pond will be a catch basin for runoff. Select a level spot; the immediate vicinity of the pond must be level, and starting out that way saves a lot of work. (Remember that you can use excavated soil to help level the site.)

Using graph paper, enlarge the outline of the pond provided on the site plan on p. 65, altering it as you wish. If you change the size or depth of the pond, or are interested in growing a wider variety of water plants or in adding fish, remember that a healthy pond must achieve a balance between the plants and fish and the volume, depth, and temperature of the water. Even if you're not altering size or pond plants and fish, it's a good idea to consult with a knowledgeable person at a nursery or pet store specializing in water-garden plants and animals.

Calculate the liner width by adding twice the maximum depth of the pool plus an additional 2 ft. to the width. Use the same formula to calculate the length. So, for a pond 2 ft. deep, 6 ft. wide, and 12 ft. long, the liner width would be 4 ft. plus 6 ft. plus 2 ft. (or 12 ft.). The length would be 4 ft. plus 12 ft. plus 2 ft. (or 18 ft.).

Small fiberglass pool

A fiberglass shell about 3 to 5 ft. in diameter and about 2 ft. deep is ideal for the small pool on p. 66. Garden centers often stock pond shells in a variety of shapes.

Dig a hole about 6 in. wider on all sides than the shell; its depth should equal that of the shell plus 1 in. for a sand base, plus the thickness of the fieldstone edging. Compact the bottom of the hole and spread the sand; then lower the shell into place. Add temporary wedges or props if necessary to orient and level the shell. Slowly fill the shell with water, backfilling around it with sand or sifted soil, keeping pace with the rising water level. Excavate a wide relief for the edging stones, laying them on as firm a base as possible, slightly overhanging the rim of the shell.

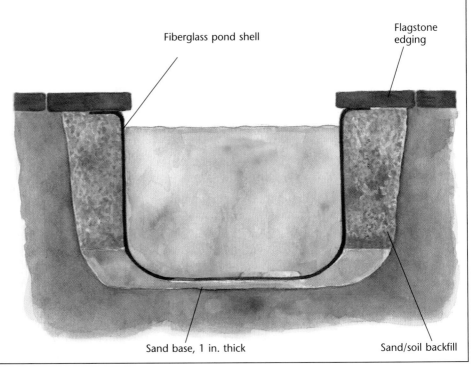

Fiberglass pond shell

Flagstone edging

Sand base, 1 in. thick

Sand/soil backfill

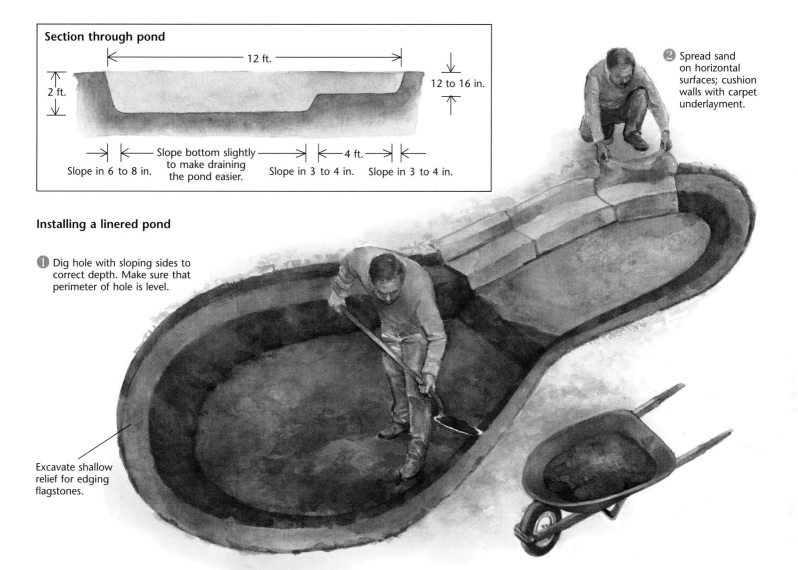

Section through pond

12 ft.

2 ft.

12 to 16 in.

Slope in 6 to 8 in.   Slope bottom slightly to make draining the pond easier.   4 ft.   Slope in 3 to 4 in.   Slope in 3 to 4 in.

Installing a linered pond

❶ Dig hole with sloping sides to correct depth. Make sure that perimeter of hole is level.

Excavate shallow relief for edging flagstones.

❷ Spread sand on horizontal surfaces; cushion walls with carpet underlayment.

Excavation

If your soil isn't too compacted or rocky, a good-size pond can be excavated with a shovel or two in a weekend ❶. (Energetic teenagers are a marvelous pool-building resource.) If the site isn't level, you can grade it using a stake-and-level system like the one described on pp. 124–125 for grading the patio.

Outline the pond's shape with garden lime, establishing the curves freehand with a garden hose or by staking out a large grid and plotting from the graph-paper plan. The pond has two levels. Most of the pond is 2 ft. deep to accommodate water lilies and other plants requiring deeper water, as well as fish. One end is only 12 to 16 in.

deep for plants requiring shallower submersion. (You can put plant pots on stacks of bricks or other platforms to vary heights as necessary.) The walls will be less likely to crumble as you dig and the liner will install more easily if you slope the walls in about 3 to 4 in. for each foot of depth. Make them smooth, removing roots, rocks, and other sharp protrusions.

Excavate a shallow relief about 1 ft. wide around the perimeter to contain the liner overlap and stone edging. (The depth of the relief should accommodate the thickness of the edging stones.) Somewhere along the perimeter, create an overflow channel to take runoff after a heavy rain. This can simply be a 1- to 2-in. depression

a foot or so wide spanned by one of the edging stones. Lengths of PVC pipe placed side by side beneath the stone (as shown in the drawing on p. 128) will keep the liner in place. The overflow channel can open onto a lower area of lawn or garden adjacent to the pond or to a rock-filled dry well.

Fitting the liner

When the hole is complete, cushion the surfaces to protect the liner ❷. Here we show an inch-thick layer of sand on the bottom surfaces and carpet underlayment on the sloping walls. Fiberglass batting insulation also works well, as do old blankets or even heavy landscaping fabric.

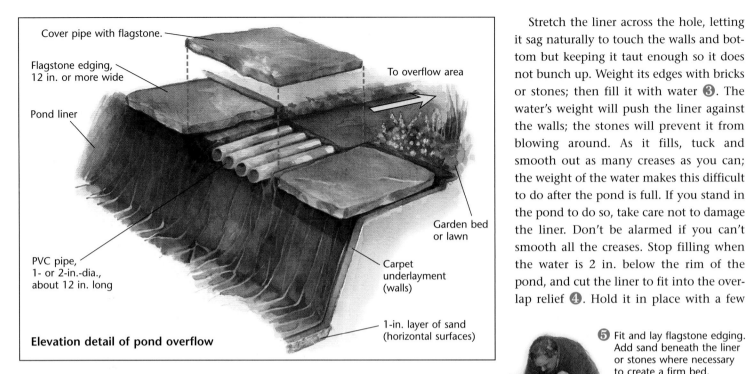

Cover pipe with flagstone.

Flagstone edging,
12 in. or more wide

Pond liner

To overflow area

PVC pipe,
1- or 2-in.-dia.,
about 12 in. long

Garden bed
or lawn

Carpet
underlayment
(walls)

1-in. layer of sand
(horizontal surfaces)

Elevation detail of pond overflow

Stretch the liner across the hole, letting it sag naturally to touch the walls and bottom but keeping it taut enough so it does not bunch up. Weight its edges with bricks or stones; then fill it with water ❸. The water's weight will push the liner against the walls; the stones will prevent it from blowing around. As it fills, tuck and smooth out as many creases as you can; the weight of the water makes this difficult to do after the pond is full. If you stand in the pond to do so, take care not to damage the liner. Don't be alarmed if you can't smooth all the creases. Stop filling when the water is 2 in. below the rim of the pond, and cut the liner to fit into the overlap relief ❹. Hold it in place with a few

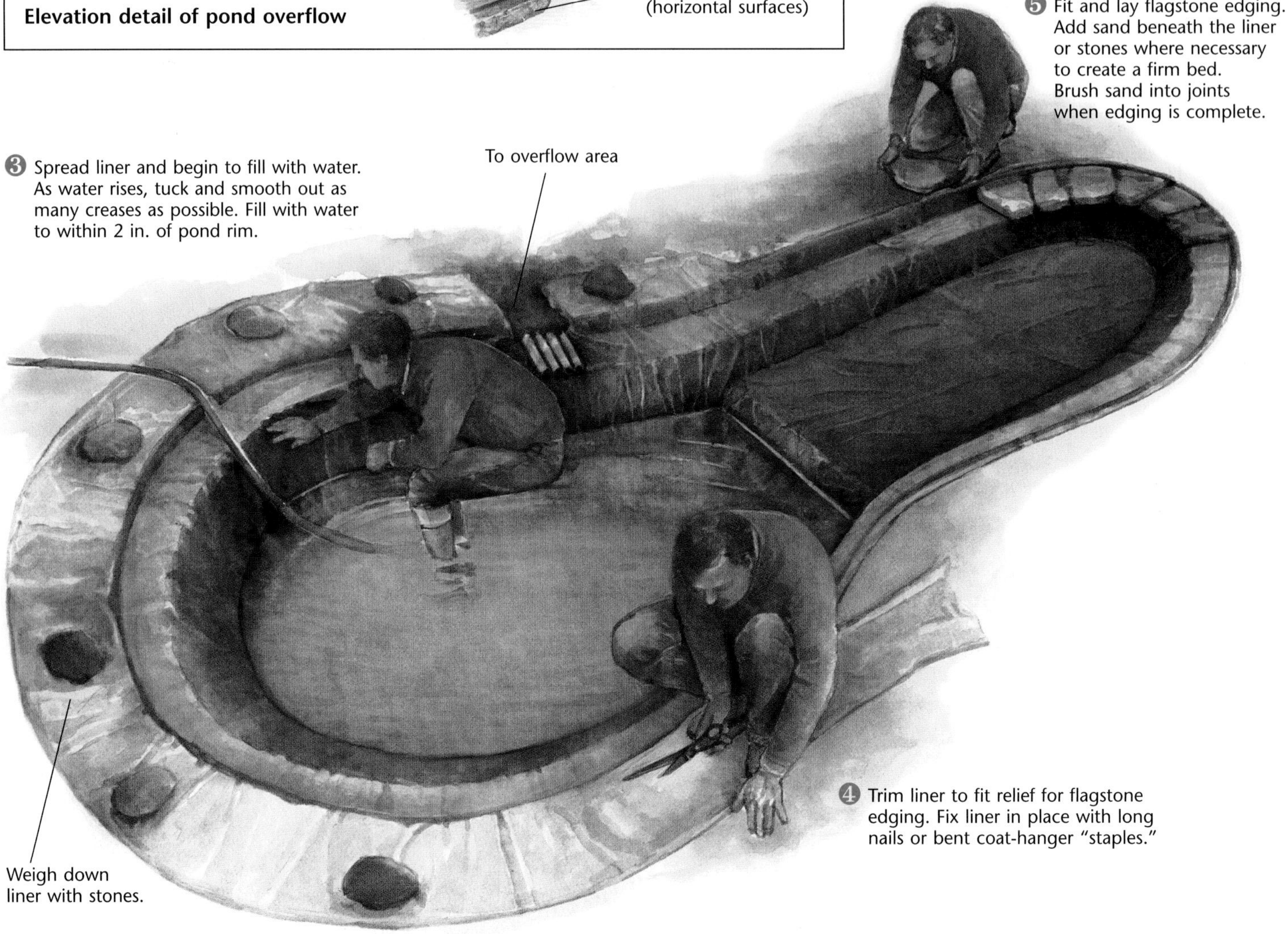

❸ Spread liner and begin to fill with water. As water rises, tuck and smooth out as many creases as possible. Fill with water to within 2 in. of pond rim.

To overflow area

❺ Fit and lay flagstone edging. Add sand beneath the liner or stones where necessary to create a firm bed. Brush sand into joints when edging is complete.

Weigh down liner with stones.

❹ Trim liner to fit relief for flagstone edging. Fix liner in place with long nails or bent coat-hanger "staples."

long nails or large "staples" made from coat hangers while you install the edging.

Edging the pond

Finding and fitting flagstones so there aren't wide gaps between them is the most time-consuming part of this task. Cantilevering the stones an inch or two over the water will hide the liner somewhat.

The stones can be laid directly on the liner, as shown ❺. Add sand under the liner to level the surface where necessary so that the stones don't rock. Such treatment will withstand the occasional gingerly traffic of pond and plant maintenance but not the wear and tear of young children or large dogs regularly running across the edging. (The liner won't go long without damage if used as a wading pool.) If you anticipate heavier traffic, you can bed the stones in 2 to 3 in. of mortar. It's prudent to consult with a landscape contractor about whether your intended use and soil require some sort of footing for mortared stones.

Water work

Unless you are a very tidy builder, the water you used to fit the liner will be too dirty to leave in the pond. (Spilled mortar can also make the water too alkaline for plants or fish.) Siphon or pump out the water, clean the liner, and refill the pond. If you're adding fish to the pond, you'll need to let the water stand for a week or so to allow any chlorine (which is deadly to fish) to dissipate. Check with local pet stores to find out if your water contains chemicals that require commercial conditioners to make the water safe for fish.

Installing the pond and plants is only the first step in water gardening. It takes patience, experimentation, and usually some consultation with experienced water gardeners to achieve a balance between plants, fish, and waterborne oxygen, nutrients, and waste that will sustain all happily, while keeping algae, diseases, insects, and predators at acceptable levels.

Growing pond plants

One water lily, a few upright-growing plants, and a bundle of submerged plants (which help keep the water clean) are enough for a medium-size pond. An increasing number of nurseries and garden centers stock water lilies and other water plants. For a larger selection, your nursery or garden center may be able to recommend a specialist supplier.

These plants are grown in containers filled with heavy garden soil (*not* potting soil, which contains ingredients that float). You can buy special containers designed for aquatic plants, or simply use plastic pails or dishpans. Line basket-like containers with burlap to keep the soil from leaking out the holes. A water lily needs at least 2 to 3 gal. of soil; the more, the better. Most other water plants, such as arrowhead and wild blue flag, need at least 2 gal. of soil.

After planting, add a layer of gravel on the surface to keep soil from clouding the water and to protect roots from marauding fish. Soak the plant and soil thoroughly; then set the container in the pond, positioning it so the water over the soil is 6 to 18 in. deep for water lilies, 0 to 6 in. for most other plants.

For maximum bloom, push a tablet of special water-lily fertilizer into the pots once or twice a month throughout the summer. Most water plants are easy to grow and carefree, although many are tropicals that die after hard frost, so you'll have to replace them each spring.

Planting water plants

Set water plants in a container of heavy garden soil. Cover soil surface with gravel to keep soil from floating away.

Gravel

1- to 3-gal. dishpan or special container lined with burlap and filled with heavy garden soil

Building a Retaining Wall

Contours and sloping terrain can add considerable interest to a home landscape. But you can have too much of a good thing. Two designs in this book employ retaining walls to alter problem slopes. The wall shown on p. 44 eliminates a small but abrupt grade change, producing two almost level surfaces and the opportunity to install attractive plantings on them. On p. 80 curving retaining walls help turn a steep slope into a showpiece.

Retaining walls can be handsome landscape features in their own right. Made of cut stone, fieldstone, brick, landscape timbers, or concrete, they can complement the materials and style of your house or nearby structures. However, making a stable, long-lasting retaining wall of these materials can require tools and skills many homeowners do not possess.

For these reasons we've instead chosen retaining-wall systems made of precast concrete for designs in this book. Readily available in a range of sizes, surface finishes, and colors, these systems require few tools and no special skills to install. They have been engineered to resist the forces that soil, water, freezing, and thawing bring to bear on a retaining wall. Install these walls according to the manufacturer's specifications, and you can be confident that they will do their job for many years.

A number of systems are available in the region through nurseries, garden centers, and local contracting suppliers (check the Yellow Pages). But they all share basic design principles. Like traditional dry-stone walls, these systems rely largely on weight and friction to contain the weight of the soil. In many systems, interlocking blocks or pegs help align the courses and increase the wall's strength. In all systems, blocks must rest on a solid, level base. A freely draining backfill of crushed stone is essential to avoid buildup of water pressure (both liquid and frozen) in the retained soil, which can buckle even a heavy wall.

The construction steps shown here are typical of those recommended by most system manufacturers for retaining walls up to 3 to 4 ft. tall; be sure to follow the manufacturer's instructions for the system you choose. (Some installation guides are excellent; others are less helpful. Weigh the quality of instructions in your decision of which system to buy.) For higher walls, walls on loose soil or heavy clay soils, and walls retaining very steep slopes, it is prudent to consult with a landscape architect or contractor.

Building a wall

Installing a wall system is just about as simple as stacking up children's building blocks. The most important part of the job is establishing a firm, level base. Start by laying out the wall with string and hose (for curves) and excavating a base trench.

As the boxed drawing shows, the position of the wall in relation to the base of the slope determines the height of the

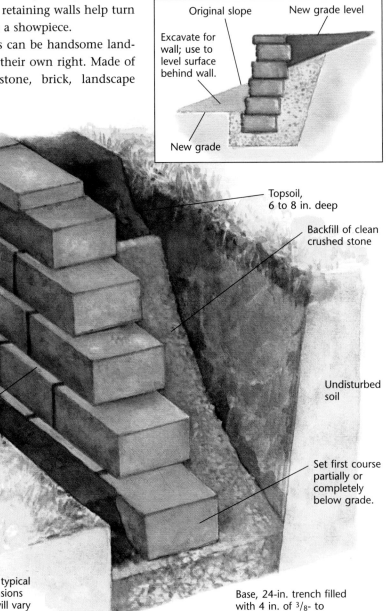

Original slope
New grade level
Excavate for wall; use to level surface behind wall.
New grade

Cap block

Topsoil, 6 to 8 in. deep

Backfill of clean crushed stone

Undisturbed soil

"Batter" wall by offsetting each course.

Set first course partially or completely below grade.

Precast-system retaining wall

Drawing represents typical construction; dimensions and specifications will vary depending on the system.

Base, 24-in. trench filled with 4 in. of $^3/_8$- to $^3/_4$-in. crushed stone wall, how much soil you move, and the leveling effect on the slope. Unless the wall is very long, it is a good idea to excavate along the entire length and fine-tune the line of the wall before beginning the base trench. Remember to excavate back far enough to accommodate the stone backfill. Systems vary, but a foot of crushed-stone backfill behind the blocks is typical.

Systems vary in the width and depth of trench and type of base material, but in all of them, the trench must be level across its width and along its length. We've shown a 4-in. layer of 3/8- to 3/4-in. crushed stone (blocks can slip sideways on rounded aggregate or pea gravel, which also don't compact as well). Depending on the system and the circumstances, a portion or all of the first course lies below grade, so the soil helps hold the blocks in place.

Add crushed stone to the trench, level it with a rake, and compact it with a hand tamper or mechanical compactor. Lay the first course of blocks carefully ❶. Check frequently to make sure the blocks are level across their width and along their length. Stagger vertical joints as you stack subsequent courses. Offset the faces of the blocks so the wall leans back into the retained soil. Some systems design this "batter" into their blocks; others allow you to choose from several possible setbacks.

As the wall rises, shovel backfill behind the blocks ❷. Clean crushed rock drains well; some systems suggest placing a barrier of landscaping fabric between the rock and the retained soil to keep soil from migrating into the fill and impeding drainage.

Thinner cap blocks finish the top of the wall ❸. Some wall systems recommend cementing these blocks in place with a weatherproof adhesive. The last 6 to 8 in.

Building a wall

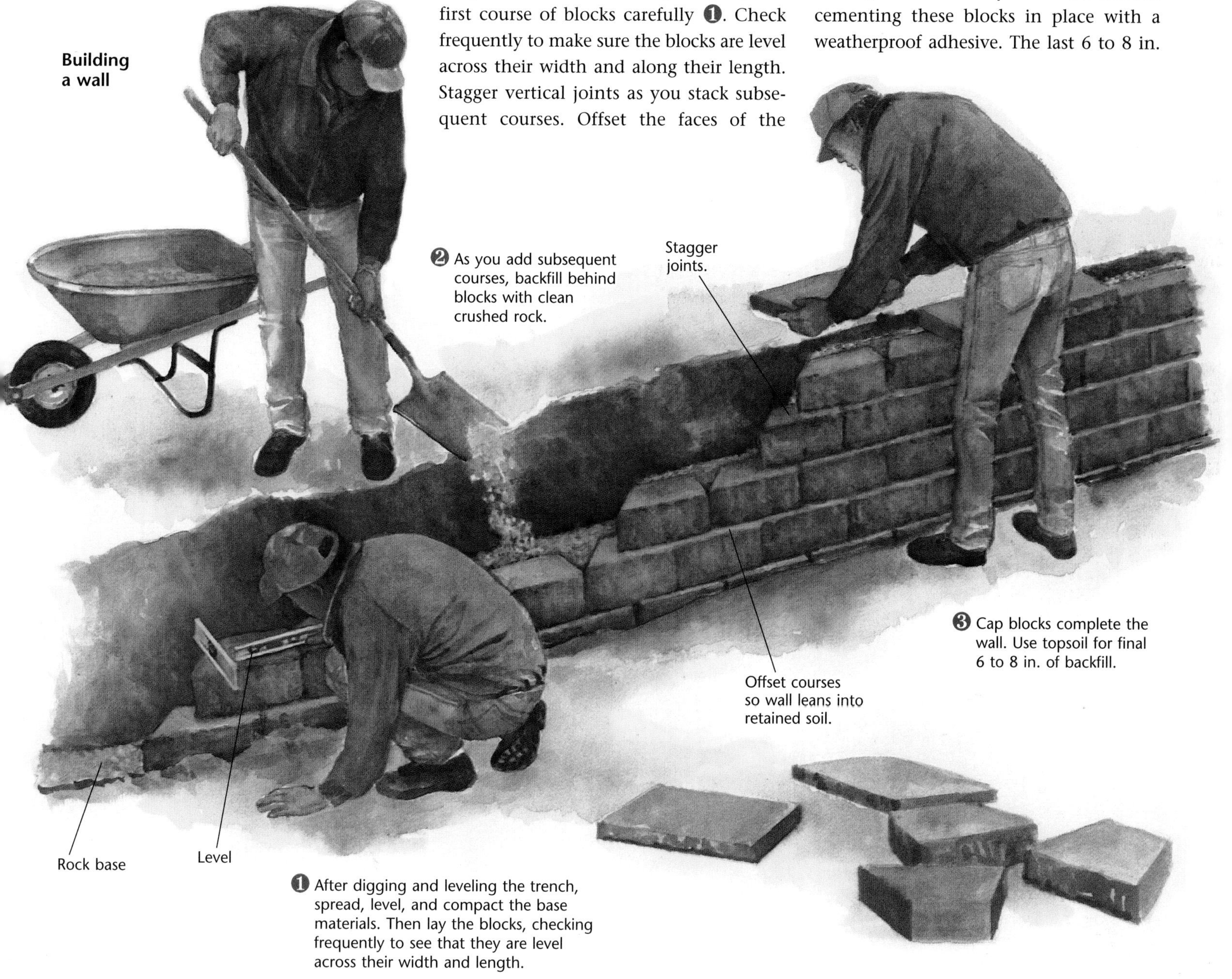

❷ As you add subsequent courses, backfill behind blocks with clean crushed rock.

Stagger joints.

❸ Cap blocks complete the wall. Use topsoil for final 6 to 8 in. of backfill.

Offset courses so wall leans into retained soil.

Rock base

Level

❶ After digging and leveling the trench, spread, level, and compact the base materials. Then lay the blocks, checking frequently to see that they are level across their width and length.

**Wall parallel to a slope:
Stepped base**

Backfill so grade behind
finishes level with top of wall.

Construct walls running
parallel to a slope in "steps,"
each with a level base.

Crushed-stone base

Finish grade
in front of wall

**Wall parallel to a slope:
Stepped cap**

Sometimes the top of a wall needs
to step up or down to accommodate
grade changes in the slope behind.

Cap block

A "return" corner

Where you want the slope to extend
beyond the end of the wall, make a
corner that cuts into the slope.

Step wall below grade
to provide solid foundation.

Line of finish
grade outside wall

of the backfill should be topsoil, firmed
into place and ready for planting.

If your site slopes along the wall's
length, you'll need to "step" the bottom of
the wall, as shown at top left. Create a
length of level trench along the lowest portion of the site; then work up the slope,
creating steps as necessary. The design
shown on p. 82 incorporates this solution.
The base starts level with an adjacent driveway, then rises up a gently sloping hill,
while the top of the wall remains level.

The top of the wall can also step if the
slope dissipates at one end (see drawing at
middle left). Here the base of the wall will
rest on level ground, but the slope behind
the wall decreases along the wall's length,
as does the height of the wall. Such slopes
are common on sites such as the one
shown on pp. 80–83, which slopes away
from the house and toward the driveway.
The design on p. 80 shows another solution to this dilemma—a wall of uniform
height with a "return" corner at one end
(see bottom left), backfilled to raise the
grade behind to the top of the wall.

Curves and corners

Wall-system blocks are designed so that
curves are easy to lay. Corners may require
that you cut a few blocks or use specially
designed blocks, but they are otherwise
uncomplicated. If your wall must fit a pre-
scribed length between corners, consider
working from the corners toward the middle (after laying a base course). Masons use
this technique, which also helps to avoid
exposing cut blocks at the corners.

You can cut blocks with a mason's chisel
and mallet or rent a mason's saw. Chiseling
works well where the faces of the blocks are
rough textured, so the cut faces blend right
in. A saw is best for smooth-faced blocks
and projects requiring lots of cutting.

Where the wall doesn't run the full
length of the slope, the best-looking and
most structurally sound termination is a
corner constructed to cut back into the
slope, as shown at bottom left.

Steps

Steps in a low retaining wall are not difficult to build, but they require forethought and careful layout. Systems differ on construction details. The drawing below shows a typical design where the blocks and stone base rest on "steps" cut into firm subsoil. If your soil is less stable or is recent fill, you should excavate the entire area beneath the steps to the same depth as the wall base and build a foundation of blocks, as shown in the boxed drawing.

These steps are independent of the adjacent "return" walls, which are vertical, not battered (stepped back). In some systems, steps and return walls are interlocked. To match a path, you can face the treads with the same stone, brick, or pavers, or you can use the system's cap blocks or special treads.

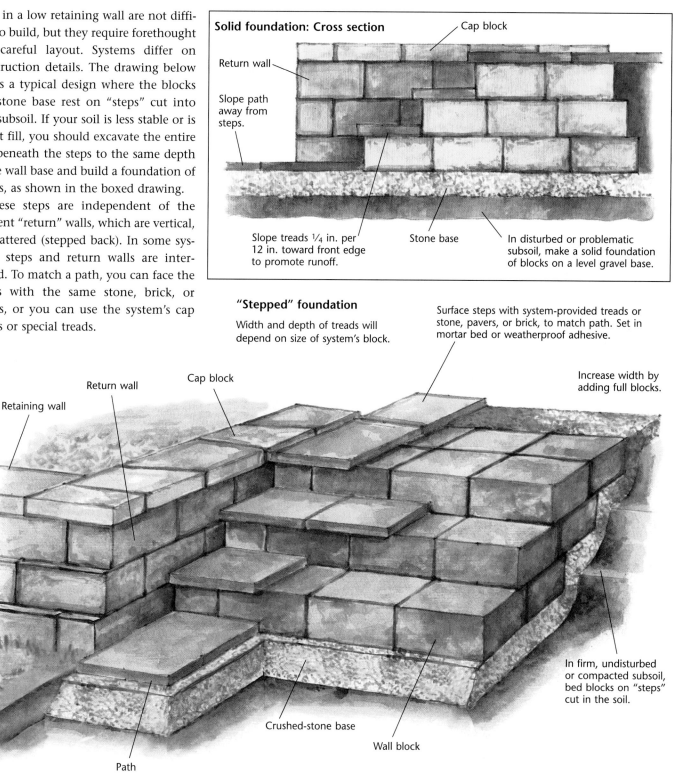

Solid foundation: Cross section

Cap block

Return wall

Slope path away from steps.

Slope treads 1/4 in. per 12 in. toward front edge to promote runoff.

Stone base

In disturbed or problematic subsoil, make a solid foundation of blocks on a level gravel base.

"Stepped" foundation

Width and depth of treads will depend on size of system's block.

Surface steps with system-provided treads or stone, pavers, or brick, to match path. Set in mortar bed or weatherproof adhesive.

Increase width by adding full blocks.

Retaining wall

Return wall

Cap block

In firm, undisturbed or compacted subsoil, bed blocks on "steps" cut in the soil.

Crushed-stone base

Wall block

Path

Fences, Arbors, and Trellises

Novices who have no trouble tackling a simple flagstone path often get nervous when it comes time to erect a fence, an arbor, or even a trellis. While such projects can require more skill and resources than others in the landscape, the ones in this book have been designed with less-than-confident do-it-yourself builders in mind. The designs are simple, the materials are readily available, and the tools and skills will be familiar to anyone accustomed to ordinary home maintenance.

First we'll introduce you to the materials and tools needed for the projects. Then we'll present the small number of basic operations you'll employ when building them. Finally, we'll provide drawings and comments on each of the projects.

Materials

Of the materials offering strength, durability, and attractiveness in outdoor settings, wood is the easiest to work and affords the quickest results. While almost all commercially available lumber is strong enough for landscape structures, most decay quickly when in prolonged contact with soil and water. Cedar, cypress, and redwood, however, contain natural preservatives and are excellent for landscape use. Alternatively, a range of softwoods (such as pine, fir, and hemlock) are pressure-treated with preservatives and will last for many years. Parts of structures that do not come in contact with soil or are not continually wet can be made of ordinary construction-grade lumber, but unless they're regularly painted, they will not last as long as treated or naturally decay-resistant material.

In addition to dimension lumber, several of the designs incorporate lattice, which is thin wooden strips crisscrossed to form patterns of diamonds or squares. Premade lattice is widely available in sheets 4 ft. by 8 ft. and smaller. Lattice comes in decay-resistant woods as well as in treated and untreated softwoods. The strips are typically from $1/8$ to $3/8$ in. thick and about $1^{1}/_{2}$ in. wide, overlapped to form squares ranging from 1 to 3 in. or more on a side. Local supplies vary, and you may find lattice made of thicker or narrower material. Lattice can be tricky to cut; if you're uneasy about this task, many suppliers will cut it for you for a small fee.

Fasteners

For millennia, even basic structures such as these would have been assembled with complicated joints, the cutting and fitting of which required long training to master. Today, with simple nailed, bolted, or screwed joints, a few hours' practice swinging a hammer or wielding a cordless electric screwdriver is all the training necessary.

All these structures can be assembled entirely with nails. But screws are stronger and, if you have a cordless screwdriver, make assembly easier. Buy common or box nails (both have flat heads) hot-dipped galvanized to prevent rust. Self-tapping screws ("deck" screws) require no pilot holes. For rust resistance, buy galvanized screws or screws treated with zinc dichromate.

Galvanized metal connectors are available to reinforce the joints used in these projects. (See the joinery drawings on pp. 138–139.) For novice builders, connectors are a great help in aligning parts and making assembly easier. (Correctly fastened with nails or screws, the joints are strong enough without connectors.)

Finishes

Cedar, cypress, and redwood are handsome when left unfinished to weather, when treated with clear or colored stains, or when painted. Pressure-treated lumber is best painted or stained to mask the greenish cast of the preservatives; weathered it turns a rather unattractive gray-green.

Outdoor stains are becoming increasingly popular. Clear or lightly tinted stains can preserve or enhance the rich reddish browns of cedar, cypress, and redwood. Stains also come in a range of colors that can be used like paint. Because they penetrate the wood rather than forming a film, stains don't form an opaque surface—you'll still need paint to make a picket fence white. On the other hand, stains won't peel or chip like paint and are therefore easier to touch up and refinish.

When choosing a finish, take account of what plants are growing on or near the structure. It's a lot of work to remove yards of vines from a trellis or squeeze between a large shrub and a fence to repaint; consider an unfinished decay-resistant wood or an initial stain that you allow to weather.

Tools

Even the least-handy homeowner is likely to have most of the tools needed for these projects: claw hammer, crosscut handsaw, brace-and-bit or electric drill, adjustable wrench, combination square, tape measure, carpenter's level, and sawhorses. You may even have Grandpa's old posthole digger. Many will have a handheld power circular saw, which makes faster (though noisier) work of cutting parts to length. A cordless drill/screwdriver is invaluable if you're substituting screws for nails. If you have more than a few holes to dig, consider renting a gas-powered posthole digger. A 12-in.-diameter hole will serve for 4x4 posts; if possible, get a larger-diameter digger for 6x6 posts.

Setting posts

All the projects are anchored by firmly set, vertical posts. In general, the taller the structure, the deeper the post should be set. For the arbors and the tallest fences, posts should be at least 3 ft. deep. Posts for fences up to 4 ft. tall can be set 2 ft. deep. To avoid post movement caused by expansion and contraction of the soil during freeze-thaw cycles, set all arbor posts below the frost line. The colder the climate, the deeper the frost line; check with local building authorities.

The length of the posts you buy depends, of course, on the depth at which they are set and their finished heights. When calculating lengths of arbor posts, remember that the tops of the posts must be level. The easiest method of achieving this is to cut the posts to length after installation. For example, buy 12-ft. posts for an arbor finishing at 8 ft. above grade and set 3 ft. in the ground. The convenience is worth the expense of the foot or so you cut off. The site and personal preference can determine whether you cut fence posts to length after installation or buy them cut to length and add or remove fill from the bottom of the hole to position them at the correct heights.

Fence posts

Lay out and set the end or corner posts of a fence first; then add the intermediate posts. Dig the holes by hand or with a power digger ❶. To promote drainage, place several inches of gravel at the bottom of the hole for the post to rest on. Checking with a carpenter's level, plumb the post vertically and brace it with scrap lumber nailed to stakes ❷. Then add a few more inches of gravel around the post's base.

If your native soil compacts well, you can fix posts in place with tamped earth. Add the soil gradually, tamping it continuously with a heavy iron bar or 2x4. Check regularly with a level to see that the post doesn't get knocked out of plumb. This technique suits rustic or informal fences, where misalignments caused by shifting posts aren't noticeable or damaging.

For more formal fences, or where soils are loose or fence panels are buffeted by winds or snow, it's prudent to fix posts in concrete ❸. Mix enough concrete to set

Setting a fence post

Post — Slope top surface for drainage.

3 ft. (typical)

Concrete and rubble (shown), or tamped earth

Coarse gravel

1 ft. (typical)

❶ Position the end or corner posts; then dig holes for them.

❷ Plumb the post, checking on adjacent faces with a level. Hold it in position with stakes and braces.

❸ Fill the hole with concrete and rubble.

④ Stretch a string between the tops of the two end posts. Then locate positions of intermediate posts with a plumb bob.

⑤ After digging the holes, stretch a string between the end posts to align intermediate posts. Use a level to plumb adjacent faces.

Fencing a slope

Whether you step the top of the fence or make it parallel to the slope, fence posts must be vertical.

the two end posts; as a rule of thumb, figure one 80-lb. bag of premixed concrete per post. As you shovel it in, prod the concrete with a stick to settle it, particularly if you've added rubble to extend the mix. Build the concrete slightly above grade and slope it away from the post to aid drainage.

Once the end posts are set, stretch a string between the posts. (The concrete should cure for 24 hours before you nail or screw rails and panels in place, but you can safely stretch string while the concrete is still wet.) Measure along the string to position the intermediate posts; drop a plumb bob from the string at each intermediate post position to gauge the center of the hole below ④. Once all the holes have been dug, again stretch a string between the end posts, near the top. Set the intermediate posts as described previously; align one face with the string and plumb adjacent faces with the carpenter's level ⑤. Check positions of intermediate posts a final time with a tape measure.

If the fence is placed along a slope, the top of the slats or panels can step down the slope or mirror it (as shown in the bottom drawing at left). Either way, make sure that the posts are plumb, rather than leaning with the slope.

Arbor posts

Arbor posts are installed just like fence posts, but you must take extra care when positioning them. The corners of the structure must be right angles, and the sides must be parallel. Locating the corners with batter boards and string is fussy but accurate. Make the batter boards by nailing 1x2 stakes to scraps of 1x3 or 1x4, and position them about 1 ft. from the approximate location of each post as shown in the boxed drawing on the facing page. Locate the exact post positions with string; adjust the string so the diagonal measurements are equal, which ensures that the corners of the structure will be at right angles.

At the intersections of the strings, locate the postholes by eye or with a plumb bob ❶. Remove the strings and dig the holes; then reattach the strings to position the posts exactly ❷. Plumb and brace the posts carefully. Check positions with the level and by measuring between adjacent posts and across diagonals. Diagonal braces between adjacent posts will stiffen them and help align their faces ❸. Then add concrete ❹ and let it cure for a day.

To establish the height of the posts, measure up from grade on one post; then use a level and straightedge to mark the heights of the other posts from the first one. Where joists will be bolted to the faces of the posts, you can install the joists and use their top edges as a handsaw guide for cutting the posts to length.

Batter boards

Set L-shaped batter boards at each corner and stretch string to position the posts exactly.

1x2 stakes and 1x3 boards

Taut string

Taut string

18 to 24 in.

For square or rectangular post layout, diagonal measurements should be equal.

Setting arbor posts

❶ Position the posts with batter boards, taut string, and a plumb bob.

Batter board

Plumb bob

❷ Remove the string to dig the holes; then reattach it and align the outer faces of the posts with the string while you plumb and brace them.

Taut string

❸ Check distances between posts at top. Add diagonal bracing between posts to fix positions.

❹ Cement posts in place.

Joints

The components of the fences, arbors, and trellises used in this book are attached to the posts and to each other with the simple joints shown below. Because all the parts are made of dimensioned lumber, the only cuts you'll need to make are to length. For strong joints, cut ends as square as you can, so the mating pieces make contact across their entire surfaces. If you have no confidence in your sawing, many lumberyards will cut pieces to length for a modest fee.

Beginners often find it difficult to keep two pieces correctly positioned while trying to drive a nail into them, particularly when the nail must be driven at an angle, called "toenailing." If you have this problem, predrill for nails, or use screws, which draw the pieces together, or metal connectors, which can be nailed or screwed in place on one piece and then attached to the mating piece.

For several designs, you need to attach lattice panels to posts. The panels are made by sandwiching store-bought lattice between frames of dimensioned lumber

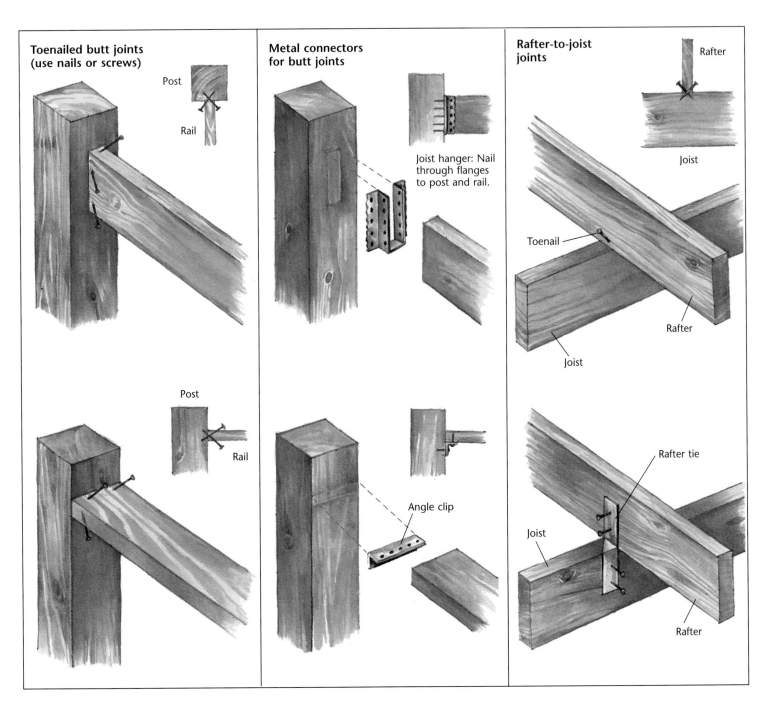

Toenailed butt joints (use nails or screws)

Post

Rail

Post

Rail

Metal connectors for butt joints

Joist hanger: Nail through flanges to post and rail.

Angle clip

Rafter-to-joist joints

Rafter

Joist

Toenail

Rafter

Joist

Rafter tie

Joist

Rafter

(construction details are given on the following pages). While the assembled panels can be toenailed to the posts, novices may find that the job goes easier using one or more types of metal connector, as shown in the drawing at below right. Attach the angle clips or angle brackets to the post; then position the lattice panel and fix it to the connectors. For greatest strength and ease of assembly, attach connectors with self-tapping screws driven by an electric screwdriver.

In the following pages, we'll show and comment on construction details of the fences, arbors, and trellises presented in the Portfolio of Designs. (The page number indicates the design.) Where the basic joints discussed here can be used, we have shown the parts but left choice of fasteners to you. Typical fastenings are indicated for other joints. We have kept the constructions shown here simple and straightforward. They are not the only possibilities, and we encourage experienced builders to adapt and alter constructions as well as designs to suit differing situations and personal preferences.

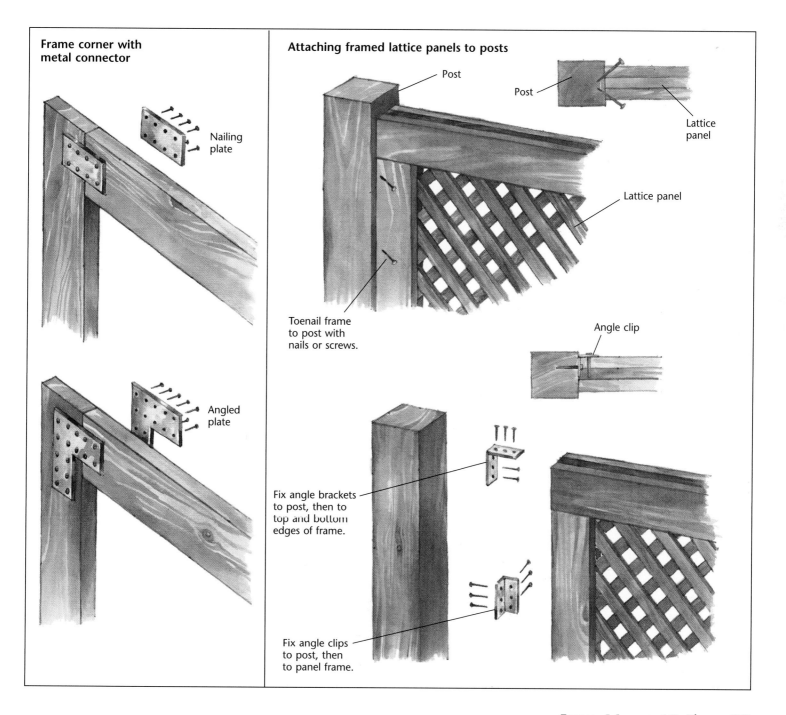

Frame corner with metal connector

Nailing plate

Angled plate

Attaching framed lattice panels to posts

Post

Post

Lattice panel

Lattice panel

Toenail frame to post with nails or screws.

Angle clip

Fix angle brackets to post, then to top and bottom edges of frame.

Fix angle clips to post, then to panel frame.

Picket fence
(pp. 50–51)

This fence, a variation of the traditional picket fence, adds a modestly formal note to a backyard entry. The hefty 6x6 posts are used for their visual weight; 4x4 posts are strong enough, if you prefer them.

To build the fence, you can set the posts first (see pp. 134–136) and make fence sections to fit between them. Or make the sections first and set posts accordingly. The pickets are sandwiched between two sets of rails top and bottom and are fixed in place with nails or screws. If you're making fence sections to fit a predetermined distance between posts, adjust the gap between pickets to ensure uniform spacing. When you lay out the pickets, make sure that there is a space between each post and the end picket.

You can fasten the rails to the posts by toenailing or with metal fasteners. Depending on your choice of attachment method, adding a spacer between the ends of the rails, as shown in the detail drawing, may make attachment easier. After the fence sections are fixed to the posts, add the cap pieces to the top rails and to the posts.

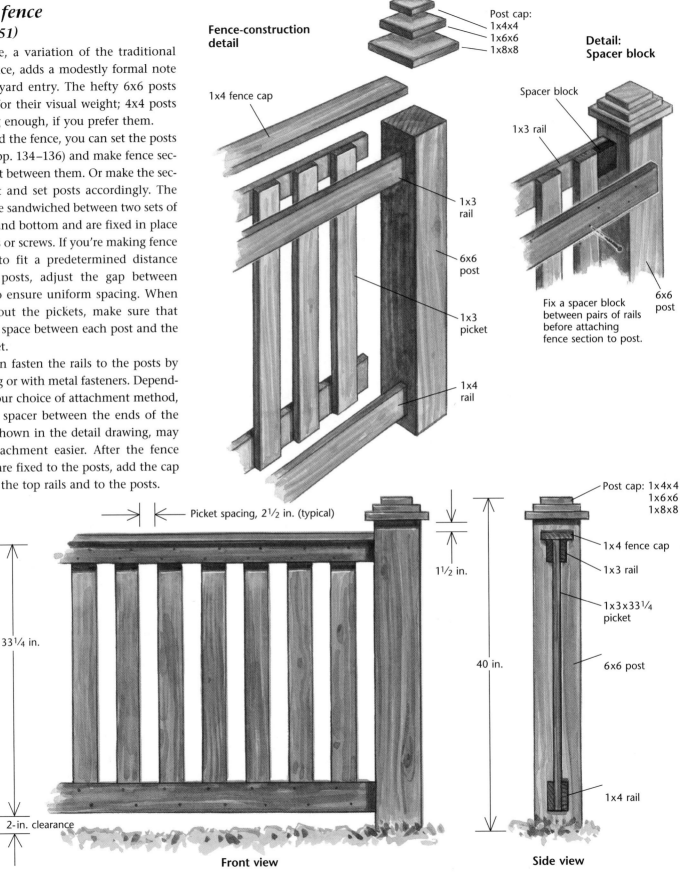

Fence-construction detail

Post cap:
1x4x4
1x6x6
1x8x8

1x4 fence cap

1x3 rail

6x6 post

1x3 picket

1x4 rail

Detail: Spacer block

Spacer block

1x3 rail

6x6 post

Fix a spacer block between pairs of rails before attaching fence section to post.

Picket spacing, 2½ in. (typical)

33¼ in.

36 in.

2-in. clearance

1½ in.

40 in.

Front view

Post cap: 1x4x4
1x6x6
1x8x8

1x4 fence cap

1x3 rail

1x3x33¼ picket

6x6 post

1x4 rail

Side view

Homemade lattice trellis

(pp. 52–53)

The trellis shown here supports climbing plants to make a vertical garden of a blank wall. The two gabled sections meet at a 90° angle, adding depth to the planting as well as height. Because of the angled assembly, the sections could stand on their own, but it's best to fix them to posts at the center and each end, as shown in the box below. The posts need extend no more than half the height of the trellis. Leave room between the trellis and the wall for access behind the trellis.

The trellis is made entirely of 1x2s. Start by cutting all the pieces to length. (Here we'll call the horizontal members "rails" and the vertical members "stiles.") Working on a large flat surface, nail or screw the two outer stiles to the top and bottom rails. Attach the remaining rails and then the intermediate stiles. You can use a piece of scrap wood 6 in. long as a spacer. Finally, cut and fix the diagonals across the top.

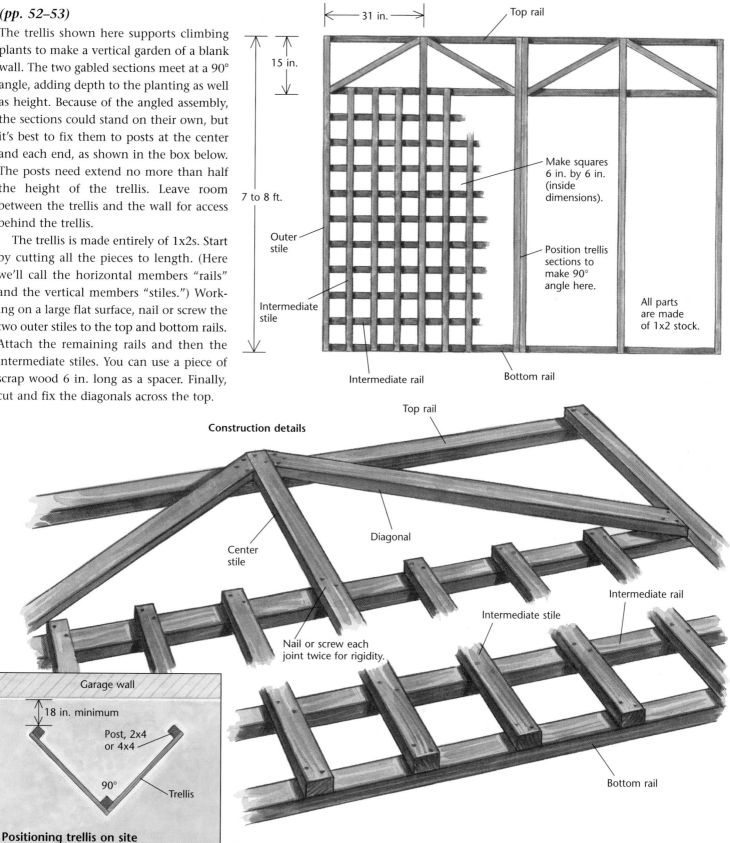

31 in.

15 in.

7 to 8 ft.

Top rail

Make squares 6 in. by 6 in. (inside dimensions).

Position trellis sections to make 90° angle here.

All parts are made of 1x2 stock.

Outer stile

Intermediate stile

Intermediate rail

Bottom rail

Construction details

Top rail

Diagonal

Center stile

Nail or screw each joint twice for rigidity.

Intermediate stile

Intermediate rail

Bottom rail

Garage wall

18 in. minimum

Post, 2x4 or 4x4

90°

Trellis

Positioning trellis on site

Hideaway arbor

(pp. 56–59)

This cozy enclosure shelters a bench and supports vines to shade the occupants. Once the posts are set in place, this project can be finished in a weekend.

Build the arbor before laying the pavers under it. After setting the 6x6 posts (see pp. 134–137), attach the 2x10 joists with carriage bolts. (The sizes of posts and joists have been chosen for visual effect; 4x4 posts and 2x6 or 2x8 joists will work, too.) Tack the joists in place with nails; then bore holes for the bolts through post and both joists with a long electrician's auger bit. Fix the rafters by toenailing or using rust-protected metal rafter ties. Nail or screw the rafters at each end to the posts for added stability.

Sandwich store-bought lattice between 1x3s to make the trellis panels for the vines, and fix them to the posts with metal connectors. Offset the corner joints, as shown in the drawing, or reinforce them with metal brackets, or both.

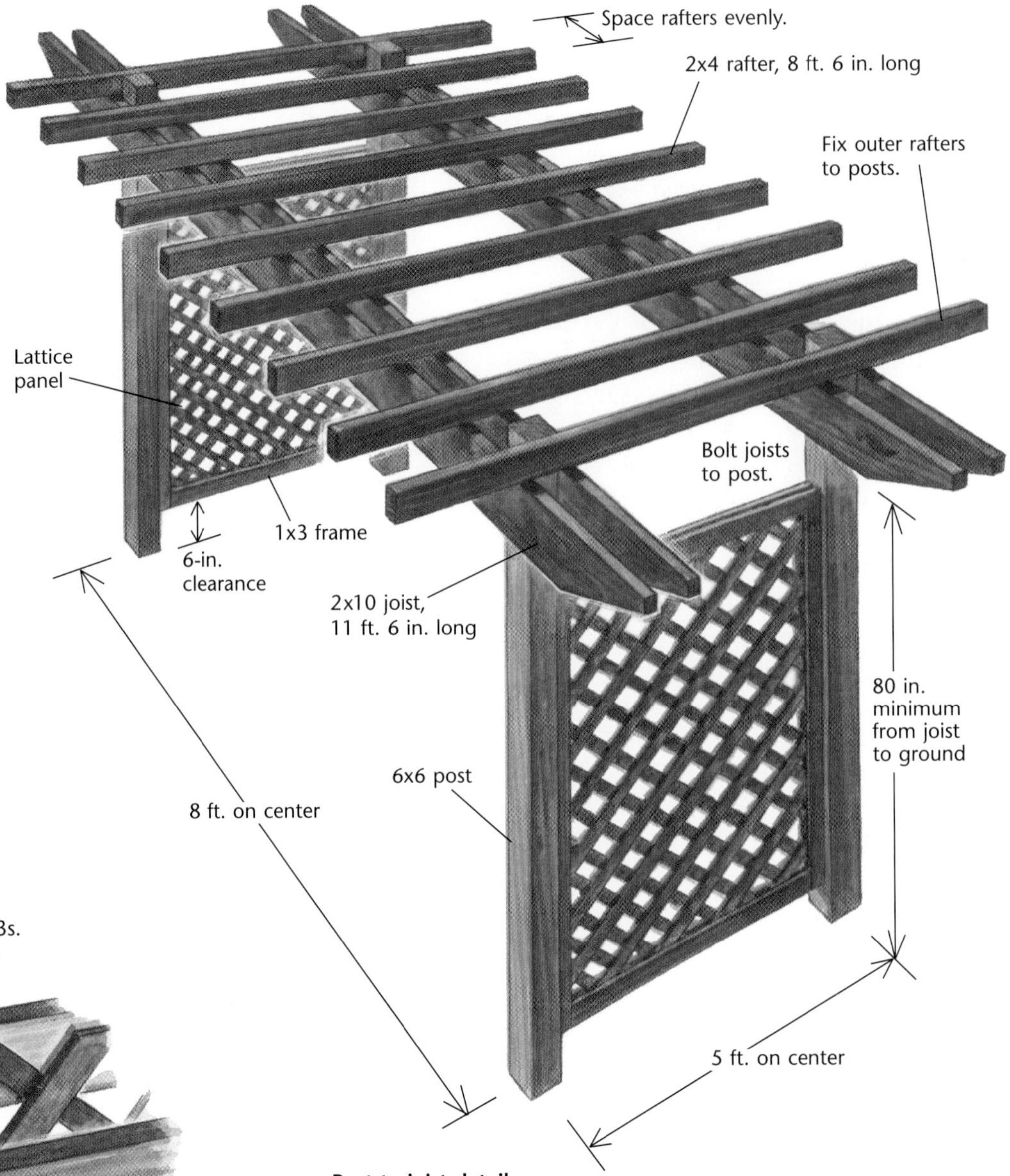

Space rafters evenly.

2x4 rafter, 8 ft. 6 in. long

Fix outer rafters to posts.

Lattice panel

Bolt joists to post.

1x3 frame

6-in. clearance

2x10 joist, 11 ft. 6 in. long

80 in. minimum from joist to ground

6x6 post

8 ft. on center

5 ft. on center

Post-to-joist detail

Trellis-panel construction

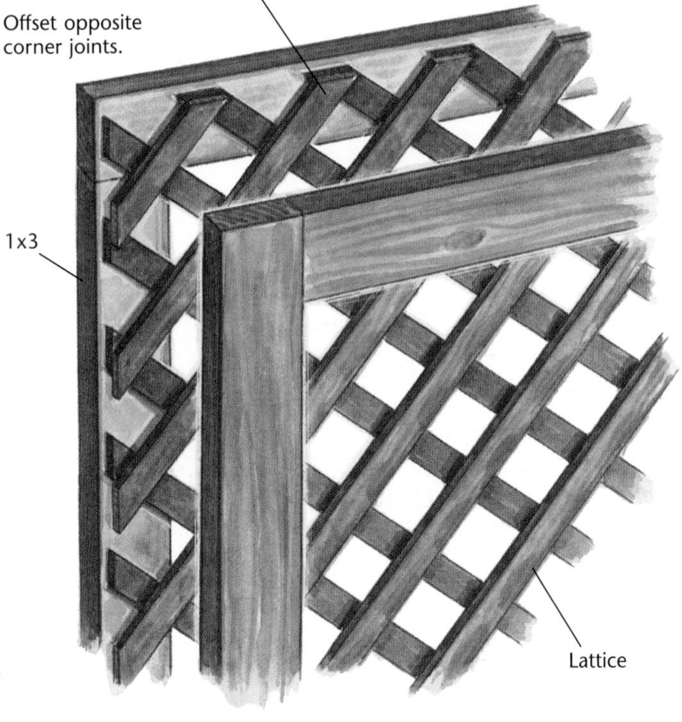

Tack lattice to one set of 1x3s. Nail or screw 1x3s together.

Offset opposite corner joints.

1x3

Lattice

2x4 rafter

Hex nut

Washer

½x10 carriage bolt

6x6 post

2x10 joist

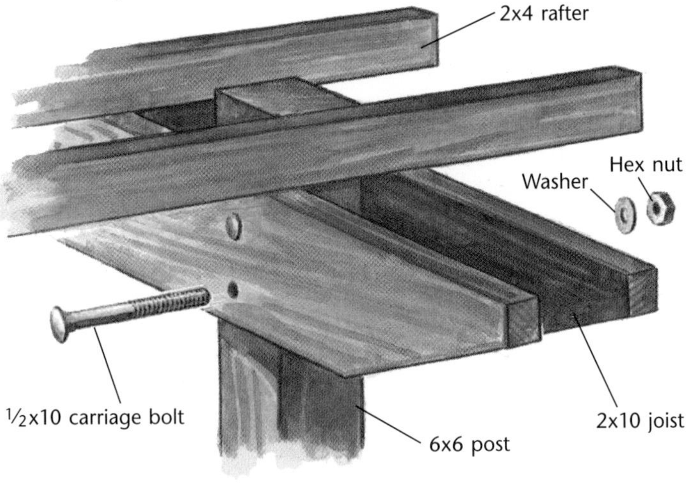

Louvered fence

(pp. 60–61)

Made of vertical slats set at an angle, this 6-ft.-tall fence allows air circulation to plants and people near the patio, while providing a privacy screen. Be sure to check local codes about height and setback from property lines.

The slats are supported top and bottom by 2x4 rails; a 2x6 beneath the bottom rail stiffens the entire structure, keeps the slat assembly from sagging, and adds visual weight to the design. Set the 4x4 posts (see pp. 134–136). Then cut the rails to fit between them. Toenailed nails or screws or metal connectors are strong enough, but you can add a 2x4 nailer between the rails (as shown in the drawing at bottom right) to make positioning and assembly easier.

Position the first 1x6 slat at 45° to the rails with a tri-square or protractor. Use a spacer block 1½ in. wide to position the other slats, as shown below. Nailing or screwing down through the top rail is easy. Nailing up through the bottom rail is more difficult; instead, you could toenail through the edges or faces of the slats into the bottom rail.

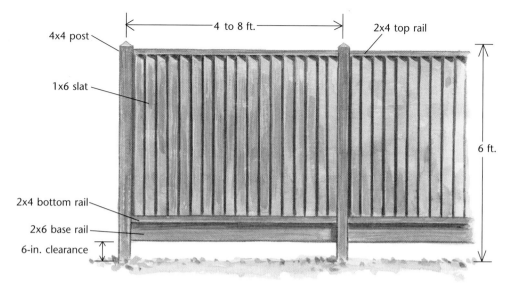

4x4 post
2x4 top rail
1x6 slat
4 to 8 ft.
6 ft.
2x4 bottom rail
2x6 base rail
6-in. clearance

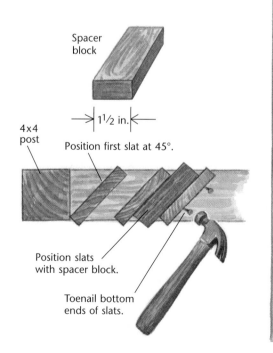

Spacer block
1½ in.
4x4 post
Position first slat at 45°.
Position slats with spacer block.
Toenail bottom ends of slats.

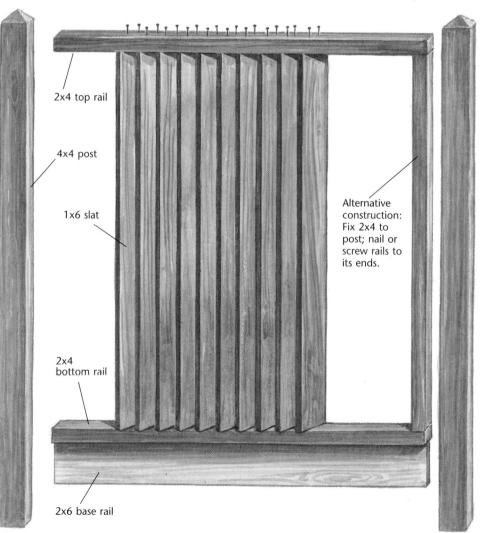

2x4 top rail
4x4 post
1x6 slat
2x4 bottom rail
2x6 base rail
Alternative construction: Fix 2x4 to post; nail or screw rails to its ends.

Board-and-lattice fence
(pp. 72–75)

Displayed in front of this tall fence, plants in a traditional border will be the center of attention, catching the eye without distractions in the background. If the fence is near a property line, remember to check local codes for rules about fence height.

This fence looks complicated, but it is easy to build. After you set the posts (see pp. 134–136), install the four horizontal rails, working from the bottom up. The support rail, a 2x6 turned on edge, provides visual weight (makes the fence look better) and keeps the bottom rail and slats from sagging if the distance between posts is 6 ft. or more.

The slats and lattice are sandwiched between two strips of wood (called "stops") nailed to each rail. These can be square or quarter-round in section. Attach one side of each pair of stops before fixing the rails to the posts. Cut lattice and slats to fit between the rails; then add the second stop. You could toenail the slats to the rail before adding the second stop to keep the slats from shifting side to side.

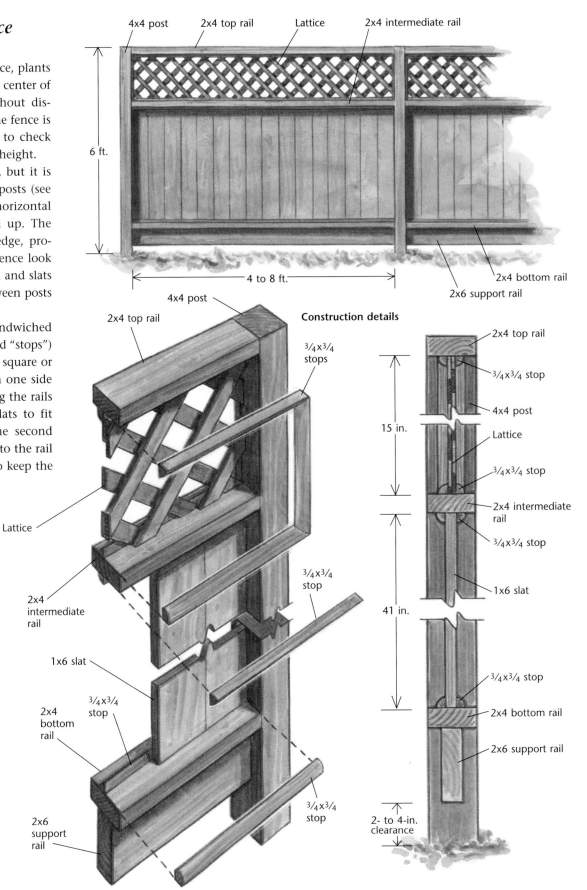

Construction details

Fixing the slats

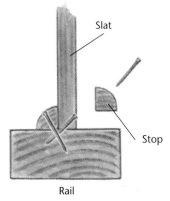

Nail the first stop, add the slats (toenailing them is optional), and then nail the second stop in place.

Passageway arbor

(pp. 90–91)

Draped with clematis, this shallow arbor welcomes visitors to a small Japanese-style stroll garden situated in a narrow side yard. Once you have gathered the materials together, you should need no more than an afternoon to build the arbor.

Set the posts first, as described on pp. 134–137. The hefty 6x6 posts shown here add presence to the arbor; but cheaper, easier-to-handle 4x4s will make an equally sturdy structure. Cut the joists and rafters to length. The 60° angles on their ends can easily be cut with a handsaw. Bolt or nail the joists in place. Then toenail the short rafters to the joists or attach them with metal fasteners.

To climb, clematis need something for their leaf petioles to wrap around. Stretching strands of coarse rope or cord between the large screw eyes fixed to the rafters and the base of the posts, as shown here, works well. The leafy vines soon hide the rope or cord from view.

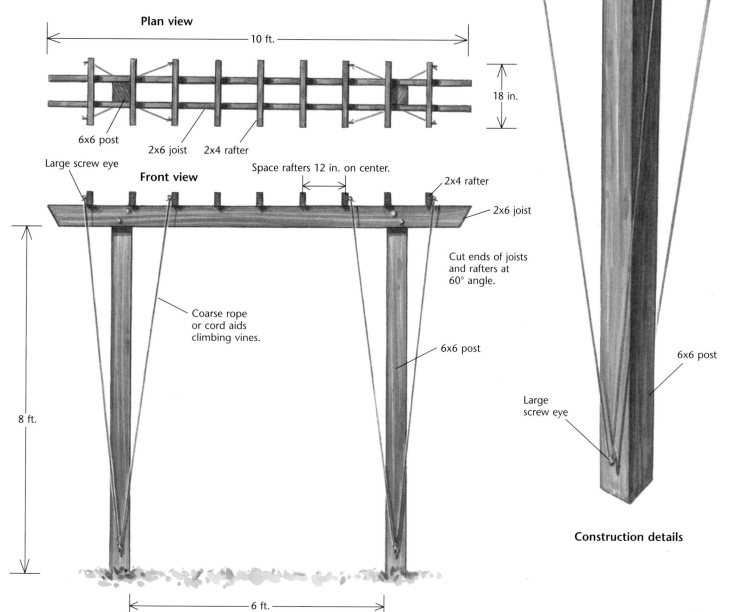

Large screw eye

2x4 rafter

2x6 joist

Stretch coarse rope or cord between screw eyes to aid climbing vines.

6x6 post

Large screw eye

Construction details

Plan view

10 ft.

18 in.

6x6 post

2x6 joist

2x4 rafter

Front view

Large screw eye

Space rafters 12 in. on center.

2x4 rafter

2x6 joist

Cut ends of joists and rafters at 60° angle.

6x6 post

Coarse rope or cord aids climbing vines.

8 ft.

6 ft.

Lattice skirting for a deck
(pp. 92–95)

The wide lattice gridwork shown here gives the base of a tall deck an airy but substantial look and creates (with a planting of sizable shrubs) a sense of enclosure for a storage area beneath the deck.

The gridwork can easily be nailed or screwed together on a large flat area and then attached to the deck posts. If you want to assemble the gridwork on the deck posts, first fix the horizontal members. Then screw the vertical members to them using an electric screwdriver. (Nailing these vertical pieces would be difficult.) To ensure equal spacing, lay out the vertical members before assembly.

We've shown a grid of 2x2s fixed to deck posts spaced 7 ft. apart. A lightweight grid made of 1x2s could be used for decks with posts spaced 4 to 6 ft. apart. Alter the size of the gridwork squares to ensure a uniform gridwork pattern between posts.

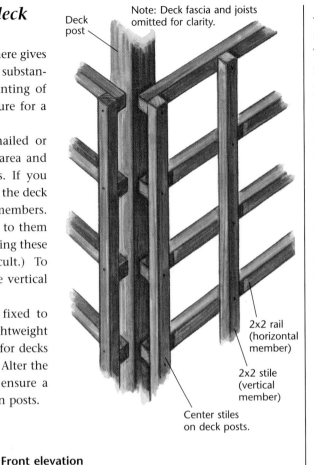

Deck post

Note: Deck fascia and joists omitted for clarity.

2x2 rail (horizontal member)

2x2 stile (vertical member)

Center stiles on deck posts.

Front elevation

Lattice attached to side of deck

Deck fascia

2x2 lattice

12 in. on center

Entry arbor and fence
(pp. 100–102)

This arbor makes an event of the passage from sidewalk to front door or from one part of your property to another. Two versions are shown on pp. 100–102. In one, the U-shaped base is extended to form a low fence on both sides of the arbor. The other features just the arbor.

Begin work on the arbor by erecting the U-shaped base sections. Note that the slats are held in place by narrow pieces of stop nailed to the rails and posts. (Slats can be 1x4s, 1x6s, or a mixture of both.) You can extend the base to make a fence as shown in the design on pp. 100–101.

To build the wide-grid lattice superstructure, first assemble the two 4-ft.-high side walls on a flat surface. Then nail them to the cap rail of the base. Fix the joists to the top plates of the side walls by toenailing or by using metal connectors. Toenail the diagonal braces in place. Assemble the 1-ft.-tall gable walls and nail them to the joists.

Use a framing square to lay out the angles on the ends of the rafters, or draw a full-scale front view of the gable and transfer the angles from the drawing. Complete the arbor by nailing the rafters to the gable walls and ridge.

Fence elevation

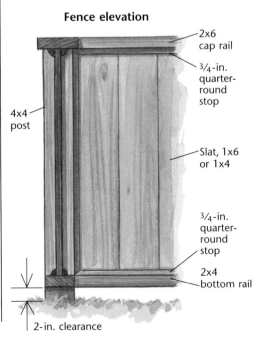

2x6 cap rail

3/4-in. quarter-round stop

4x4 post

Slat, 1x6 or 1x4

3/4-in. quarter-round stop

2x4 bottom rail

2-in. clearance

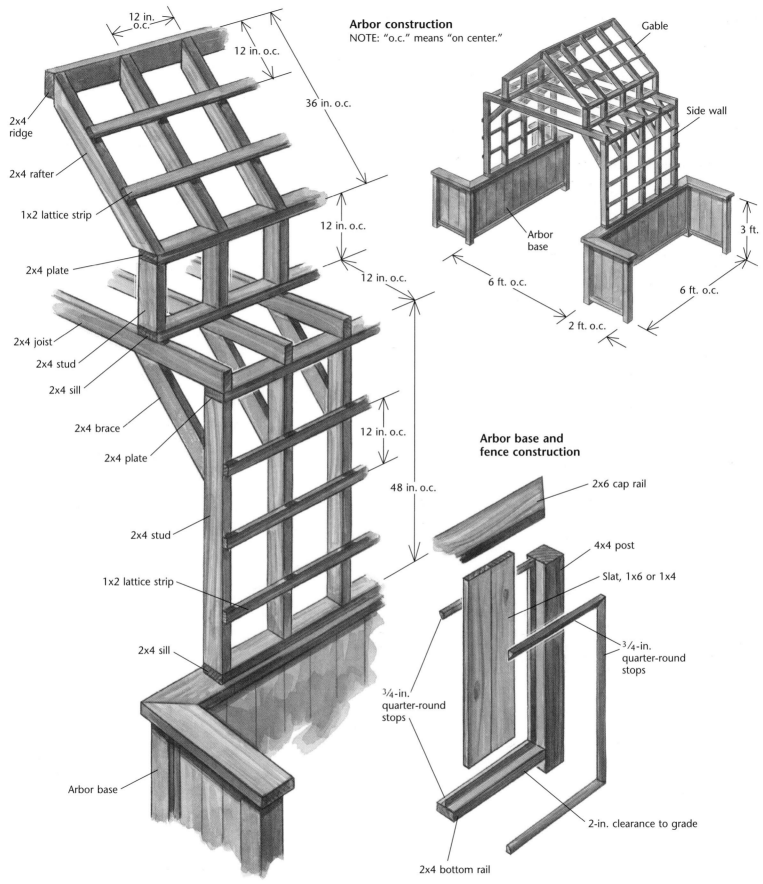

Arbor construction
NOTE: "o.c." means "on center."

12 in. o.c.

12 in. o.c.

36 in. o.c.

2x4 ridge

2x4 rafter

1x2 lattice strip

2x4 plate

12 in. o.c.

12 in. o.c.

2x4 joist

2x4 stud

2x4 sill

2x4 brace

2x4 plate

12 in. o.c.

2x4 stud

48 in. o.c.

1x2 lattice strip

2x4 sill

Arbor base

Gable

Side wall

Arbor base

3 ft.

6 ft. o.c.

6 ft. o.c.

2 ft. o.c.

Arbor base and fence construction

2x6 cap rail

4x4 post

Slat, 1x6 or 1x4

¾-in. quarter-round stops

¾-in. quarter-round stops

2-in. clearance to grade

2x4 bottom rail

Preparing the Soil for Planting

The better the soil, the better the plants. Soil quality affects how fast plants grow, how big they get, how good they look, and how long they live. But on many residential lots, the soil is shallow and infertile. Unless you happen to be lucky enough to have a better-than-average site where the soil has been cared for and amended over the years, perhaps for use as a vegetable garden or flower bed, you should plan to improve your soil before planting in it.

If you were planting just a few trees or shrubs, you could prepare individual planting holes for them and leave the surrounding soil undisturbed. However, for nearly all the plantings in this book, digging individual holes is impractical, and

it's much better for the plants if you prepare the soil throughout the entire area that will be planted. (The major exception is when you're planting under a tree, which we'll discuss on p. 150.)

For most of the situations shown in this book, you could prepare the soil with hand tools—a spade, digging fork, and rake. The job goes faster, though, if you use a rototiller, and a rototiller is better than hand tools for mixing amendments into the soil. Unless you grow vegetables, you probably won't use a rototiller often enough to justify buying one yourself, but you can easily borrow or rent a rototiller or hire someone with a tiller to come and prepare your site.

Loosen the soil

After you've removed any sod or other vegetation from the designated area (see pp. 116–117), the first step is digging or tilling to loosen the soil ❶. Do this on a day when the soil is moist—not so wet that it sticks to your tools or so dry that it makes dust. Start at one end of the bed and work back and forth until you reach the other end. Try to dig down at least 8 in., or deeper if possible. If the ground is very compacted, you'll need to make repeated passes with a tiller to reach 8 in. deep. Toss aside any large rocks, roots, or debris that you encounter as you dig. When working near a house or other buildings, be sure to locate buried wires, cables, and pipes. (This

Preparing the soil for planting

❶ Use a spade, digging fork, or tiller to dig at least 8 in. deep and to break the soil into rough clods. Discard rocks, roots, and debris. Watch out for underground utilities.

❷ Spread a 2- to 3-in. layer of organic matter on top of the soil.

❸ Sprinkle measured amounts of fertilizer and mineral amendments evenly across the entire area, and mix thoroughly into the soil.

is required by law in some towns.) Most local governments have a number you can call to request help locating buried utilities.

After this initial digging, the ground will probably be very rough and lumpy. Whump the clods with the back of a digging fork or make another pass with the tiller. Continue until you've reduced all the clumps to the size of apples.

After loosening the existing soil and digging it as deeply as possible, you may need to add topsoil to fill in low spots, refine the grade, or raise the planting area above the surrounding grade for better drainage or to make it easier to see a favorite plant. Unless you need just a few bags of it, order topsoil by the cubic yard from a landscape contractor; make sure it has been screened to remove big lumps.

Add organic matter

Common dirt (and purchased topsoil, too) consists mainly of rock and mineral fragments of various sizes—which are mostly coarse and gritty in sandy soil, and dust-fine in clay soil. One of the best things you can do to improve any kind of soil for garden plants is to add some organic matter.

Sold in bags or in bulk at nurseries and garden centers, organic materials include all kinds of composted plant parts and animal manures. Whatever you choose, be sure that it has already been composted or stored in a pile for several months. Fresh, raw manure can "burn" plant roots. Fresh sawdust or chipped bark can "steal" nitrogen from the soil. Fresh hay can contain weed seeds.

How much organic matter should you use? Spread a layer 2 to 3 in. thick across the entire area you're working on ❷. At this thickness, a cubic yard (about one heaping pickup-truck load) of bulk material, or six bales of peat moss, will cover 100 to 150 sq. ft. If you're working on a large area and need several cubic yards of organic matter, have it delivered. Ask the driver to dump the pile as close to your project area as possible; it's worth allowing

---

Common fertilizers and soil amendments

The following materials serve different purposes. Follow soil-test recommendations or the advice of an experienced gardener in choosing which amendments would be best for your soil. If so recommended, you can apply two or three of these amendments at the same time, using the stated rate for each one.

Material	Description	Amount for 100 sq. ft.
Bagged steer manure	A weak all-purpose fertilizer.	6–8 lb.
Dried poultry manure	A high-nitrogen fertilizer.	2 lb.
5-5-5 all-purpose fertilizer	An inexpensive and popular synthetic fertilizer.	2 lb.
Superphosphate or rock phosphate	Supplies phosphorus. Work into the soil as deep as possible.	2–4 lb.
Greensand	Supplies potassium and many trace elements.	2–4 lb.
Regular or dolomitic limestone	Used primarily to sweeten acid soil.	5 lb.
Gypsum	Helps loosen clay soil. Also helps reduce salt buildup in roadside soil.	2 lb.
Wood ash	Supplies potassium, phosphorus, and lime.	2–4 lb.

---

the truck to drive across your lawn to get there. You can spread a big truckload of material in just a few hours if you don't have to cart it very far.

Add fertilizers and mineral amendments

Organic matter improves the soil's texture and helps it retain water and nutrients, but it doesn't actually supply many nutrients. To provide the nutrients that plants require, you need to use organic or synthetic fertilizers and powdered minerals. It's most helpful if you mix these materials into the soil before you do any planting, putting them down into the root zone as shown in the drawing ❸, but you can also sprinkle them on top of the soil in subsequent years to maintain a planting.

Getting a sample of soil tested (a service that's usually available free or at low cost through your County Extension Service) is the most accurate way to determine how much of which nutrients is needed. Less precise, but often adequate, is asking the advice of an experienced gardener in your neighborhood. Test results or a gardener's advice will point out any significant deficiencies in your soil, but these are uncommon. Most soil just needs a moderate, balanced dose of nutrients.

Most important is to avoid using too much of any fertilizer or mineral. Don't guess at this; measure and weigh carefully. Calculate your plot's area. Follow your soil-test results, instructions on a commercial product's package, or the general guidelines given in the chart above, and weigh out the appropriate amount, using a kitchen or bathroom scale. Apply the material evenly across the plot with a spreader or by hand.

Mix and smooth the soil

Finally, use a digging fork or tiller and go back and forth across the bed again until the added materials are mixed thoroughly into the soil and everything is broken into nut-size or smaller lumps ❹. Then use a rake to smooth the surface ❺.

At this point, the soil level may look too high compared with adjacent pavement or lawn, but don't worry. It will settle a few inches over the next several weeks and end up close to its original level.

Working near trees

Plantings under the shade of stately old trees can be cool lovely oases, like the ones shown on pp. 84–87. But to establish the plants, you'll need to contend with the tree's roots. Contrary to popular belief, most tree roots are in the top few inches of the soil, and they extend at least as far away from the trunk as the limbs do. If you dig anyplace in that area, you'll probably cut or bruise some of the tree's roots. When preparing for planting beneath a tree, therefore, it is important to disturb as few roots as possible.

It is natural for a tree's trunk to flare out at the bottom and for the roots near the trunk to be partly above ground. Don't bury them. However, if the soil has eroded away from roots farther out from the trunk, it's okay to add a layer of soil up to several inches deep and top the new soil with a thinner layer of mulch. Adding some soil like this makes it easier to start ground covers or other plants underneath a tree. (See p. 157 for planting instructions.) Just don't overdo it—covering roots with too much soil can starve them of oxygen, damaging or killing them, and piling soil close to the trunk can rot the bark.

❹ Use a tiller or digging fork to mix everything together, again working as deep as possible.

❺ Finish by smoothing the surface with a rake.

Making neat edges

All but the most informal landscapes look best if you define and maintain neat edges between the lawn and any adjacent plantings. There are several ways to do this, varying in appearance, effectiveness, cost, and convenience. For the Midwest region, the best methods are cut edges, dry-laid brick or stone, and wood or timber. (Several prefabricated edging systems that you may see in stores or catalogs work well only in warmer climates; they tend to frost-heave in cold winters.) The time to install an edging is after you prepare the soil but before you plant the bed.

Cut edge

Lay a hose or rope on the ground to mark the line where you want to cut. Then cut along the line with a sharp spade or edging tool. Lift away any grass that was growing into the bed (or any plants that were running out into the lawn). Use a rake or hoe to smooth out a shallow trench on the bed side of the cut. Keep the trench empty; don't let it fill up with mulch.

Pros and cons: Free. Good for straight or curved edges, level or sloped sites. You have to recut the edge at least twice a year, in spring and late summer, but you can cut 50 to 100 ft. in an hour or so. Don't cut the trench too deep; if a mower wheel slips down into it, you'll scalp the lawn. Crabgrass and other weeds may sprout in the exposed soil.

Brick or stone mowing strip

Dig a trench about 8 in. wide and 4 in. deep around the edge of the bed. Fill it halfway with sand; then lay bricks on top, setting them level with the soil on the lawn side. You'll need three bricks

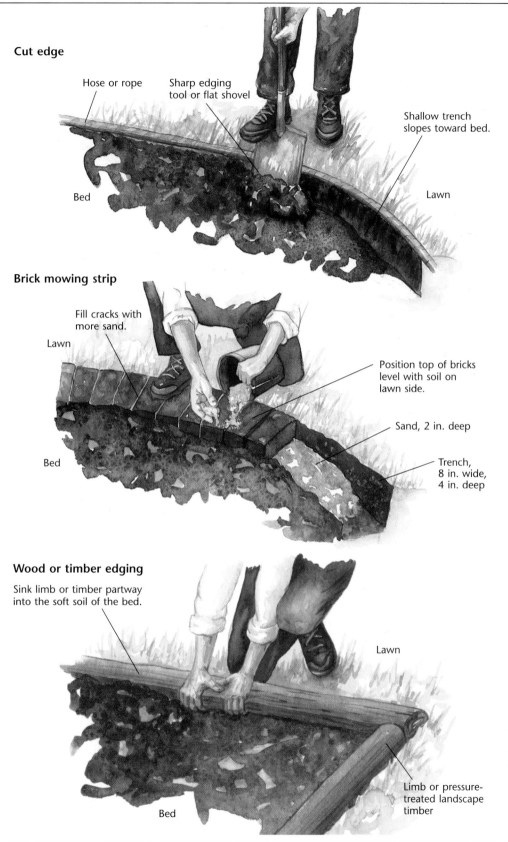

Cut edge

Hose or rope

Sharp edging tool or flat shovel

Shallow trench slopes toward bed.

Bed

Lawn

Brick mowing strip

Fill cracks with more sand.

Lawn

Position top of bricks level with soil on lawn side.

Sand, 2 in. deep

Bed

Trench, 8 in. wide, 4 in. deep

Wood or timber edging

Sink limb or timber partway into the soft soil of the bed.

Lawn

Limb or pressure-treated landscape timber

Bed

per foot of edging. Sweep extra sand into any cracks between the bricks. You'll probably have to reset a few frost-heaved bricks each spring. You can substitute cut stone blocks or concrete pavers for bricks.

Pros and cons: Good for straight or curved edges on level or gently sloped sites. Looks good in combination with brick walkways or a brick house. Fairly easy to install and maintain. Some kinds of grass and plants will grow under, between, or over the bricks.

Wood or timber edging

You can make a sturdy edging quickly by laying pressure-treated 3x4 landscape timbers from the lumberyard around the edge of the bed. For a rustic look, use tree trunks or limbs about 4 to 6 in. in diameter. Sink the limbs or pressure-treated timbers partway into the soft soil of the bed so they won't roll out of place. Simply butt ends together to extend the edging's length or to form a corner. You can't mow right up to a wood edging, but you can cut the lawn there with a string trimmer.

Pros and cons: Keeps mulch from drifting out of the bed but doesn't confine vigorous plants. Works best for straight edges on level sites, unless you choose curved limbs and fit them to the contours of the bed and the ground. Liable to frost-heave, but you can easily push timbers back into place in the spring. Natural wood is free or cheap, is easy to work with, and looks pleasingly rustic, but it decays after several years and needs to be replaced. Pressure-treated timbers cost more but look more formal and last for decades.

Buying Plants

Once you have chosen and planned a landscape project, make a list of the plants you want and start thinking about where to get them. You'll need to locate the kinds of plants you're looking for, choose good-quality plants, and get enough of the plants to fill your design area.

Where and how to shop

You may already have a favorite place to shop for plants. If not, look in the Yellow Pages under Nursery Stock, Nurserymen, Garden Centers, and Landscape Contractors, and choose a few places to visit. Take your shopping list, find a salesperson, and ask for help. The plants in this book are commonly available in most parts of the Midwest region, but you may not find everything you want at one place. The salesperson may refer you to another nursery, offer to special-order plants, or recommend similar plants as substitutes.

If you're buying too many plants to carry in your car or truck, ask about delivery—it's usually available and sometimes free. Some nurseries offer to replace plants that fail within a limited guarantee period, so ask about that, too.

The staff at a good nursery or garden center will usually be able to answer most of the questions you have about which plants to buy and how to care for them. If you can, go shopping on a rainy weekday when business is slow so staff will have time to answer your questions.

Don't be lured by the low prices of plants for sale at supermarkets or discount stores unless you're sure you know exactly what you're looking for and what you're looking at. The salespeople at these stores rarely have the time or knowledge to offer you much help, and the plants are often disorganized, unlabeled, and stressed by poor care.

If you can't find a plant locally or have a retailer order it for you, you can always order it yourself from a mail-order nursery. Most mail-order nurseries produce good plants and pack them well, but if you haven't dealt with a business before, be smart and place a minimum order first. Judge the quality of the plants that arrive; then decide whether or not to order larger quantities from that firm.

Choosing particular plants

If you need, for example, five boxwoods and the nursery or garden center has a whole block of them, how do you choose which five to buy? Because the sales staff may be too busy to help you decide, you may need to choose by yourself.

Most plants today are grown in containers, so it's possible to lift them one at a time and examine them from all sides. Following the guidelines shown in the drawings below, evaluate each plant's shape, size, health and vigor, and root system.

Trees and shrubs are sometimes sold "balled-and-burlapped," that is, with a ball

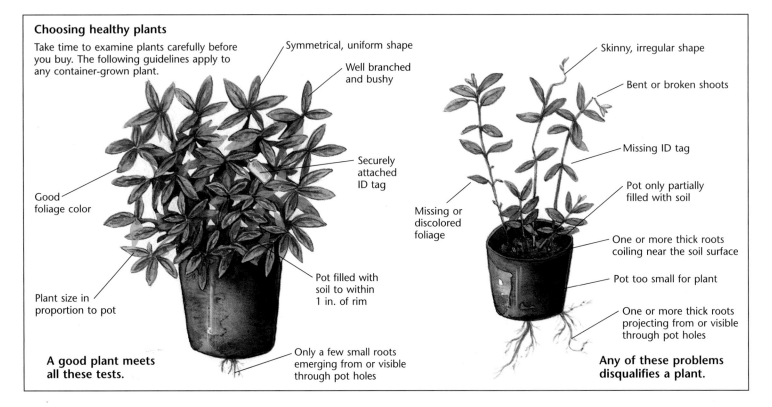

Choosing healthy plants

Take time to examine plants carefully before you buy. The following guidelines apply to any container-grown plant.

Symmetrical, uniform shape

Well branched and bushy

Securely attached ID tag

Good foliage color

Pot filled with soil to within 1 in. of rim

Plant size in proportion to pot

Only a few small roots emerging from or visible through pot holes

A good plant meets all these tests.

Skinny, irregular shape

Bent or broken shoots

Missing ID tag

Pot only partially filled with soil

Missing or discolored foliage

One or more thick roots coiling near the soil surface

Pot too small for plant

One or more thick roots projecting from or visible through pot holes

Any of these problems disqualifies a plant.

of soil and roots wrapped tightly in burlap. For these plants, look for strong limbs with no broken shoots, an attractive profile, and healthy foliage. Then press your hands against the burlap-covered root ball to make sure that it feels firm, solid, and damp, not loose or dry. (If the ball is buried within a bed of wood chips, carefully pull the chips aside; then push them back after inspecting the plant.)

To make the final choice when you're considering a group of plants, line them up side by side and select the ones that are most closely matched in height, bushiness, and foliage color. If your design includes a hedge or mass planting where uniformity is very important, it's a good idea to buy a few extra plants as potential replacements in case of damage or loss. It's easier to plan ahead than to find a match later. Plant the extras in a spare corner so you'll have them if you need them.

Sometimes a plant will be available in two or more sizes. Which is better? That depends on how patient you are. The main reason for buying bigger plants is to make a landscape look impressive right away. If you buy smaller plants and set them out at the same spacing, the planting will look sparse at first, but it will soon catch up. A year after planting, you can't tell if a perennial came from a quart- or gallon-size pot: the plants will look the same. For shrubs, the difference between one size pot and the next usually represents a year's growth.

Timing

It's a good idea to plan ahead and start shopping for plants before you're ready to put them in the ground. That way, if you can't find everything on your list, you'll have time to keep shopping around, place special orders, or choose substitutes. Most nurseries will let you "flag" an order for later pickup or delivery, and they'll take care of the plants in the meantime. Or you can bring the plants home; just remember to check the soil in the containers every day and water if needed.

The Planting Process

Throughout the Midwest region, spring is the best season for planting. You can start planting as soon as the soil thaws and the nurseries open, and continue through mid-June with good results. Planting in spring gives the plants a whole growing season to send out roots and get established before facing the rigors of winter. The second-best time for planting in the Midwest is from mid-August through late September, after the heat of summer but before hard frosts. If you want to plant during the summer, do it on a cloudy day when rain is forecast.

Compared with preparing the soil, putting plants in the ground goes quite quickly. If you're well prepared, you can plant a whole bed in just an hour or two. On the following pages we'll give an overview of the process and discuss how to handle individual plants.

Try to stay off the soil

Throughout the planting process, do all you can by reaching in from outside the bed—don't step on the newly prepared soil if you can help it, because that compacts the soil and makes it harder to dig planting holes. Use short boards or scraps of plywood as temporary steppingstones if you do need to step on the soil. As soon as you can decide where to put them, lay permanent steppingstones for access to plants that need regular maintenance.

Check placement and spacing

The first step in planting is to mark the position of each plant. The simplest way to do this is to arrange the plants themselves on the bed. Use an empty pot or a stake to represent any plant that's too heavy to move easily. Follow the site plan for the design, use a yardstick to check the spacing, and set the plants in place.

Then step back and take a look. Walk around and look from all sides. Go into the house and look out the window. What do you think? Should any of the plants be adjusted a little—moved to the left or right, to the back or front, a little closer together or farther apart? Don't worry if the planting looks a little sparse now. It *should* look that way at first. Plants almost always grow faster and get bigger than you can imagine when you're first setting them out, and it's almost always better to allow space and wait a few years for them to fill in than to crowd them too close together at first and then need to keep pruning and thinning them later. (You might fill between them with low-growing annuals, as suggested in the box on page 154.)

Planting pointers   When working on top of prepared soil, kneel on a piece of plywood to distribute your weight.

Use empty pots or stakes to mark positions of plants not yet purchased or too heavy to move frequently.

Moving through the job

When you're satisfied with the arrangement, mark the position of each plant with a stake or stone, and set the plants aside, out of the way, so you won't knock them over or step on them as you proceed. Start planting in order of size. Do the biggest plants first; then move on to the medium-size and smaller plants. If all the plants are about the same size, start at the back of the bed and work toward the front, or start in the center and work to the edges.

Using annuals as fillers

The plants in our designs have been spaced so they will not be crowded at maturity. Buying more plants and spacing them closer may fill things out faster, but in several years (for perennials; longer for shrubs) you'll need to remove plants or prune them frequently.

If you want something to fill the gaps between newly planted perennials, shrubs, or ground covers for that first year or two, use some annuals. The best annual fillers are compact plants that grow only 6 to 10 in. tall. These plants will hide the soil or mulch and make a colorful carpet. Avoid taller annuals, because they can shade or smother your permanent plantings.

The following annuals are all compact, easy to grow, readily available, and inexpensive. Seeds of those marked with a symbol (❀) can be sown directly in the garden. For the others, buy six-packs or flats of plants. Thin seedlings or space plants 8 to 12 in. apart.

❀ **Annual phlox:** Red, pink, or white flowers. Good for hot dry sites.

❀ **China pink:** Red, pink, white, or bicolor flowers. Blooms all summer.

Dusty miller: Silvery foliage, often lacy-textured. No flowers.

Edging lobelia: Dark blue, magenta, or white flowers. Likes afternoon shade.

Flossflower: Fluffy blue, lavender, or white flowers. Choose dwarf types.

Garden verbena: Bright red, pink, purple, or white flowers. Good for sunny dry sites.

❀ **Indian blanket:** Bright red-and-yellow flowers. Blooms all summer.

Moss rose: Bright flowers in many colors. Good for sunny dry sites.

Pansy and viola: Multicolored flowers. Grow best in cool weather.

❀ **Sweet alyssum:** Fragrant white or lilac flowers. Blooms for months. Very easy.

Wax begonia: Rose, pink, or white flowers. Good for shady sites but also takes sun.

Position trees and shrubs to show their best side

Most trees and shrubs are slightly asymmetric. There's usually enough irregularity in their branching or shape that one side looks a little fuller or more attractive than the other sides do. After you've set a tree or shrub into its hole, step back and take a look. Then turn it partway, or try tilting or tipping it a little to one side or the other. Once you've decided which side and position looks best, start filling in the hole with soil. Stop and check again before you firm the soil into place.

The fine points of spacing

When you're planting a group of the same kind of plants, such as perennials, bulbs, ferns, or ground covers, it normally looks best if you space them informally, in slightly curved or zigzag rows, with the plants in one row offset from those of the next row. Don't arrange plants in a straight row unless you want to emphasize a line, such as the edge of a bed. In that case, make the row perfectly straight by sighting down it and adjusting any plants that are out of line. (Stretch a string for long rows.) After planting, step back and evaluate the effect. If you want to adjust the placement or position of any plant, now is the time to do so.

Rake, water, and mulch

Use a garden rake to level out any high and low spots that remain after planting. Water enough to settle the soil into place around the roots. You can use a hose or watering can and water each plant individually, or you can set up a sprinkler to do the whole planting at once. Mulch the entire planting area with 1 to 3 in. of composted bark, wood chips, or other organic matter. Mulch is indispensable for controlling weeds and regulating the moisture and temperature of the soil. If you're running out of time, you don't have to spread the mulch right away, but try to get it done within the next week or so.

Planting Basics

Planting container-grown plants

1 Dig a hole a little wider than the container but not as deep.

2 Remove the plant from the container.

3 Unwind any large, coiled roots and cut them off short. Cut vertical slits through masses of fine roots.

4 Position the plant in the hole and fill around it with soil.

Most of the plants that you buy for a landscaping project today are grown and sold in individual plastic containers, but large shrubs and trees may be balled-and-burlapped. Mail-order plants may come bare-root. And ground covers are sometimes sold in flats. In any case, the basic concern is the same: Be careful what you do to a plant's roots. Spread them out; don't fold or coil them or cram them into a tight hole. Keep them covered; don't let the sun or air dry them out. And don't bury them too deep; set the top of the root ball level with the surrounding soil.

Planting container-grown plants

The steps are the same for any plant, no matter what size container it's growing in. Dig a hole that's a little wider than the container but not quite as deep **1**. Check by setting the container into the hole—the top of the soil in the container should be slightly higher than the surrounding soil. Dig several holes at a time, at the positions that you've already marked out.

Remove the container **2**. With one hand, grip the plant at the base of its stems or leaves, like pulling a ponytail, while you tug on the pot with the other hand. If the pot doesn't slide off easily, don't pull harder on the stems. Try whacking the pot with your trowel; if it still doesn't slide off, use a strong knife to cut or pry it off.

Examine the plant's roots **3**. If there are any thick, coiled roots, unwind them and cut them off close to the root ball, leaving short stubs. If the root ball is a mass of fine, hairlike roots, use the knife to cut three or four slits from top to bottom, about 1 in. deep. Pry the slits apart and tease the cut roots to loosen them. This cutting or slitting may seem drastic, but it's actually good for the plant because it forces new roots to grow out into the surrounding soil. Work quickly. Once you've taken a plant out of its container, get it in the ground as soon as possible. If you want to prepare several plants at a time, cover them with an old sheet or tarp to keep the roots from drying out.

Set the root ball into the hole **4**. Make sure that the plant is positioned right, with its best side facing out, and that the top of the root ball is level with or slightly higher than the surface of the bed. Then add enough soil to fill in the hole, and pat it down firmly.

Planting a balled-and-burlapped shrub or tree

Local nurseries often grow shrubs and trees in fields, then dig them with a ball of root-filled soil and wrap a layer of burlap snugly around the ball to keep it intact. The main drawback with this system is that even a

Balled-and-burlapped

The top of the ball should be level with the surrounding soil. Cut twine that wraps around the trunk. Fold down the burlap, but don't remove it.

Ground covers in flats

Remove a clump of little plants, tease their roots apart, and plant them quickly.

Bare-root plants

Dig a hole wide enough that you can spread out the roots. A stick helps you gauge the plant's correct depth as you fill the hole with soil.

Bulbs

Plant bulbs with the pointed end up, at a depth and spacing determined by the size of the bulb.

small ball of soil is very heavy. If the ball is more than a foot wide, moving the plant is usually a two-person job. If you're buying a tree with a ball bigger than that, ask the nursery to deliver and plant it. Here's how to proceed with plants that are small enough that you can handle them.

Dig a hole several inches wider than the root ball but not quite as deep as the root ball is high. Step in the bottom of the hole to firm the soil so the plant won't sink. Set the plant into the hole, and lay a stick across the top of the root ball to make sure it's at or a little higher than grade level.

Rotate the plant until its best side faces out. Be sure to cut or untie any twine that wraps around the trunk. Fold the burlap down around the sides of the ball, as shown in the drawing. Don't try to pull the burlap out altogether—roots can grow out through it, and it will eventually decompose. Fill soil all around the sides of the ball and pat it down firmly. Spread only an inch of soil over the top of the ball.

Planting bare-root plants

Mail-order nurseries sometimes dig perennials, roses, and other plants when the plants are dormant; cut back the tops; and wash all the soil off the roots, to save space and weight when storing and shipping them. If you receive a plant in bare-root condition, unwrap it, trim away any roots that are broken or damaged, and soak the roots in a pail of water for several hours.

To plant, dig a hole large enough that you can spread the roots across the bottom without folding them. Start covering the roots with soil, and then lay a stick across the top of the hole and hold the plant against it to check the planting depth, as shown in the drawing. Raise or lower the plant if needed in order to bury just the roots, not the buds. Add more soil, firming it down around the roots, and continue until the hole is full.

Planting ground covers from flats

Sometimes ground covers are sold in flats of 25 or more rooted cuttings. Start at one corner, reach underneath the soil, and lift out a portion of the flat's contents. Working quickly, because the roots are exposed, tease the cuttings apart, trying not to break off any roots, and plant them individually. Then lift out the next portion and continue planting.

Planting bulbs

Plant daffodils, tulips, crocuses, and other spring-blooming bulbs from September to November, when fresh bulbs are available at local garden centers or delivered by catalog merchants. If the soil in the bed was well prepared, you can use a trowel to dig holes for planting individual bulbs; where you have room, you can dig a wider hole or trench for planting a group of bulbs all at once. The perennials, ground covers, shrubs, and trees you planted earlier in the fall or in the spring will still be small enough that planting bulbs among them won't unduly disturb their root systems. As a rule of thumb, plant small (grape- or cherry-size) bulbs about 2 in. deep and 3 to 5 in. apart, and large (walnut- or egg-size) bulbs 4 to 6 in. deep and 6 to 10 in. apart.

Confining perennials

Yarrow, bee balm, artemisia, and various other perennials, grasses, and ferns are described as invasive because they spread by underground runners. To confine these plants to a limited area, install a barrier when you plant them. Cut the bottom off a 5-gal. or larger plastic pot, bury the pot so its rim is above the soil, and plant the perennial inside. You'll need to lift, divide, and replant part of the perennial every second or third year.

Position rim above soil surface.

Remove bottom of pot.

Planting under a tree

When planting beneath a mature tree, as for the designs on pp. 84–87, remember that most tree roots are in the top few inches of the soil, and they extend at least as far away from the trunk as the limbs do. For areas of ground cover and most container-grown perennials, you can add topsoil and organic amendments up to about 6 in. deep over the entire area; then set the plants out in the new soil. Larger plants need deeper holes. Whether you dig their planting holes in existing soil or through a layer of added topsoil, dig carefully, disturbing as few tree roots as possible. If you encounter a large root, move the planting hole rather than sever the root.

Basic Landscape Care

The landscape plantings in this book will grow increasingly carefree from year to year as the plants mature, but of course you'll always need to do some regular maintenance. Depending on the design you choose, this ongoing care may require as much as a few hours a week during the season or as little as a few hours a year. No matter what you plant, you'll have to control weeds, use mulch, water as needed, and do spring and fall cleanups. Trees, shrubs, and vines may need staking or training at first and occasional pruning or shearing afterward. Perennials, ground covers, and grasses may need to be cut back, staked, deadheaded, or divided. Performing these tasks, which are explained on the following pages, is sometimes hard work, but for many gardeners it is enjoyable labor, a chance to get outside in the fresh air. Also, spending time each week with your plants helps you identify and address problems before they become serious.

Mulches and fertilizers

Covering the soil in all planted areas with a layer of organic mulch does several jobs at once: it improves the appearance of your garden while you're waiting for the plants to grow, reduces the number of weeds that emerge, reduces water loss from the soil during dry spells, moderates soil temperatures, and adds nutrients to the soil as it decomposes. Inorganic mulches such as landscape fabric and gravel also provide some of these benefits, but their conspicuous appearance and the difficulty of removing them if you ever want to change the landscape are serious drawbacks.

Many materials are used as mulches; the box on p. 158 presents the most common, with comments on their advantages and disadvantages. Consider appearance, availability, cost, and convenience when you're comparing different products. Most garden centers have a few kinds of bagged mulch materials, but for mulching large areas, it's easier and cheaper to have a landscape contractor or other supplier deliver a truckload of bulk mulch. A landscape looks best if you see the same mulch throughout the entire planting area, rather than a patchwork of different mulches. You can achieve a uniform look by spreading a base layer of homemade compost, rotten hay, or other inexpensive material and topping that with a neater-looking material such as bark chips or shredded bark.

It takes at least a 1-in. layer of mulch to suppress weeds, but there's no need to spread it more than 3 in. deep. As you're spreading it, don't put any mulch against the stems of any plants, because that can lead to disease or insect problems. Put most of the mulch *between* plants, not right *around* them. Check the mulch each spring when you do an annual garden inspection and cleanup. Be sure it's pulled back away from the plant stems. Rake the surface of the mulch lightly to loosen it, and top it up with a fresh layer if the old material has decomposed.

Fertilizer

Decomposing mulch frequently supplies enough nutrients to grow healthy plants, but using fertilizer helps if you want to boost the plants—to make them grow faster, get larger, or produce more flowers. There are dozens of fertilizer products on the market—liquid and granular, fast-acting and slow-release, organic and synthetic. All give good results if applied as directed. And observe the following precautions: Don't overfertilize, don't fertilize when the soil is dry, and don't fertilize after midsummer, because plants need to slow down and finish the season's growth before cold weather comes.

Controlling weeds

Weeds are not much of a problem in established landscapes. Once the "good" plants have grown big enough to merge together, they tend to crowd or shade out all but the most persistent undesirable plants. But weeds can be troublesome in a new landscape unless you take steps to prevent and control them.

There are two main types of weeds: those that mostly sprout up as seedlings and those that keep coming back from perennial roots or runners. Try to identify and eliminate any perennial weeds before you start a landscaping project (see p. 116). Then you'll only have to deal with new seedlings later, which is a much easier job.

Annual and perennial weeds that commonly grow from seeds include crabgrass, chickweed, dandelions, plantain, purslane, ragweed, and violets. Trees and shrubs such

---

Mulch materials

Bark products. Bark nuggets, chipped bark, shredded bark, and composted bark, usually from conifers, are available in bags or in bulk. All are attractive, long-lasting, medium-price mulches.

Chipped tree trimmings. The chips from utility companies and tree services are a mixture of wood, bark, twigs, and leaves. These chips cost less than pure bark products (you may be able to get a load for free), but they don't look as good and you have to replace them more often, because they decompose fast.

Sawdust and shavings. These are cheap or free at sawmills and woodshops. They make good path coverings, but they aren't ideal mulches, because they tend to pack down into a dense, water-resistant surface.

Hulls and shells. Cocoa hulls, buckwheat hulls, peanut shells, and nut shells are available for pickup at food-processing plants and are sometimes sold in bags or bulk at garden centers. They're all attractive, long-lasting mulches. Price varies from free to quite expensive, depending on where you get them.

Tree leaves. A few big trees may supply all the mulch you need, year after year. You can just rake the leaves onto a bed in fall, but they'll probably blow off it again. It's better to chop them up with the lawn mower, pile them in compost bins for the winter, and spread them where needed in late spring. If you have the space for two sets of compost bins, give leaves an extra year to decompose before spreading them. Pine needles make good mulch, too, especially for azaleas, mountain laurels, and other acid-loving shrubs. You can spread pine needles in fall, because they cling together and don't blow around.

Grass clippings. A 1- to 2-in. layer of dried grass clippings makes an acceptable mulch that decomposes within a single growing season. Don't pile clippings too thick, though. If you do, the top surface dries and packs into a water-resistant crust, and the bottom layer turns into nasty slime.

Hay and straw. Farmers sell hay that's moldy, old, or otherwise unsuitable for fodder as "mulch" hay. This hay is cheap, but it's likely to include weed seeds, particularly seeds of weedy grasses such as barnyard grass. Straw—the stems of grain crops such as wheat—is usually seed-free but more expensive. Both hay and straw are more suitable for mulching vegetable gardens than landscape plantings because they have to be renewed each year. They are bulky at first but decompose quickly. They also tend to attract rodents.

Gravel. A mulch of pea gravel or crushed rock, spread 1 to 2 in. thick, helps keep the soil cool and moist, and many plants grow very well with a gravel mulch. However, compared with organic materials such as bark or leaves, it's much more tiring to apply a gravel mulch in the first place; it's harder to remove leaves and litter that accumulate on the gravel or weeds that sprout up through it; it's annoying to dig through the gravel if you want to replace or add plants later; and it's extremely tedious to remove the gravel itself, should you ever change your mind about having it there.

Landscape fabrics. Various types of synthetic fabrics, usually sold in rolls 3 to 4 ft. wide and 20, 50, or 100 ft. long, can be spread over the ground as a weed barrier and topped with a layer of gravel, bark chips, or other mulch. Unlike plastic, these fabrics allow water and air to penetrate into the soil. It's useful to lay fabric under paths, but not in planted areas. In a bed, it's a two-person job to install the fabric in the first place, it's inconvenient trying to install plants through holes cut in the fabric, and it's hard to secure the fabric neatly and invisibly at the edges of the bed. The fabric lasts indefinitely, and removing it—if you change your mind— is a messy job.

Clear or black plastic. Don't even think about using any kind of plastic sheeting as a landscape mulch. The soil underneath a sheet of plastic gets bone-dry, while water accumulates on top. Any loose mulch you spread on plastic slips or floats around and won't stay in an even layer. No matter how you try to secure them, the edges of plastic sheeting always pull loose, appear at the surface, degrade in the sun, and shred into tatters.

as silver maple, wild cherry, euonymus, black locust, buckthorn, and honeysuckle produce weedy seedlings, too. For any of these weeds that grow from seeds, the strategy is twofold: try to keep the weed seeds from sprouting, and eliminate any seedlings that do sprout as soon as you see them, while they are still small.

Almost any patch of soil includes weed seeds that are ready to sprout whenever that soil is disturbed. You have to disturb the soil to prepare it before planting, and that will probably cause an initial flush of weeds, but you won't see that many weeds again if you leave the soil undisturbed in subsequent years. You don't need to hoe, rake, or cultivate around perennial plantings. Leave the soil alone, and fewer weeds will appear. Using mulch helps even more; by shading the soil, it prevents weed seeds from sprouting. And if weed seeds blow in and land on top of the mulch, they'll be less likely to germinate there than they would on bare soil.

Pull or cut off any weeds that appear while they're young and small, just a few inches tall. Don't let them mature and go to seed. Most weed seedlings emerge in late spring and early summer. If you get rid of them then, you won't see many more seedlings for the rest of the growing season.

Using herbicides

Two kinds of herbicides can be very useful and effective in maintaining home landscapes, but only if used correctly. You must choose the right product for the job and follow the directions on the label regarding dosage and timing of application exactly.

Preemergent herbicides. Usually sold in granular form, these herbicides are designed to prevent weed seeds, particularly crabgrass and other annual weeds, from sprouting. One application is usually enough to last through the growing season, but it must be done in early spring, at the time the forsythias start blooming. If you wait until later, many weeds will

Weeds that sprout from seeds
Simple root systems can easily be pulled while still small.

Plantain

Maple seedling

Dandelion

Weeds that sprout back from perennial roots or runners
Connected by underground runners, the shoots of these weeds need to be pulled repeatedly, smothered with a thick mulch, or killed with an herbicide.

Mother plant

Ground ivy

Runner

Using herbicides on perennial weeds
Ready-to-use spot-weeder sprays are convenient, but you must aim carefully. Try using a sheet of cardboard as a backdrop to protect desirable plants from herbicide drift.

Use a disposable, sponge-type paintbrush to apply the herbicide selectively, painting only the weeds. Prepare the solution as directed for spray application. Use only enough to wet the leaves, so none drips off.

already have sprouted, and a preemergent herbicide will not stop them then.

Read the label carefully, and make sure the herbicide you buy is registered for use around the kinds of ground covers, perennials, shrubs, or other plants you have. Measure the area of your bed, weigh out the appropriate amount of granules, and sprinkle them as evenly as possible across the soil. Wear heavy rubber gloves that are rated for use with farm chemicals, not common household rubber gloves, and follow the safety precautions on the product label.

Postemergent herbicides. These chemicals are used to kill plants. Some kinds kill only the aboveground parts of a plant; other kinds are absorbed into the plant and kill it, roots and all. Postemergent herbicides are typically applied as sprays, which you can buy ready-to-use or prepare by mixing a concentrate with water. Look for those that break down quickly, and read the label carefully for registered applications, specific directions, and safety instructions.

Postemergent herbicides work best if applied when the weeds are growing vigorously. You usually have to apply enough to thoroughly wet the plant's leaves and to do it during a spell of dry weather. Applying an herbicide is an effective way to get rid of a perennial weed that you can't dig or pull up, but it's really better to do this before you plant a bed, as it's hard to spray herbicides in an established planting without getting some on your good plants. Aim carefully, shielding nearby plants as shown in the drawing on p. 159, and don't spray on windy days. Brushing or sponging the herbicide on the leaves is slower than spraying, but you're sure to avoid damaging adjacent plants.

Using postemergent herbicides in an established planting is a painstaking job, but it may be the only way to get rid of a persistent perennial weed. For young weed seedlings, it's usually easier and faster to pull them by hand than to spray them.

Watering

Watering is less of a concern for gardeners in the Midwest region than in some parts of the country, but even here there are dry spells and droughts when plants could use more water than nature provides. New plantings, in particular, almost always need water more often than rain supplies it.

Deciding if water is needed

Usually only experienced gardeners can judge whether plants need water simply by looking at their leaves. The appearance of the leaves can be misleading. Fortunately, there are two very reliable ways of deciding whether you should water.

One is to check the soil. Get a paint stirrer or similar piece of unfinished, light-colored wood and use it like the dipstick that monitors oil in an automobile. Push it down through the mulch and a few inches into the soil, leave it there for an hour or so, and pull it out to see if moisture has discolored the wood. If so, the soil is moist enough for plants. If not, it's time to water.

You have to let the stick dry out before you use it again; it's handy to have several of these sticks around the garden shed.

The other method is to make a habit of monitoring rainfall by having your own rain gauge or listening to the weather reports, and marking a calendar to keep track of rainfall amounts. In the Midwest region, most landscape plants thrive if they get 3 in. of rain a month. You should make every effort to water new plantings if there's been less than 1 in. of rain in two or three weeks. In subsequent years, after the plants have had time to put down roots, they can endure three or more weeks with no rain at all; even so, you should water them if you can. In this region, established plants rarely die from drought, but they do show many signs of the stress caused by too little water—wilting leaves, premature leaf drop, failure to bloom or to set fruit, and increased susceptibility to insect and disease attacks.

Pay attention to soil moisture or rainfall amounts from April through October,

Checking soil moisture
Stick a paint stirrer or similar piece of light-colored, unfinished wood down through the mulch and into the soil. Pull it up after an hour. If the bottom of the stick looks and feels damp, the soil is moist enough for plants.

Monitoring a sprinkler
Set several tuna-fish cans throughout the area, and let the sprinkler run until about 1 in. of water has collected in each can.

because plants can suffer from dryness throughout that entire period, not just in the heat of summer, and water whenever the soil is dry. As for time of day, you can water whenever the plants need it and you get the chance—morning, afternoon, evening, or night. Gardening books sometimes warn against watering plants late in the day, saying that plants are more vulnerable to fungal infections if the leaves stay wet at night. That's true, but in this region plants get wet with dew most nights anyway, whether you water or not.

How much to water

It's easy to overwater a houseplant but hard to overwater a plant that is growing in the ground. Outdoors, you're much more likely to water too little than too much. You could spend an hour with hose in hand, watering the plants in a flower bed, and supply the equivalent of $1/4$ in. of rain or less. Holding a hose or carrying a bucket is practical for watering new plantings only where the plants are few, small, or relatively widely spaced. To thoroughly water an area that's filled with plants, you need a system that allows you to turn on the water, walk away, and come back later. An oscillating sprinkler on the end of a hose works fine, or you can weave a soaker hose through the bed. Inexpensive timers that turn water on and off automatically make it easier for people with busy schedules to get their watering done.

No matter how you water, you should monitor how much water you have applied and how evenly it was distributed. If you're hand-watering or using a soaker hose, the watering pattern may be quite uneven. Put several wooden "dipsticks" in different parts of the bed to make sure that all areas have received enough water to moisten the sticks. Monitor the output of a sprinkler by setting tuna-fish cans around the bed and checking to see how much water they catch, like measuring rainfall. Let the sprinkler run until there's about an inch of water in each can.

Caring for Woody Plants

A well-chosen garden tree, such as the ones recommended in this book, grows naturally into a pleasing shape, won't get too large for its site, is resistant to pests and diseases, and doesn't drop messy pods or other litter. Once established, these trees need very little care from year to year.

Regular watering is the most important concern in getting a tree off to a good start. Don't let it suffer from drought for the first few years. To reduce competition, don't plant ground covers or other plants within 2 ft. of the tree's trunk. Just spread a thin layer of mulch there.

Arborists now dismiss other care ideas that once were common practice. According to current thinking, you don't need to fertilize a tree when you plant it (in fact, most landscape trees never need fertilizing). Keep pruning to a minimum at planting time; remove only dead or damaged twigs, not healthy shoots. Finally, if a tree is small enough that one or two people can carry and plant it, it doesn't need staking and the trunk will grow stronger if unstaked. Larger trees that are planted by a nursery may need staking, especially on windy sites, but the stakes should be removed within a year.

Shaping young trees

As a tree grows, you can direct its shape by pruning once a year, in winter or summer. (See the box below.) Take it easy, though. Don't prune just for the sake of pruning; that does more harm than good. If you

---

Pruning to direct growth

Pruning shapes plants not only by removing stems, branches, and leaves but also by inducing and directing new growth. All plants have a bud at the base of every leaf. New shoots grow from these buds. Cutting off the end of a stem encourages the lower buds to shoot out and produces a bushier plant. This type of pruning makes a hedge fill out and gives an otherwise lanky perennial or shrub a better rounded shape.

The same response to pruning also allows you to steer the growth of a plant. The bud immediately below the cut will produce a shoot that extends in the direction the bud was pointing. To direct a branch or stem, cut it back to a bud pointing in the direction you want to encourage growth. This technique is useful for shaping young trees and shrubs and for keeping their centers open to light and air.

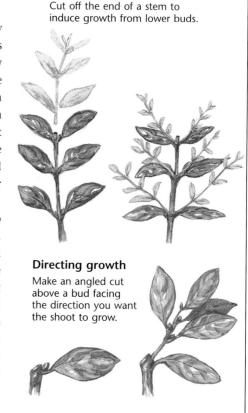

Bushier growth
Cut off the end of a stem to induce growth from lower buds.

Directing growth
Make an angled cut above a bud facing the direction you want the shoot to grow.

Pruning roses

Roses are vigorous, fast-growing shrubs that need regular pruning to keep them shapely and attractive. Most of this pruning should be done in early spring, just as the buds start to swell but before the new leaves start to unfold. All roses need similar care at this time. Prune off any shoots frozen or broken during the winter, remove old or weak shoots and crossing or crowded stems, and trim back any asymmetric or unbalanced shoots.

Don't be afraid of cutting back too hard; it's better to leave just a few strong shoots than a lot of weak ones. If you cut old stems off at ground level, new ones will grow to replace them. Cut damaged or asymmetric stems back partway and they will branch out.

Always use sharp pruning shears and cut back to a healthy bud, leaving no stub. Right after pruning you can add fresh mulch around the plant.

An annual spring pruning is enough to keep shrub roses such as 'Bonica' and 'Frau Dagmar Hartop' fairly neat and compact, but you may want to remove or trim an errant or too-vigorous shoot during the summer. You can do that anytime.

Climbing roses don't need as much spring pruning as shrubs do—just remove weak or damaged shoots—but they need more attention throughout the summer, because their stems or canes can grow a foot or more in a month. Check regularly and tie this new growth to the trellis while it's still supple and manageable. When the canes grow long enough to reach the top of the trellis or arbor, cut off their tips and they will send out side shoots, from which the flowers will form.

It's up to you whether to prune off the flower stalks as the roses fade. If you don't, many kinds of roses will proceed to form small red or orange fruits, called rose hips. These are decorative throughout the late summer and fall, and they sometimes last into the winter. Roses are so vigorous that it doesn't hurt the plant to let it set plenty of fruits. On the other hand, roses often look messy as the petals fade, so you might prefer to remove the spent blossoms. Also, most roses bloom more abundantly and over a longer season if you keep pruning off the flowers to keep the hips from developing. If you decide to remove the flowers, use your pruning shears to cut the stem back to a healthy leaf or bud. If you prefer to let the hips form, prune them off in late winter or early spring by cutting in the same way.

Pruning a shrub rose

Every spring, remove old, weak, frozen, or damaged shoots; stems that are crossing or crowded; and stems that stick out too far and look asymmetric. Don't be afraid to cut a lot away.

Cut blackened winter-damaged shoots back to healthy, green tissue.

Removing flowers or hips

If the roses look messy as they fade, cut them off by pruning the stem back to a healthy leaf.

If you prefer to let the hips develop, leave the flowers alone. Remove the old bunches of hips in winter or spring, cutting back to a healthy bud.

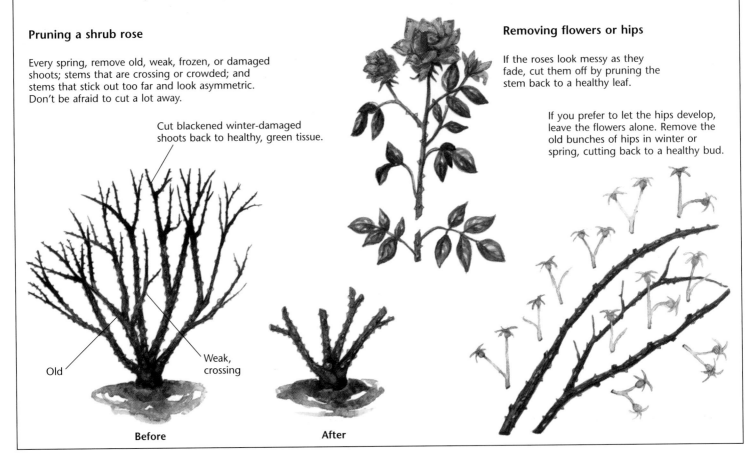

Old

Weak, crossing

Before

After

(Continued from p. 161)

don't have a good reason for making a cut, don't do it. Follow these guidelines:

• *Use sharp pruning* shears, loppers, or saws, which make clean cuts without tearing the wood or bark.

• *Cut branches back* to a healthy shoot, leaf, or bud, or cut back to the branch collar at the base of the branch, as shown at right. Don't leave any stubs; they're ugly and prone to decay.

• *Remove any dead* or damaged branches and any twigs or limbs that are very spindly or weak.

• *Where two limbs* cross over or rub against each other, save one limb—usually the thicker, stronger one—and prune off the other one.

• *Prune or widen* narrow crotches. Places where a branch and trunk or two branches form a narrow V are weak spots, liable to split apart as the tree grows. Where the trunk of a young tree exhibits such a crotch or where either of two shoots could continue the growth of a branch, prune off the weaker of the two. Where you wish to keep the branch, insert a piece of wood as a spacer to widen the angle, as shown in the drawings below. Leave the spacer in place for a year or so.

One trunk or several?

If you want a young tree to have a single trunk, identify the leader or central shoot and let it grow straight up, unpruned. The

Where to cut

When removing the end of a branch, cut back to a healthy leaf, bud, or side shoot. Don't leave a stub. Use sharp pruning shears to make a neat cut that slices the stem rather than tears it.

trunk will grow thicker faster if you leave the lower limbs in place for the first few years, but if they're in the way, you can remove them. At whatever height you choose—usually about 8 ft. off the ground if you want to walk or see under the tree—select the shoots that will become the main limbs of the tree. Be sure they are evenly spaced around the trunk, pointing outward at wide angles. Remove any lower or weaker shoots. As the tree matures, the only further pruning required will be an annual checkup to remove dead, damaged, or crossing shoots.

Several of the trees in this book, including Amur maple, Japanese tree lilac, serviceberry, and Washington hawthorn, are

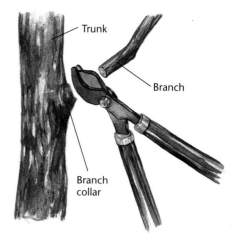

When removing an entire branch, cut just outside the slightly thickened area, called the branch collar, where the branch grows into the trunk.

often grown with multiple (usually two to four) trunks, for a graceful, clumplike appearance. When buying a multiple-trunk tree, choose one with trunks that diverge at the base. The more space between them, the better, so they can grow without squeezing each other. Prune multiple-trunk trees as previously described for single-trunk trees. Remove some of the branches that are growing toward the center of the clump, so the center doesn't get too dense and tangled.

Pruning shrubs

Shrubs are generally carefree plants, but they almost always look better if you do some pruning at least once a year. As a

Avoiding narrow crotches

A tree's limbs should spread wide, like outstretched arms. If limbs angle too close to the trunk or to each other, there isn't room for them to grow properly and they may split apart after a few years, ruining the tree.

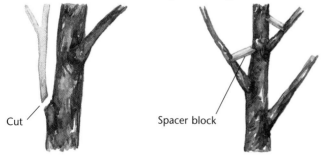

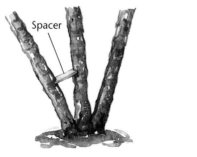

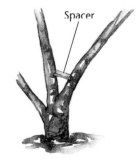

Single-trunk trees: Correct narrow crotches on a young tree by removing the less desired limb or by widening the angle with a wooden spacer block. Choose well-spaced shoots to become the main limbs of a shade tree.

Multiple-trunk trees: Whether the stems of a multiple-trunk tree emerge from the ground or from a single trunk near the ground, widen angles if necessary to keep the trunks from touching.

Selective pruning

Remove weak, spindly, bent, or broken shoots (red). Where two branches rub on each other, remove the weakest or the one that's pointing inward (orange). Cut back long shoots to a healthy, outward-facing bud (blue).

Severe pruning

In late winter or early spring, before new growth starts, cut all the stems back close to the ground.

Shearing

Trim with hedge clippers to a neat profile.

minimum, remove dead twigs from time to time, and if any branches are broken by storms or accidents, remove them as soon as convenient, cutting back to a healthy bud or to the plant's crown. Also, unless the shrub produces attractive seedpods or berries, it's a good idea to trim off the flowers after they fade.

Beyond this routine pruning, some shrubs require more attention. (The entries in Plant Profiles, pp. 172–197, give more information on when and how to prune particular shrubs.) Basically, shrub pruning falls into three categories: selective pruning, severe pruning, and shearing.

Selective pruning means using pruning shears to remove or cut back individual shoots, in order to refine the shape of the bush and to maintain its vigor, as well as to limit its size. (See the drawing at left.) This job takes time but produces a very graceful and natural-looking bush. Cut away weak or spindly twigs and any limbs that cross or rub against each other, and cut all the longest shoots back to a healthy, outward-facing bud or to a pair of buds. You can do selective pruning on any shrub, deciduous or evergreen, at any time of year.

Severe pruning means using pruning shears or loppers to cut away most of a shrub's top growth, leaving just short stubs or a gnarly trunk. This kind of cutting back is usually done once a year in late winter or early spring. Although it seems drastic, severe pruning is appropriate with a number of plants and in some landscaping situations.

It keeps potentilla and spirea compact and bushy. It stimulates red-twig dogwood to produce canelike stems with bright red bark. And on smoke tree it promotes the growth of bold, unbranched stems with larger-than-average leaves.

One or two severe prunings done when a shrub is young can make it branch out at the base, producing a bushier specimen or a fuller hedge plant. Nurseries often do this pruning as part of producing a good plant,

and if you buy a shrub that's already bushy, you don't need to cut it back yourself.

Older shrubs that have gotten tall and straggly sometimes respond to a severe pruning by sprouting out with renewed vigor, sending up lots of new shoots that bear plenty of foliage and flowers. This strategy doesn't work for all shrubs, though—sometimes severe pruning kills a plant. Don't try it unless you know it will work (check with a knowledgeable person at a nursery) or are willing to take a chance.

Shearing means using hedge shears or an electric hedge trimmer to trim the surface of a shrub, hedge, or tree to a neat, uniform profile, producing a solid mass of greenery. Both deciduous and evergreen shrubs and trees can be sheared; those with small, closely spaced leaves and a naturally compact growth habit usually look best. A good time for shearing most shrubs is early summer, after the new shoots have elongated but before the wood has hardened, but you can shear at other times of year, and you may need to shear some plants more than once a year.

If you're planning to shear a plant, start when it is young and establish the shape—cone, pyramid, flat-topped hedge, or whatever. Looking at the profile, always make the shrub wider at the bottom than on top; otherwise the lower limbs will be shaded and won't be as leafy. Shear off as little as needed to maintain the shape as the shrub grows. Once the shrub gets as big as you want it, shear as much as necessary to keep it that size.

Making a hedge

To make a hedge that's dense enough that you can't see through it, choose shrubs that have many shoots at the base. If you can only find skinny shrubs, prune them severely the first spring after planting to stimulate bushier growth.

Hedge plants are set in the ground as described on pp. 155–156 but are spaced closer together than they would be if planted as individual specimens. We took that into account in creating the designs and plant lists for this book; just follow the spacings recommended in the designs. If you're impatient for the hedge to fill in, you can space the plants closer together, but don't put them farther apart.

A hedge can be sheared, pruned selectively, or left alone, depending on how you want it to look. Slow-growing, small-leaved plants such as boxwood and Japanese holly make rounded but natural-looking hedges with no pruning at all, or you can shear them into any profile you choose and make them perfectly neat and uniform. (Be sure to keep them narrower at the top.) Choose one style and stick with it. Once a hedge is established, you can neither start nor stop shearing it without an awkward transition that may last a few years before the hedge looks good again.

Getting a vine off to a good start

Nurseries often sell clematis, honeysuckle, and other vines as young plants with a single stem fastened to a stake. To plant them, remove the stake and cut off the stem right above the lowest pair of healthy leaves, usually about 4 to 6 in. above the soil ❶. This forces the vine to send out new shoots low to the ground. As soon as those new shoots begin to develop (a month or so after planting), cut them back to their first pairs of leaves ❷. After this second pruning, the plant will become bushy at the base. Now as new shoots form, use sticks or strings to direct them toward the base of the support they are to climb ❸.

Engelman ivy doesn't need any further attention. It can climb any trellis or support, because its stems form special rootlets that cling to the surface. Once they're started, both clematis and honeysuckle scramble up a lattice trellis, although it helps if you tuck in any stray ends from time to time. The plants can't climb a smooth surface, however. To help them cover a fence with wide vertical slats or a porch post, you have to provide something the vine can wrap around. Screw a few eyebolts to the top and bottom of such a support and stretch wire, nylon cord, or polypropylene rope between them. (The wires or cords should be a few inches out from the fence, not flush against it.)

'Zéphirine Drouhin' and other so-called climbing roses don't really climb at all by themselves—you need to fasten them to a support. Twist-ties are handy for this job. Roses grow fast, so you'll have to tie in the new shoots every few weeks from spring to fall.

After the first year, the vines in this book don't need regular pruning, but you should remove any dead, damaged, or straggly stems whenever you see them. If vines grow too long, you can cut them back any time during the season. They will branch out from below the cut.

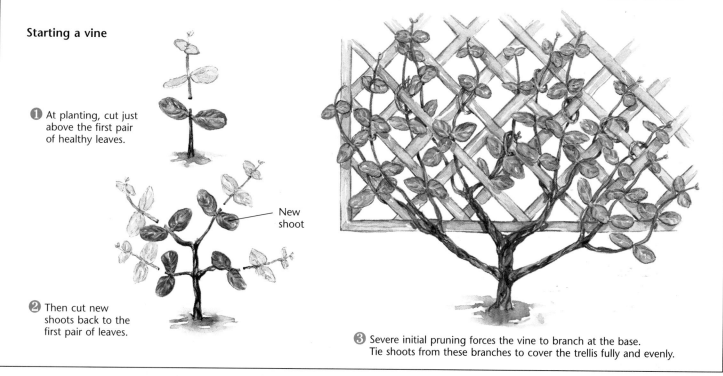

Starting a vine

❶ At planting, cut just above the first pair of healthy leaves.

New shoot

❷ Then cut new shoots back to the first pair of leaves.

❸ Severe initial pruning forces the vine to branch at the base. Tie shoots from these branches to cover the trellis fully and evenly.

Caring for Perennials

Perennials are simply plants that send up new growth year after year. A large group, perennials include flowering plants such as daylilies and astilbes as well as grasses, ferns, and hardy bulbs. Although some perennials need special conditions and care, most of the ones in this book are adaptable and easygoing. Get them off to a good start by planting them in well-prepared soil, adding a layer of mulch, watering as often as needed throughout the first year, and keeping weeds away. After that, keeping perennials attractive and healthy typically requires just a few minutes per plant each year.

Routine annual care

Some of the perennials that are used as ground covers, such as lily-of-the-valley, periwinkle, sweet woodruff, and sweet violet, need virtually no care. On a suitable site, they'll thrive for decades even if you pay them no attention at all.

Most garden perennials, though, look and grow better if you clean away the old leaves and stems at least once a year. When to do this depends on the plant. Perennials such as aster, daylily, dwarf fountain grass, hosta, iris, and peony have leaves and stalks that turn tan or brown after they're frosted in fall. Cut these down to the ground in late fall or early spring; either time is okay.

Perennials such as beach wormwood, bigroot geranium, dianthus, and coralbells have foliage that is more or less evergreen, depending on the severity of the winter. For those plants, wait until early spring; then cut back any leaves or stems that are discolored or shabby-looking. Don't leave cuttings lying on the soil, because they may contain disease spores. Do not compost diseased stems or leaves.

Right after you've cleared away the dead material is a good time to renew the mulch on the bed. Use a fork, rake, or cultivator to loosen the existing mulch, and add some fresh mulch if needed. Also, if you want to sprinkle some granular fertilizer on the bed, do that now, when it's easy to avoid getting any on the plants' leaves. Fertilizing perennials is optional, but it does make them grow bigger and bloom more than they would otherwise.

Pruning and shearing perennials

Some perennials that bloom in summer or fall respond well to being pruned earlier in the growing season. Bee balm, boltonia, New England aster, and 'Autumn Joy' sedum all form tall clumps of stems topped with lots of little flowers. Unfortunately, tall stems are liable to flop over in stormy

Pruning a perennial

Prune to create neater, bushier clumps of some summer- and fall-blooming perennials such as garden phlox, chrysanthemums, 'Autumn Joy' sedum, and boltonia. When the stalks are about 1 ft. tall, cut them all back by one-third. Remove the weakest stalks at ground level.

weather, and even if they don't, too-tall clumps can look leggy or top-heavy. To prevent floppiness, prune these plants when the stems are about 1 ft. tall. Remove the weakest stems from each clump by cutting them off at the ground, then cut all the remaining, strong stems back by about one-third. Pruning in this way keeps these plants shorter, stronger, and bushier, so you don't need to bother with stakes to keep them upright.

Remove faded flowers

Removing flowers as they fade (called "deadheading") makes the garden look neater, prevents unwanted self-sown seedlings, and often stimulates a plant to continue blooming longer than it would if you left it alone, or to bloom a second time later in the season. (This is true for shrubs and annuals as well as for perennials.)

Pick large flowers such as daisies, daylilies, irises, and lilies one at a time, snapping them off by hand. Use pruning shears on perennials such as astilbe, bleeding heart, hosta, lady's mantle, and yarrow that produce tall stalks crowded with lots of small flowers, cutting the stalks back to the height of the foliage. Use hedge shears on bushy plants that are covered with lots of small flowers on short stalks, such as catmint, dianthus, and snow-in-summer, cutting the stems back by about one-half.

Instead of removing them, you may want to let the flowers remain on coneflower, purple coneflower, false indigo, Siberian iris, 'Autumn Joy' sedum, and the various grasses. These plants all bear conspicuous seedpods or seed heads on stiff stalks that remain standing and look interesting throughout the fall and winter.

Dividing perennials

Most perennials send up more stems each year, forming denser clumps or wider patches. Dividing is the process of cutting or breaking apart these clumps or patches. This is an easy way to make more plants to expand your garden, to control a plant that might otherwise spread out of bounds, or to renew an old specimen that doesn't look good or bloom well anymore.

Most perennials can be divided as often as every year or two if you're in a hurry to make more plants, or they can go for several years if you don't have any reason to disturb them. You can divide them in early spring, just as new growth is starting, or in late summer and early fall, up until a month before hard frost.

There are two main approaches to dividing perennials, as shown in the drawings at right. You can leave the plant in the ground and use a sharp shovel to cut it apart, like slicing a pie, then lift out one chunk at a time. Or you can dig around and underneath the plant and lift it out all at once, shake off the extra soil, and lay the plant on the ground or a tarp where you can work with it.

Some plants, such as boltonia, yarrow, and most ferns, are easy to divide. They almost fall apart when you dig them up. Others, such as astilbe, daylily, and most grasses, have very tough or tangled roots and you'll have to wrestle with them, chop them with a sharp butcher knife, pry them apart with a strong screwdriver or garden fork, or even cut through the roots with a hatchet or pruning saw. However you approach the job, before you insert any tool, take a close look at the plant right at ground level, and be careful to divide *between*, not *through*, the biggest and healthiest buds or shoots. Using a hose to wash loose mulch and soil away makes it easier to see what you're doing.

Don't make the divisions too small; they should be the size of a plant that you'd want to buy, not just little scraps. If you have more divisions than you need or want, choose just the best-looking ones to replant and discard or give away the others. Replant new divisions as soon as possible in freshly prepared soil. Water them right away, and water again whenever the soil dries out over the next few weeks or months, until the plants are growing again.

Divide hardy bulbs such as daffodils and crocuses every few years by digging up the clumps after they have finished blooming but before the foliage turns yellow. Shake the soil off the roots, pull the bulbs apart, discard any that are damaged or diseased, and replant the rest promptly, setting them as deep as they were buried before.

Dividing perennials

You can divide a clump or patch of perennials by cutting down into the patch with a sharp spade, like slicing a pie or a pan of brownies, then lifting out the separate chunks.

Or you can dig up the whole clump, shake the extra soil off the roots, then pull or pry it apart into separate plantlets.

Problem Solving

Some plants are much more susceptible than others to damage by severe weather, pests, or diseases. In this book, we've recommended plants that are generally trouble-free, especially after they have had a few years to get established in your landscape. But even these plants are subject to various mishaps and problems. The challenge is learning how to distinguish which problems are really serious and which are just cosmetic, and deciding how to solve—or, better yet, prevent—the serious problems.

Identify, then treat

Don't jump to conclusions and start spraying chemicals on a supposedly sick plant before you know what (if anything) is actually wrong with it. That's wasteful and irresponsible, and you're likely to do the plant as much harm as good. Pinpointing the exact cause of a problem is difficult for even experienced gardeners, so save yourself frustration and seek out expert help from the beginning.

If it seems that there's something wrong with one of your plants—for example, if the leaves are discolored, have holes in them, or have spots or marks on them—cut off a sample branch, wrap it in damp paper towels, and put it in a plastic bag (so it won't wilt). Take the sample to the nursery or garden center where you bought the plant, and ask for help. If the nursery can't help, contact the nearest office of your state's Cooperative Extension Service or a public garden in your area and ask if they have a staff member who can diagnose plant problems.

Meanwhile, look around your property and around the neighborhood, too, to see if any other plants (of the same or different kinds) show similar symptoms. If a problem is widespread, you shouldn't have much trouble finding someone who can

identify it and tell you what, if anything, to do. If only one plant is affected, it's often harder to diagnose the problem, and you may just have to wait and see what happens to it. Keep an eye on the plant, continue with watering and other regular maintenance, and see if the problem gets worse or goes away. If nothing more has happened after a few weeks, stop worrying. If the problem continues, intensify your search for expert advice.

Plant problems stem from a number of causes: insect and animal pests, diseases, and poor care, particularly in winter. Remember that plant problems are often caused by a combination of these; all the more reason to consult with experts about their diagnosis and treatment.

Pests, large and small

Deer, rabbits, and woodchucks are liable to be a problem if your property is surrounded by or adjacent to fields or woods. You may not see them, but you can't miss the damage they do—they bite the tops off or eat whole plants of hostas, daylilies, and many other perennials. Deer also eat the leaves and stems of maples, yews, arborvitae, and many other trees and shrubs. Commercial or homemade repellents that you spray on the foliage may be helpful if the animals aren't too hungry. (See the box at right for plants that deer seem to avoid.) But in the long run, the only solution is to fence out deer and to trap and remove smaller animals.

Chipmunks and squirrels are cute but naughty. They normally don't eat much foliage, but they do eat some kinds of flowers and several kinds of bulbs, they dig up new transplants, and they plant nuts in your flower beds and lawns. Voles and field mice can kill trees and shrubs by stripping the bark off the trunk, usually in the winter when the ground is covered with snow,

and they eat away at many perennials, too. Moles don't eat plants, but their digging makes a mess of a lawn or flower bed. Persistent trapping is the most effective way to control all of these little critters.

Insects and related pests can cause minor or devastating damage. Most plants can afford to lose part of their foliage or sap without suffering much of a setback, so don't panic if you see a few holes chewed in a leaf. However, whenever you suspect that insects are attacking one of your plants, try to catch one of them in a glass jar and get it identified, so you can decide what to do.

There are several new kinds of insecticides that are quite effective but much safer to use than the older products. You must read the fine print on the label to determine whether an insecticide will control your particular pest. Carefully follow the directions for how to apply the product, or it may not work.

Deer-resistant plants

Deer may nibble these plants, but they're unlikely to strip them bare. If you live in an area where deer populations are high, consider substituting some of these plants for others that are specified in a design.

Trees and shrubs

Andromeda	Forsythia	Pine
Barberry	Holly	Smoke tree
Boxwood	Lilac	Spirea
Dogwood	Magnolia	Spruce

Perennials

Astilbe	Geranium	Lenten rose
Bee balm	Grasses	Peony
Blazing star	Heuchera	Russian sage
Bluebeard	Iris	Sage
Daffodil	Lamb's ears	Veronica
Ferns	Lavender	Yarrow

Diseases

Several types of fungal, bacterial, and viral diseases can attack garden plants, causing a wide range of symptoms such as disfigured or discolored leaves or petals, powdery or moldy-looking films or spots, mushy or rotten stems or roots, and overall wilting. As with insect problems, if you suspect that a plant is infected with a disease, gather a sample of the plant and show it to someone who can identify the problem before you do any spraying.

In general, plant diseases are hard to treat, so it's important to take steps to prevent problems. These steps include choosing plants adapted to your area, choosing disease-resistant plants, spacing plants far enough apart so that air can circulate between them, and removing dead stems and litter from the garden.

Perennials that would otherwise be healthy are prone to fungal infections during spells of hot humid weather, especially if the plants are crowded together or if they have flopped over and are lying on top of each other or on the ground. Look closely for moldy foliage, and if you find any, prune it off and discard (don't compost) it. It's better to cut the plants back severely than to let the disease spread. Plan to avoid repeated problems by dividing the perennials, replanting them farther apart, and pruning them early in the season so they don't grow so tall and floppy again. Crowded shrubs are also subject to fungal problems in the summer and should be pruned so that air can flow around them.

Winter protection

More plants are damaged or killed in the winter than in any other season. They may freeze during a severe cold spell, get broken by snow or ice, dry out, or be drowned. There are a few steps you can take to prevent winter damage.

Plant shrubs far enough away from a street, driveway, or building that they won't get crushed by the extra snow that accumulates from shoveling or slides off a roof. (Where designs in this book call for plantings in these kinds of areas, we've selected plants that hold up well.) Use stakes to mark the edge or corners of any planting that's adjacent to a walk or driveway, so you can avoid hitting the plants with a snowblower or shovel.

Spray evergreen shrubs with an antitranspirant such as Wilt-Pruf™ in late fall to keep their leaves from dehydrating in the cold, dry, winter winds. Alternatively, you can erect burlap tents around young shrubs, to protect them from November until April. Drive four stakes in the ground, then wrap burlap around them and staple it in place, leaving the top open.

Any small or medium-size perennial or shrub that is planted in the fall is liable to be pushed up out of the ground, or frost-heaved, if the soil repeatedly freezes and thaws, and that means its roots get dried out. To prevent this, cover the ground around these plants with a loose mulch such as evergreen boughs (limbs from discarded Christmas trees are good) as soon as the soil has frozen hard, and don't remove the covering until midspring.

Many more plants die from being too wet in winter than from getting too cold. Any plants growing where water collects and the ground stays saturated in winter are liable to rot. If you're thinking about planting in a low spot, prevent this kind of loss by preparing the site before you plant. Dig deep to loosen compacted subsoil, and add more topsoil to raise the surface of the bed, so that water will drain both down and away from the root zone.

Winter protection

To avoid hitting plants with a snowblower or shovel, mark plantings near sidewalks and driveways before they are snow-covered.

Erect burlap tents around small to medium-size shrubs to protect them from cold dry winds in winter.

Plant Profiles

Plants are the heart of the designs in this book. In this section you'll find descriptions of all the plants used in the designs, along with information on planting and maintaining them. These trees, shrubs, perennials, grasses, bulbs, and vines have all proven themselves as dependable performers in the region. They offer a wide spectrum of lovely flowers and fruits, handsome foliage, and striking forms. Most contribute something of note in at least two seasons. You can use this section as an aid when installing the designs in this book and as a reference guide to desirable plants for other home landscaping projects.

Using the plant profiles — All of these plants are proven performers in many of the soils, climates, and other conditions commonly found in the Midwest region. But they will perform best if planted and cared for as described in the Guide to Installation. In these descriptions and recommendations, the term "garden soil" means soil that has been prepared for planting by digging or tilling and adding some organic matter, so that it's loose enough for roots and water to penetrate easily. Here also, "full sun" means a site that gets at least eight hours a day of direct sun throughout the growing season. "Partial sun" and "partial shade" both refer to sites that get direct sun for part of the day but are shaded the rest of the time by a building, fence, or tree. "Full shade" means sites that don't receive direct sunlight.

The plants are organized here alphabetically by their scientific name. If you're browsing, page references direct you to the designs in which the plants appear. Those in ***bold italic*** type indicate the page where a photo of the plant can be found.

Ajuga reptans
CARPET BUGLE

Acer ginnala
AMUR MAPLE. A small deciduous tree, usually grown with multiple trunks as a bushy specimen about 15 to 25 ft. tall and wide. Has conspicuous, sweet-scented, pale-colored flowers in spring; showy clusters of red fruits in summer; and crimson fall foliage. Needs full sun and a well-drained site. Tolerates poor, dry soil. Prune in summer, removing weak or crossing limbs. Pages: 30, ***31,*** 36.

Acer rubrum
RED MAPLE. An adaptable native tree that makes a good shade tree. Grows fast and reaches 40 ft. or taller. Deciduous leaves with three-pointed lobes turn bright red in the fall. Clusters of small red flowers dangle from the bare twigs in early spring. 'Red Sunset' and 'October Glory' are popular cultivars with outstanding fall color. Needs full sun. This tree is native to swampy sites, but it adapts to drier soil. Pages: 77, ***79.***

Achillea 'Moonshine'
'MOONSHINE' YARROW. A perennial with flat clusters of small lemon yellow flowers on stiff stalks about 2 ft. tall. Finely divided gray-green leaves have a pungent aroma. Spreads to form a patch 2 to 3 ft. wide. Needs full sun. Cut off old flower stalks when the blossoms fade. Divide every few years in spring or fall. Pages: 21, ***23,*** 81, 102.

Aegopodium podagraria 'Variegatum'
GOUTWEED. A perennial ground cover that spreads fast by underground runners and soon forms a dense patch of green-and-white foliage about 1 ft. tall. White flowers like those of Queen Anne's lace bloom in early summer. Pick them off as soon as they fade, because self-sown seedlings have plain green foliage and look weedy. Adapts to sun or shade; grows in almost any soil. Pages: 77, 99, ***99.***

Ajuga reptans
CARPET BUGLE. A low, mat-forming perennial used as a ground cover. Erect, 6-in. spikes densely packed with blue flowers are very showy for a few weeks in May or June. The glossy leaves can be dark green, purple-bronze, or variegated, depending on the cultivar. All forms are attractive and easy to grow. Adapts to sun or shade. After the flowers fade, cut them off with a string trimmer, lawn mower, or hedge shears. Spreads quickly and will invade a lawn unless you keep cutting along the edge or install a mowing strip. Pages: 23, ***23,*** 41, 77.

Amelanchier × grandiflora

SERVICEBERRY. A small deciduous tree, usually under 25 ft. tall, with multiple trunks. Attractive all year, it has white flowers in early spring, blue or purplish berries in summer, bright red-orange fall foliage, and smooth gray bark. 'Cole's Select' is a popular cultivar with vivid fall color. Needs full or partial sun. Grows fairly slowly, so buy a good-size specimen to start with. Needs little pruning: just remove any crossing branches. Pages: 22, 68, 70, **71**, 77.

Anemone

JAPANESE ANEMONE. Perennials with small daisylike flowers on branching stalks held well above a bushy clump of large, dark green leaves. *A. japonica* (also listed as *A. × hybrida*) 'Alba' (pp. 84, **86**) has clear white single flowers on 3-ft. stalks in September; 'Honorine Jobert' is similar. *A. vitifolia* 'Robustissima' (pp. 25, **62**, 63, 69) has single pink flowers on 42-in. stalks in August and September. Other cultivars are good, too. All need partial shade and rich, moist soil. Cut down old stalks in fall. Divide every few years in spring.

Aquilegia 'Biedermeier'

'BIEDERMEIER' COLUMBINE. A compact form of this popular perennial, with lovely spurred flowers in shades of blue, pink, yellow, or white on stalks 12 to 18 in. tall. Forms a neat mound of blue-green, scalloped leaves. Prefers partial or full sun. Carefree. Individual plants live only a few years, but replacements will pop up here and there if you let the seeds mature and scatter naturally. Page: 45.

Aristolochia durior

DUTCHMAN'S PIPE. A vigorous vine with large heart-shaped leaves that provide cool shade all summer and drop in winter. Bears pipe-shaped flowers in early summer. Climbs by twining and grows at least 10 ft. tall. Tolerates sun or shade. Prune young plants so they branch out at the base. Prune older plants to limit their size. Page: 94.

Aronia melanocarpa

BLACK CHOKEBERRY. A deciduous native shrub that grows 4 to 8 ft. tall and wide. It bears clusters of white flowers in spring and has dark blue-black berries that attract robins and other songbirds in late summer. The leaves are glossy dark green in summer, turning red in fall. Adapts to sun or shade and grows in almost any soil. Needs minimal pruning or care. Pages: 77, 81, 82, **83**, 91.

Aquilegia 'Biedermeier'
COLUMBINE

Aristolochia durior
DUTCHMAN'S PIPE

Artemisia ludoviciana 'Valerie Finnis'

'VALERIE FINNIS' ARTEMISIA. A perennial that forms a patch of erect stems 2 to 3 ft. tall. Grown for its foliage, which is bright silvery white. Needs full sun, average garden soil. Cut the stems back partway in late spring to encourage branching and to discourage blooming (the flowers aren't very attractive). Spreads to form a patch at least 2 to 3 ft. wide. Divide every second or third year in spring or fall. Pages: 57, 81, 106, *107.*

Artemisia stelleriana 'Silver Brocade'

'SILVER BROCADE' BEACH WORMWOOD. A sprawling perennial, often used as an edging or ground cover, with deeply lobed, silver-gray leaves. Also bears clusters of small yellow blossoms on 1-ft. stalks, but most gardeners shear these off as soon as they appear. Needs full sun, well-drained soil. If decayed spots appear on the leaves in hot humid summers, cut the stems back halfway. The plants will recover in cooler weather. Pages: 47, 81, *83.*

Aruncus dioicus

GOATSBEARD. A perennial wildflower that forms an impressive clump 4 to 6 ft. tall, with finely divided compound leaves and fluffy clusters of creamy white flowers in early summer. Prefers full or partial shade. Easy to grow. Cut off the flowers when they fade if you think they look shabby; otherwise, needs no care. Pages: *62,* 63, 95.

Asarum canadense
WILD GINGER

Asarum

WILD GINGER. Perennials grown for their foliage and used as ground covers. *A. canadense* (pp. 41, 78) is a native species with dull green, slightly fuzzy, deciduous, heart-shaped leaves 6 to 8 in. wide, on stalks about 6 in. tall. It spreads fairly quickly and is hardy throughout the Midwest region. European wild ginger, *A. europaeum* (pp. 66, *67*), has glossy evergreen leaves 3 to 5 in. wide, on stalks about 4 in. tall. Though very lovely, it spreads more slowly and is hardy only to Zone 5. Both species need full or partial shade and rich, moist, well-drained soil. Once established, they are carefree and can grow for many years without needing any attention.

Asclepias tuberosa

BUTTERFLY WEED. A perennial wildflower with flat heads of bright orange flowers in early summer and attractive seedpods in fall. Grows slowly for the first few years, but once established, thrives for decades and requires minimal care. Forms a clump up to 2 ft. tall and wide, with more stems each year. Needs full sun and well-drained soil. Pages: 75, *75.*

Aster novae-angliae 'Purple Dome'

'PURPLE DOME' NEW ENGLAND ASTER. A compact form of the popular perennial wildflower, this aster forms a dense mound of dark green foliage all summer, then bears thousands of dark purple flowers with yellow "eyes." Blooms for a month or so in early fall. Grows about 2 ft. tall and wide. Needs full sun and good air circulation. In shady or overly sheltered sites the foliage is subject to mildew diseases, which don't hurt the plant but do look ugly. Grows best in rich, moist soil. Divide every year or two in early spring. Pages: 42, 60, 64, 72, 75, *75,* 77.

Astilbe

ASTILBE. Among the best perennials for shady or partly shady sites, astilbes have fluffy plumes of tiny flowers and healthy, glossy, compound leaves all season. There is a wide selection of hybrid astilbes, *A.* × *arendsii*, sold by cultivar name, that grow from 18 to 42 in. tall and have white, pale pink, rose, or red flowers (pp. 82, *83*). 'Deutschland' and 'White Gloria' are popular cultivars with erect clusters of white flowers on stalks about 2 ft. tall in early summer (p. 84). 'Ostrich Plume' (pp. 24, 95) has drooping clusters of pink flowers on 3-ft. stalks in midsummer. A related plant, *A. simplicifolia* 'Sprite' (pp. *62,* 63, 66), is more compact, with pale pink flowers on 1-ft. stalks in mid- to late summer.

All astilbes prefer rich, moist, well-drained soil and need shade from midday sun. Cut off flower stalks when the blooms turn brown (or leave them in place, if you like the looks of the dried flowers). Cut foliage to the ground in late fall or early spring. Divide every three to five years in spring or late summer, using a sharp spade or ax to cut the tough, woody rootstock into a few large chunks.

Aurinia saxatilis

BASKET-OF-GOLD. One of the first perennials to bloom in spring, bearing masses of gold flowers at the time when daffodils and forsythias bloom. Gray foliage is attractive for the rest of the summer and fall. Needs full sun and well-drained soil. Cut stems back halfway after it blooms and again in summer if the leaves get diseased during a spell of hot, humid weather. Fast-growing but short-lived, so buy replacements every few years. Grows about 6 to 8 in. tall, spreads 2 to 3 ft. wide. Pages: 21, 53, *55.*

Baptisia australis

FALSE INDIGO. A perennial prairie wildflower that's unusually carefree and long-lived. Forms a mushroom-shaped mound of blue-green foliage, topped in early summer with showy spikes of indigo blue flowers, followed by clusters of decorative seedpods that last through the fall. Cut stalks to the ground in winter. Grows about 3 ft. tall. The clump grows wider every year, eventually reaching 3 to 6 ft. wide, but plants never need division. Adapts to full sun or partial shade. Pages: 69, *71,* 72, 77.

Berberis thunbergii

JAPANESE BARBERRY. A deciduous shrub with stiff, spiny stems and small leaves. Can grow into a broad mound 6 ft. tall and 8 ft. wide but is typically kept smaller by shearing. Leaves are green in summer, bright red in fall. Small red berries hang on most of the fall and winter. 'Crimson Pygmy' (pp. 36, *38,* 64, 74, 101) is a dwarf form that reaches about 2 ft. tall and spreads 3 to 5 ft. wide, with foliage that is purplish all summer and turns crimson in fall. Barberries need full sun and well-drained soil. Shear anytime, if desired. Pages: 101, *103.*

Boltonia asteroides 'Snowbank'

'SNOWBANK' BOLTONIA. A perennial wildflower that blooms for many weeks in fall, bearing thousands of

Astilbe × arendsii

small white asterlike blossoms. Forms a clump 3 to 4 ft. tall, 2 to 4 ft. wide, with many erect stems. The slender, pale green leaves look neat and healthy all summer. Takes full or partial sun. Cut stems back partway in late spring to reduce height of clump, if desired. Cut to the ground in winter. Divide every few years in early spring. Pages: 49, 72, 75, *75.*

Recommended bulbs

Crocus, Crocus
Cup-shaped flowers on 4-in. stalks in April. Available in white, yellow, lilac, and purple. Plant bulbs 4 in. deep, 4 in. apart. Pages: 33, 49.

Galanthus nivalis, Snowdrop
Bright white flowers droop from 6-in. stems in March or April. Plant 3 in. deep, 3 in. apart. Pages: 33, 49.

Muscari armeniacum, Grape hyacinth
Grapelike clusters of sweet-scented purple flowers last for several weeks in April and May. Plant bulbs 3 in. deep, 3 in. apart. Don't be surprised to see the grassy foliage appear in fall; it lasts through the winter. Pages: 33, 49, 51, 77.

Narcissus, Daffodil
The most popular spring bulb. There are hundreds of cultivars, with flowers in shades of yellow and white on stalks 6 to 24 in. tall, blooming in sequence from early to late spring. Some kinds have a lovely fragrance. 'February Gold' and 'Tête-à-Tête' are two of the first to bloom; 'Baby Moon' is one of the last. All have yellow flowers on stalks under 12 in. tall and are good for interplanting in flower beds, because their flowers are large enough to be showy but their leaves are short enough to be inconspicuous after the flowers bloom. Plant the bulbs 4 to 6 in. deep, 6 in. apart. Pages: 33, 51, 77.

Scilla siberica, Squill
Loose clusters of small bell-shaped flowers on 5-in. stalks in March. 'Spring Beauty', the most popular cultivar, has sky blue flowers; other kinds have dark blue, pink, or white flowers. Plant bulbs 3 in. deep, 3 in. apart. Page: 77.

Tulipa, Tulip
Large cup- or bell-shaped flowers on short or tall stalks in April or May. 'Red Riding Hood' (red) and 'Lilac Wonder' (pink-and-yellow) are small tulips with stalks 6 to 8 in. tall. They combine easily with other plants and live longer than most tulips do. Plant the bulbs 3 to 4 in. deep, 3 to 4 in. apart. Pages: 33, 49.

Narcissus
DAFFODIL

Bulbs

The bulbs recommended in this book are all perennials that come up year after year and bloom in spring. After they flower, their leaves keep growing and stay green until sometime in summer, when they gradually turn yellow and die down to the ground. Interplanting bulbs among daylilies, hostas, ferns, grasses, or other perennials has two benefits: the bulb flowers add color to the garden before the other plants start growing, and the other plants hide the withering bulb foliage later.

You can buy bulbs from a garden center in September or order them from catalogs earlier (in which case they'll be delivered at the proper time for planting). Either way, plant bulbs promptly in a sunny or partly sunny bed with well-prepared soil.

In subsequent years, all you have to do is pick off the faded flowers in spring and remove (or ignore, if you choose) the old leaves after they turn brown in summer. Most bulbs spread fast and form big clumps or patches. They can be divided every few years if you want to make more. Dig them up as the foliage is turning yellow, shake or pull the bulbs apart, and replant them right away. For more information on specific bulbs, see the box at left.

Buxus
BOXWOOD. Very popular and highly prized shrubs that form a dense mass of neat, small, glossy, evergreen leaves. The leaves, and also the small flowers in spring, have a distinct fragrance. Boxwood forms soft, mounded shapes if left alone or can be sheared into formal globes, cones, hedges, or topiary. There are many kinds of boxwood, differing in rate of growth, size of leaf, natural habit (upright or spreading), and winter foliage color (green or bronzy). 'Green Velvet' boxwood has small leaves that stay bright green in winter and forms a globe about 3 ft. tall (pp. 24, 60, 95, 111). 'Wintergreen' littleleaf boxwood (*B. microphylla*) is similar, growing about 3 ft. tall and wide (pp. 26, 109). Boxwoods grow slowly, so buy the largest plants you can afford. They need well-drained soil and grow best in full or partial sun. Use mulch to protect their shallow roots. Shear in early summer, if desired.

Calamagrostis × acutiflora 'Karl Foerster'
'KARL FOERSTER' FEATHER REED GRASS. A perennial grass that forms narrow, erect clumps. Fresh green leaves develop early in the season. Slender stalks topped with flower spikes that resemble pipe cleaners form in midsummer. Flower stalks reach 5 to

6 ft. tall, foliage spreads about 2 ft. wide. The whole plant gradually turns beige or tan by late summer, but it stands up well into the winter. Cut it all down to the ground before new growth starts in spring. Divide every few years if you want more plants. Otherwise, leave it alone. Adapts to most soils but needs full or partial sun. Pages: 42, 105, *107.*

Campanula carpatica

CARPATHIAN BELLFLOWER. A short, compact perennial, about 1 ft. tall and wide, that blooms for most of the summer. 'Blue Clips' has sky blue flowers; 'White Clips' has white flowers. Both have medium green foliage. Prefers full sun and well-drained soil. Divide clumps every few years in spring. Pages: 34, 45, 60, *62,* 109, 111.

Cerastium tomentosum

SNOW-IN-SUMMER. A perennial often used as a ground cover, with evergreen silvery foliage and masses of white flowers in June. Forms a low mat, with stems that trail along the ground. Needs full sun and well-drained soil. Shear off the top of the plant, cutting it back by about one-half, right after it blooms. Pages: 26, *27.*

Chamaecyparis obtusa 'Nana Gracilis'

DWARF HINOKI CYPRESS. A slow-growing conifer with graceful, glossy, emerald green foliage. Grows naturally into a narrow cone and doesn't need any pruning or shearing. Prefers partial sun and moist, well-drained soil. Buy the largest plant you can afford to start with. It may someday reach 8 ft. or taller and spread 3 to 4 ft. wide. Not hardy in Zone 4; substitute 'Holmstrup' arborvitae, *Thuja occidentalis.* Pages: *90,* 91.

Chrysanthemum × superbum

SHASTA DAISY. A popular perennial with large daisy blossoms, good for bouquets as well as in the garden. 'Alaska' (pp. *58,* 59) has flower stalks 24 to 30 in. tall; 'Silver Princess' (pp. 45, 57) has stalks only 12 in. tall. Blooms in July. Forms a low mat of glossy foliage that looks good all season. Needs full sun. Cut down the flower stalks after it blooms. Divide every year or two in early spring. Sometimes listed as *Leucanthemum × superbum.*

Clematis

CLEMATIS. Deciduous vines with large, velvety flowers in summer and dark green leaves divided into three oval leaflets. Jackman clematis, *C. × jackmanii*

Campanula carpatica 'White Clips' CARPATHIAN BELLFLOWER

Buxus 'Green Velvet' BOXWOOD

Clematis tangutica
GOLDEN CLEMATIS

(pp. 60, 72, **75**), has dark blue-purple flowers; 'Niobe' (p. 91) has ruby red flowers. Either can cover a trellis or support up to 8 ft. tall and needs full or partial sun and good garden soil amended with a cupful of ground limestone. When planting, dig the planting hole deep enough to cover the root ball and the base of the stem with about 2 in. of soil. Cut the stem back to the lowest set of healthy leaves to encourage branching near the base. Use twist-ties to secure new stems to the support. In subsequent years, prune all stems down to 1 ft. tall in spring, just as the buds begin to swell.

Clematis tangutica

GOLDEN CLEMATIS. A deciduous vine that climbs about 10 ft. tall. Small nodding yellow flowers bloom throughout the summer, followed by fluffy, silvery seed heads that last into the winter. Foliage is fine-textured. Needs full or partial sun. Prune in early spring, removing older shoots and cutting others back partway. Page: 74.

Clematis terniflora

SWEET AUTUMN CLEMATIS. A vigorous deciduous vine that can climb 25 ft. or higher, with fine-textured foliage. Bears countless clusters of small, starry, fra-

Convallaria majalis
LILY-OF-THE-VALLEY

grant white flowers in August and September. Needs full or partial sun. Prune in early spring, cutting back partway or close to the ground, depending on how far you want it to climb. Often sold under the name *C. paniculata*. Pages: 60, 77, 88, 92, **94.**

Convallaria majalis
LILY-OF-THE-VALLEY. A perennial that spreads to form a patch, with large smooth leaves held in a vertical position and very fragrant white flowers in spring. Prefers a shady site; tolerates moist soil. Makes a good ground cover, although in hot, dry years the leaves may wither early, leaving the ground bare until the next spring. Needs no routine care. Can be (but doesn't have to be) divided every few years in spring or summer. Grows about 8 in. tall. Spreads indefinitely. Pages: 41, 77, 88, 99.

Coreopsis verticillata
THREAD-LEAVED COREOPSIS. A long-blooming perennial that bears hundreds of small daisylike blossoms from July into September. 'Moonbeam' (pp. 21, 34, 60, 69, 73) has lemon yellow flowers. 'Zagreb' (pp. *38,* 39) has gold flowers. The dark green leaves are short and threadlike. Spreads to form a patch but isn't invasive. Needs full sun. Grows about 18 in. tall and wide.

Cornus
RED-TWIG DOGWOOD. Deciduous shrubs with stems that turn bright red in winter, lacy clusters of small white flowers in spring, pale blue or white berries in late summer, and large smooth leaves that are dark green in summer and turn crimson in fall. *C. alba* 'Sibirica' (p. 64) is a popular cultivar that forms a vase-shaped clump 6 to 8 ft. tall. *C. sericea* (pp. 96, *99*) can grow 8 to 10 ft. tall and spreads by suckers to form a colony. If these are unavailable, other cultivars are good substitutes. All need full or partial sun and prefer moist soil. Cut all the stems down close to the ground every few years (or every year, if you want to) in early spring. After a few weeks, the plant will send up vigorous new shoots. These young shoots develop the brightest bark.

Cotinus coggygria 'Royal Purple'
'ROYAL PURPLE' SMOKE TREE. A deciduous shrub with rounded leaves that open red, turn dark purple for the summer, then turn gold or orange in fall. Fluffy pink flower plumes are showy for many weeks in summer and fall. Grows about 10 ft. tall and wide if unpruned, or you can prune it hard every year to

Coreopsis verticillata
'Moonbeam'
THREAD-LEAVED COREOPSIS

have a smaller shrub with larger leaves; this makes a very dramatic specimen. Needs full sun for good color; turns green if shaded. If 'Royal Purple' is unavailable, 'Velvet Cloak' has similar foliage and makes a good substitute. Pages: 64, *67.*

Cotoneaster apiculatus
CRANBERRY COTONEASTER. A deciduous shrub with low, spreading limbs. Grows only 1 to 3 ft. tall, spreads 4 to 6 ft. wide. Small glossy leaves appear in early spring and turn bright red before dropping in fall. Dainty pale pink flowers mature into red berries that last until November. Needs full or partial sun and fertile, well-drained soil. Requires little regular care. You can prune as desired to control size and shape. Pages: 33, 34, **35.**

Crataegus phaenopyrum

WASHINGTON HAWTHORN. A small native tree that grows upright with a rounded crown, reaching about 25 ft. tall and 15 to 20 ft. wide. It has very thorny twigs, deciduous leaves that are glossy green all summer and sometimes turn red in fall, clusters of white flowers in June, and small bright red fruits that ripen in early fall and last into the winter. Needs full or partial sun. Requires only minimal pruning. A trouble-free, adaptable tree. Pages: 77, **79.**

Dianthus deltoides 'Brilliant'

'BRILLIANT' MAIDEN PINK. A perennial with small bright pink flowers, held on stalks about 6 in. tall above a dense mat of grassy green foliage that is semievergreen. Blooms from early summer until fall if you keep picking off the older flowers as they fade. Needs full sun and well-drained soil. Divide every few years in early spring. Pages: **46,** 47.

Dicentra spectabilis 'Alba'

WHITE BLEEDING HEART. A perennial that forms rounded clumps, about 2 to 3 ft. tall and wide, of soft-textured, lacy foliage topped with heart-shaped white flowers that dangle from delicate stalks. Blooms in May and June. May die down in summer, especially in hot, dry years. Needs partial shade and fertile, moist, well-drained soil. Divide every few years in spring or fall. Pages: 78, 84.

Dicentra spectabilis 'Alba'
WHITE BLEEDING HEART

Diervilla lonicera

DWARF BUSH HONEYSUCKLE. A deciduous native shrub that spreads by suckers to form small colonies of stems about 3 ft. tall, with neat dark green foliage that sometimes turns bright colors in fall. Bears clusters of honeysuckle-like yellow flowers in July. Takes sun or shade and grows in almost any soil. You may have to ask your nursery to order this shrub for you. It's not commonly stocked because it's less showy than other shrubs, but it's adaptable and carefree. Pages: 82, **83.**

Echinacea purpurea

PURPLE CONEFLOWER. A prairie wildflower that thrives in gardens and blooms for several weeks in July and August. Large daisylike blossoms are held on stiff branching stalks above a basal mound of dark green foliage. Normally this plant has pink-purple flowers, but there are a few cultivars with white flowers (pp. 93, **94**). Needs full sun. Cut back flower stalks if you choose, or let the seed heads ripen to feed the birds and to provide winter interest. May self-sow but isn't weedy. Older plants can be divided in early spring. Grows about 3 ft. tall, 2 ft. wide. Pages: 34, **35,** 60, 69, 77.

Epimedium grandiflorum

BISHOP'S HAT. A slow-growing but long-lived perennial with very attractive foliage. The compound leaves have glossy, heart-shaped leaflets that change from coppery to green to maroon over the course of the summer and don't die down until late fall. Sprays of small, pale pink or white flowers appear in early spring. Needs partial or full shade. Spreads slowly, forming a patch about 1 ft. tall and up to several feet wide. Makes a good ground cover under trees or shrubs. Pages: 66, 84, **86.**

Euonymus alatus 'Compactus'

COMPACT BURNING BUSH. A deciduous shrub with unusually colorful fall foliage, turning from green in midsummer to coppery in September and vivid crimson in October. Grows naturally into a neat sphere, about 6 ft. tall and wide, with branches that spread horizontally in overlapping layers, but can be sheared if you want to keep it smaller. Needs full sun or partial shade for best color. Adapts to almost any soil. Carefree. Pages: 26, 29, **31,** 33, 34, 68.

Euonymus fortunei

WINTER CREEPER, EUONYMUS. A versatile shrub or vine with glossy evergreen leaves. There are many

Recommended ferns

Adiantum pedatum, Maidenhair fern

Spreads slowly, forming a continuous patch of lacy-textured, deciduous fronds. Grows 1 to 2 ft. tall, spreads 2 to 3 ft. wide. Pages: 23, 41, *43.*

Athyrium goeringianum 'Pictum', Japanese painted fern

A colorful fern that forms rosettes of finely cut fronds marked in shades of green, silver, and maroon. They look almost iridescent. Deciduous. Grows about 1 ft. tall, 2 ft. wide. Pages: 41, *43,* 66.

Dennstaedtia puntilobula, Hay-scented fern

A native fern with finely divided deciduous fronds that develop a vanilla-like fragrance when they are damaged by mowing or frost.

Spreads by underground runners to form a patch about 2 ft. tall and at least 2 to 3 ft. wide. Pages: 64, *67.*

Dryopteris marginalis, Marginal wood fern

A native fern with glossy, evergreen, finely divided fronds. Forms clumps about 2 to 3 ft. tall, 1 ft. wide. Pages: 23, 66, *94,* 95, 99.

Matteuccia struthiopteris, Ostrich fern

An especially luxurious fern that forms large clumps of bright green deciduous fronds. Needs moist soil or it will turn yellow and go dormant before the end of summer. Grows 3 to 5 ft. tall. Over time, spreads to form a patch 3 to 5 ft. wide. Pages: *90,* 91.

Matteuccia struthiopteris
OSTRICH FERN

---

fine cultivars. 'Emerald Gaiety' (pp. 24, *27*) has small green-and-white leaves that turn pink in cold weather. It grows slowly, forming a mounded shrub at least 3 ft. tall and wide and sometimes climbing up a tree or fence. 'Canadale Gold' (p. 41) has green leaves edged with a broad yellow stripe and grows about 2 ft. tall and 3 ft. wide or wider. Both cultivars adapt to sun or shade and need well-drained soil. You can shear or prune them at any time to control size or shape. Where deer are a problem, plant pachysandra or periwinkle instead of euonymus. Quite cold-hardy if protected by a layer of snow, but leaves and stems may freeze back in snowless winters. Trim off damaged shoots in spring, and new growth will follow.

Ferns

Ferns are carefree, long-lived perennials for shady sites. Despite their delicate appearance, they're among the most durable and trouble-free plants you can grow. Almost all ferns need shade from the mid-day and afternoon sun. They grow best in soil that's been amended with extra organic matter. You can divide them every few years in early spring if you want more plants, or leave them alone for decades. They need no routine care. See the box above for more information on specific ferns.

Galium odoratum

SWEET WOODRUFF. A deciduous perennial ground cover that spreads quickly, needs very little care, and lasts for decades. Fine-textured foliage is bright green throughout the growing season, then turns beige or tan in late fall. Thousands of tiny white flowers sparkle above the fresh new foliage in May. Adapts to most soils, prefers partial or full shade. Shear or mow close to the ground in early spring and rake away the old foliage. Easily divided in spring or fall to make more plants. Buy just a few plants to start with and you'll have all you want in a year or two. Grows about 6 in. tall, spreads indefinitely. Pages: 25, *27*, 77, 84, 96.

Geranium endressii 'Wargrave Pink'

'WARGRAVE PINK' GERANIUM. A perennial that forms a large, sprawling mound, 18 in. tall and 2 to 3 ft. wide, of rich green foliage topped with pink flowers. Blooms heavily for a few weeks in early summer, with scattered flowers off and on until fall. Cut it back hard after the first bloom if it looks too floppy, and it will regrow in a more compact mound. Prefers full or partial sun. Pages: 45, *46*.

Geranium macrorrhizum

BIGROOT GERANIUM. A short, compact perennial that forms bushy clumps of fragrant semievergreen foliage topped with clusters of magenta or pink flowers in June. Grows about 12 in. tall, 18 to 24 in. wide, and makes a good ground cover. Prefers partial shade and well-drained soil. Divide crowded clumps every few years in spring or late summer. Pages: 57, *58*, 63.

Hamamelis virginiana

WITCH HAZEL. A deciduous native tree or shrub. Usually has multiple trunks and grows 15 to 20 ft. tall. Clusters of small but very sweet-scented yellow flowers line the twigs in fall, appearing at about the same time as the large rounded leaves turn gold and fall off. Prefers partial shade and moist, well-drained soil. Grows quickly. Needs minimal pruning or care. Pages: 96, *99*.

Helictotrichon sempervirens

BLUE OAT GRASS. A clump-forming grass with slender blue-gray leaves that are more or less evergreen, depending on the winter. Forms a rounded specimen 18 to 24 in. tall and wide. Blooms sparsely, with thin flower spikes that turn beige or tan. Needs full sun and well-drained or dry soil. Do not cut down in spring. Simply comb your fingers through the clump to pull out any loose, dead leaves. Old

Hamamelis virginiana
WITCH HAZEL

clumps may die out in the middle; if so, divide them in early spring. Pages: **38,** 39, 57, 74.

Hemerocallis

DAYLILY. Some of the most reliable and popular perennials, with large lilylike flowers in summer, held above dense clumps or patches of grassy, arching leaves. There are hundreds of cultivars, with orange, gold, yellow, creamy white, pink, or purplish flowers on stalks 12 to 40 in. tall. In situations where no particular cultivar is specified, go to a nursery in summer when the plants are in bloom and choose the colors and types you want (pp. 50, 54, 93). 'Stella d'Oro' (pp. 21, 45, 49, 59, 72, 101, 102, **103**) is special because it blooms over a much longer season than most daylilies do, from early June until October, bearing golden yellow flowers on stalks 18 to 24 in. tall. Most daylilies are unscented, but 'Hyperion' (pp. 72, 74, **75**) has sweet-scented, pale yellow flowers in late July on stalks 40 in. tall. 'Ice Carnival' (p. 72) has large, nearly white flowers on 28-in. stalks in mid-July. 'Mary Todd' (pp. 39, 45) has very large, heavy-textured yellow flowers on 26-in. stalks in early to mid-July.

All daylilies prefer full sun and thrive in well-prepared garden soil. Remove faded flowers every day, and cut the flower stalks off at ground level after blooming is finished. Divide every few years in late summer. When planting, space shorter daylilies about 1 ft. apart, taller kinds 2 ft. apart.

Heuchera

CORALBELLS. Perennials that form low clumps of almost evergreen foliage and bloom for most of the summer, bearing clouds of tiny red, coral, pink, or white flowers on slender stalks about 18 in. tall. Most cultivars are hybrids, and nurseries may list them as *H. × brizoides* or *H. sanguinea*. 'June Bride' and 'White Cloud' are popular cultivars with white flowers (pp. 53, **55**). 'Chatterbox' (p. 45) has deep pink flowers. All coralbells prefer partial sun and moist, well-drained soil. Remove flower stalks as the blossoms fade. Cut old leaves to the ground in early spring. Divide every few years, and contrary to normal rules, replant the divisions an inch or two deeper than they were growing before.

Heuchera micrantha 'Palace Purple'

'PALACE PURPLE' HEUCHERA. A clumping perennial with dark bronzy purple leaves, shaped like maple leaves, and sprays of tiny white flowers in summer. Grows about 1 ft. tall and wide. Looks best in par-

Hemerocallis 'Stella d'Oro' DAYLILY

Hemerocallis DAYLILY

tial shade, because the leaves tend to scorch or fade if exposed to too much sun. Grow like coralbells (see previous page). Pages: *38*, 39, 109.

Hosta

HOSTA. Hostas are long-lived, carefree, shade-tolerant perennials with beautiful leaves in a wide variety of colors and sizes. They form dome-shaped clumps or spreading patches of foliage that looks good from spring to fall and dies down in winter. Stalks of lavender, purple, or white flowers appear in mid- to late summer. Some hostas tolerate full sun, but most grow better in partial or full shade. All need fertile, moist, well-drained soil. Cut off flower stalks before seedpods ripen. Clumps can be divided in early spring if you want to make more plants; otherwise, leave them alone. Where deer are a problem, plant astilbes or ferns instead of hostas. See the box on the facing page for more information on specific hostas.

Hydrangea arborescens 'Annabelle'

'ANNABELLE' HYDRANGEA. A deciduous shrub with large, heart-shaped, solid green leaves. Basketball-sized clusters of papery white flowers form at the end of each 4-ft. stem in early summer and last

Ilex verticillata
WINTERBERRY HOLLY

through the season, gradually darkening from white to green and then fading to beige. The weight of the flowers causes the stems to arch over. Prefers partial shade. Prune off old stems at ground level in late winter or early spring. Flowers form on new growth. A long-lived and trouble-free plant. Pages: 22, *23*, 94.

Hydrangea paniculata 'Grandiflora'

PEEGEE HYDRANGEA. A deciduous shrub often trained to grow as a small, single-trunk tree, with oval light green leaves. Big clusters of papery flowers form at the tip of each branch in mid- to late summer, opening white and gradually aging to pink and finally turning tan in late fall. The dried flowers last at least partway through the winter; prune them off in spring. Can reach 15 to 20 ft. tall and wide or be kept smaller by annual pruning. Takes full or partial sun. A vigorous, trouble-free plant. Pages: 82, *83.*

Ilex crenata 'Hetzii'

'HETZII' JAPANESE HOLLY. A compact shrub with dense, twiggy growth and small evergreen leaves, good for formal specimens, hedges, and foundation plantings. Can grow up to 6 ft. tall and wide but is usually pruned or sheared to a smaller size. Adapts to full sun or partial shade, needs well-drained soil. Use a thick layer of mulch to protect the roots from cold temperatures. Not hardy in colder parts of Zone 5 or in Zone 4; substitute compact inkberry holly (*I. glabra* 'Compacta') or a boxwood (*Buxus*) there. Pages: 88, *90.*

Ilex opaca

AMERICAN HOLLY. A native tree with evergreen leaves that have a few spines around the edge. The leaves are typically olive green, but selected cultivars have glossy emerald green foliage. Female trees bear heavy crops of bright red berries if there is a male tree nearby. Has a conical shape and retains its lower limbs unless you prune them away. Grows to 30 ft. or taller. Prefers a site that's protected from sun and wind in winter. Some cultivars are hardier than others; ask a local nursery to recommend the best for your area. Pages: 77, *79.*

Ilex verticillata

WINTERBERRY HOLLY. A deciduous native shrub with many twiggy stems and soft, spineless leaves. Female cultivars such as 'Winter Red', 'Sunset', and 'Red Sprite' bear clusters of small, bright red berries that ripen in September and last until the birds eat

Recommended hostas

'August Moon' hosta
A medium-size hosta with rounded, corrugated, golden yellow leaves and white flowers. Forms a clump 30 in. wide, 20 in. tall. Page: 41.

'Francee' hosta
A medium-size hosta with heart-shaped leaves that are dark green edged with white. Lavender flowers. Forms a clump 36 in. wide, 24 in. tall. Pages: 41, 86, *86.*

'Ginko Craig' hosta
A small hosta with narrow, lance-shaped leaves that are dark green edged in white. Dark lavender flowers. Spreads fast and makes a good ground cover. Forms a clump 10 in. wide, 4 in. tall. Page: 82.

'Gold Standard' hosta
A medium-size hosta with heart-shaped leaves that change color with the seasons. They start pale green with a dark green margin in spring and turn gold with a light green margin in summer. Pale lavender flowers. A vigorous grower. Forms a clump 36 in. wide, 20 in. tall. Page: 86.

'Honeybells' hosta
A large hosta with oblong pale green leaves and fragrant lilac flowers. A vigorous grower. Forms a clump 46 in. wide, 26 in. tall. Pages: 23, 41, 82, 87.

Hosta fortunei 'Aureo-marginata'
A medium-size hosta with large, heart-shaped leaves that are dark green in the center, edged with a broad band that is gold in spring, fading to cream in summer. Lilac flowers. A vigorous grower. Forms a clump 24 in. wide, 18 in. tall. Pages: 23, *23,* 82, 86.

H. lancifolia
A small hosta with narrow, lance-shaped, solid green leaves and lilac flowers. Spreads fast and makes a good ground cover. Forms a clump 17 in. wide, 12 in. tall. Pages: 23, 87.

H. sieboldiana 'Elegans'
A large hosta with huge, round, puckered, blue-gray leaves. White flowers barely peek above the foliage. Grows slower than some hostas but matures into a fine specimen. Forms a clump 48 in. wide, 30 in. tall. Page: 41.

'Krossa Regal' hosta
A large hosta with long, arching, powder blue leaves. Forms a distinctive, erect, vase-shaped clump about 30 in. wide, 30 in. tall. Lilac flowers are held on 5-ft. stalks. Pages: 41, *43,* 87.

'Royal Standard' hosta
A medium-size hosta with glossy, solid green, heart-shaped leaves and large white flowers that have a lovely sweet aroma. A vigorous grower. Tolerates almost full sun without scorching. Forms a clump 38 in. wide, 18 in. tall. Pages: 25, *62,* 63, 82, 95.

'Sum and Substance' hosta
A large hosta with very large, thick-textured, glossy gold leaves and lavender flowers. Forms a magnificent clump of foliage extending up to 60 in. wide, 30 in. tall. Page: 25.

Hosta 'Honeybells'

Hosta sieboldiana 'Elegans'

Hosta lancifolia

Iris
BEARDED IRIS

them. To get berries, there has to be a male planted within 200 yards. Adapts to sun or shade. Rather slow-growing, so start with the largest, fullest plants you can find. Prune only to remove dead or damaged shoots. Eventually reaches 8 to 12 ft. high, depending on the site, and usually spreads wider than tall. Pages: 70, 77, *79*, 96.

Iris

BEARDED OR GERMAN IRIS. A popular perennial with large, elegant flowers in shades of blue, purple, pink, yellow, or white, on stalks 1 to 3 ft. tall. Most kinds bloom for just a week or so in May or June, but 'Immortality', with white flowers on 3-ft. stalks, reblooms in the fall. Bearded irises form a patch of stiff, bladelike, gray-green leaves about 1 ft. tall. They need full sun and well-drained soil. Divide in late summer, cutting the thick fingerlike rhizomes into sections with three or four buds or fans of foliage. When planting, bury the roots but lay the rhizome at the surface of the soil. Point the leaf fan in the direction you want the patch to grow. Page: 45.

Iris cristata

DWARF CRESTED IRIS. A perennial wildflower with lovely blue or white blossoms on 6-in. stalks in early spring and fans of pale green, bladelike leaves 6 in. tall. Spreads quickly to form a dense patch. Prefers partial shade and well-drained soil. Divide and replant like bearded iris (above). Pages: 66, *67.*

Iris ensata

JAPANESE IRIS. A perennial with spectacular flowers 8 to 10 in. wide on stalks about 3 ft. tall. The broad, ruffled petals have a fragile, velvety texture and come in bright shades of blue, purple, yellow, or white. Forms a clump of dark green, straplike leaves about 2 ft. tall. Needs full sun and very rich, fertile, moist soil. Divide every few years in late summer, cutting the clump into three or four large chunks. Page: 64.

Iris sibirica

SIBERIAN IRIS. A perennial that forms a large arching clump of tall slender leaves and blooms for a few weeks in June, with scores of showy flowers on stalks 2 to 3 ft. tall. 'Caesar's Brother' (pp. 68, *71*, 111) has dark blue-purple flowers. Other cultivars, equally lovely, have pale blue, yellow, or white flowers. Needs full or partial sun and moist, fertile, well-drained soil. Remove flower stalks after the blooms fade, or let the seedpods develop if you like their looks. Divide every few years in late summer, cutting the clump into three or four large chunks. Pages: 26, 45, 64.

Juniperus

JUNIPER. A large group of shrubs and trees with scaly or needlelike evergreen foliage, often quite fragrant, and small berrylike fruits. All need full sun and well-drained soil. They rarely need pruning but can be pruned or sheared if you want to control their size or shape. Subject to various insects and diseases but generally carefree. See the box on the facing page for more information on specific junipers.

Kalmia latifolia

MOUNTAIN LAUREL. A native shrub with smooth evergreen leaves and very showy clusters of white, pale pink, or rosy flowers in June. Slow-growing at first but faster in subsequent years. Adapts to shade but blooms much more profusely in partial or full sun. Needs moist, well-drained, acid soil amended with plenty of peat moss and topped with mulch. Snap off flower stalks as soon as the petals drop, and do any pruning at the same time. Normally reaches 10 ft. tall and wide after many years, but there are new cultivars that have brighter-colored flowers and get only about 6 ft. tall. Pages: *90,* 91.

Lamium maculatum 'White Nancy'

'WHITE NANCY' LAMIUM. A creeping perennial, often used as a ground cover. Low mats of foliage, under 6 in. tall, spread to 2 ft. or wider. Heart-shaped leaves are silver with a thin green band around the edge. Clusters of white flowers bloom in early summer. 'Beacon Silver' is a good substitute that has pink flowers. Prefers partial shade and garden or moist soil. Cut off flower stalks after it blooms. Divide every few years in spring or fall. Pages: 41, *43.*

Liatris spicata 'Kobold'

'KOBOLD' BLAZING STAR. A compact cultivar of a popular perennial prairie wildflower. Blooms in late July and August, with dense spikes of small magenta flowers on stiff stalks about 2 ft. tall arising from a clump or tuft of grassy dark green foliage. Needs full sun. Cut off the flower stalks after it blooms. Needs no other care. Pages: 34, *35,* 72, 77.

Lilium

HYBRID LILY. There are hundreds of wonderful lily cultivars, all with large flowers on leafy stalks ranging from 2 to 6 ft. tall. Flower colors include white, yellow, gold, orange, pink, red, and magenta. Different kinds bloom in sequence from early to late summer. 'Casablanca' (pp. 69, 72, 84, 109, 111, *111*) has large, flat, sweet-scented, clear white flowers on stalks 3 to 4 ft. tall. 'Stargazer' (pp. 26, *27,* 34, 111) flowers are dark crimson-pink edged with white, on stalks 2 to 3 ft. tall. Both bloom in August.

All lilies prefer full sun and deep, fertile, well-drained soil. Plant bulbs when they are available in

Recommended junipers

Juniperus chinensis 'Maney'

Juniperus chinensis, 'Maney' juniper
A vase-shaped shrub about 6 ft. tall and wide, with prickly foliage. Pages: 53, 58, 101, *103.*

J. chinensis, 'Sea Green' juniper
A broad shrub with arching limbs, usually growing about 4 ft. tall, 6 ft. wide. Foliage is dark green. Pages: 20, 50, *51,* 81, 102.

J. chinensis var. sargentii, Sargent juniper
A low shrub, usually grown as a ground cover. Forms a patch of short, upright stems. Normally has dark green foliage, but 'Glauca' is blue-green. Grows 1 to 2 ft. tall, at least 3 ft. wide. Pages: 68, 70, *71,* 93.

J. sabina, 'Arcadia' juniper
A low, spreading shrub, 12 to 18 in. tall and 3 to 4 ft. wide, with scaly, bright green foliage. Pages: 29, 31.

J. sabina, 'Broadmoor' juniper
A low, spreading shrub that forms a flat mound of feathery gray-green foliage. Grows 1 to 2 ft. tall, can reach 8 to 10 ft. wide. Pages: 53, *55.*

J. scopulorum, 'Pathfinder' juniper
A slender cone, 15 to 20 ft. tall, that's not as skinny as 'Skyrocket', with sprays of blue-gray foliage. Pages: 31, 74.

J. scopulorum, 'Skyrocket' juniper
A narrow, upright shrub, 10 to 15 ft. tall but only 2 ft. wide at the base, with blue-green foliage. Pages: 30, *31,* 88.

J. squamata, 'Blue Star' juniper
A small, slow-growing shrub that makes an irregular mound of sparkling blue, prickly-textured foliage. Reaches 1 to 2 ft. tall, 2 to 4 ft. wide after several years. Pages: 36, 74, 106, *107.*

late fall or early spring, burying them about 6 in. deep. Lilies multiply slowly and can remain in the same place for years (unless they get eaten by deer, voles, woodchucks, or other varmints). Sprinkle some bulb fertilizer on the soil each fall.

Liriope spicata

CREEPING LILYTURF. A perennial that spreads fast by underground runners to form a dense patch of dark green, grassy-looking foliage. Grows about 6 in. tall, spreads indefinitely. Makes a good ground cover for shady sites. Mow or shear off old foliage in early spring. Can be divided every few years to make more plants. Pages: 66, *67*.

Lonicera × *brownii* 'Dropmore Scarlet'

'DROPMORE SCARLET' HONEYSUCKLE. A woody vine that grows fast enough to make an impressive display in just a few years but is not aggressive and will not take over your garden. Grows 10 to 15 ft. high. Blooms from early summer until hard frost, with drooping clusters of scarlet flowers that attract hummingbirds. Needs full or partial sun. Prune young plants hard, repeating two or three times the first year if needed to encourage lots of branching near the base. Prune older plants once a year in late winter, removing deadwood and trimming back too-long stems. Pages: 54, *55,* 57, 101.

Magnolia × *loebneri* 'Dr. Merrill'

'DR. MERRILL' MAGNOLIA. A deciduous tree that's covered with fresh white flowers in early spring, before the leaves appear. The smooth leaves look fresh all summer and don't turn yellow and drop until late fall. Smooth bark and fuzzy flower buds are attractive in winter. Grows quickly, reaching 25 to 30 ft. tall and wide. Needs full or partial sun, well-drained soil. Plant in spring. Prune in early summer, removing weak or crossing limbs. Pages: *38,* 39.

Malus

CRAB APPLE. Small deciduous trees with showy flowers in May and bright-colored fruits that ripen in early fall and last all winter. 'Pink Spires' (pp. 50, *51,* 52) grows about 25 ft. tall and has lavender-pink flowers, purple-red fruits, and foliage tinged with red. 'Spring Snow' also reaches about 25 ft. and has lovely white flowers but bears few if any fruits.

Molinia arundinacea 'Windspiel' PURPLE MOOR GRASS

There are many other fine cultivars; ask a local nursery to recommend one if you can't find either of these. All need full sun. Train young trees by spreading narrow crotches and removing lower limbs to form a crown you can walk underneath. Prune off any suckers that sprout from the base of the tree, and any shoots that grow straight up.

Malva alcea 'Fastigiata'

HOLLYHOCK MALLOW. A perennial that blooms abundantly in midsummer, bearing hundreds of clear pink hollyhock-like flowers on flower stalks 3 to 4 ft. tall. In spring and fall, it forms a low mound, about 2 ft. wide, of large, bright green leaves. Needs full or partial sun. Cut flower stalks to the ground after it blooms. Often self-sows but isn't weedy. Pages: 45, *46*, 53.

Miscanthus sinensis 'Gracillimus'

MAIDEN GRASS. A showy grass that forms vase-shaped clumps 5 to 6 ft. tall of long, arching leaves that are very narrow, with a white stripe up the middle and gray-green edges. Blooms in September or October and has fluffy seed heads that last through the winter. If you can't find 'Gracillimus', 'Sarabande' is a good substitute that has similar foliage and flowers earlier in the season. Needs full sun. Cut old leaves and stalks close to the ground in late winter or early spring. Divide clumps in early spring every few years. Pages: 34, 64, 109, *111*.

Molinia arundinacea 'Windspiel'

'WINDSPIEL' PURPLE MOOR GRASS. A perennial grass that forms dense clumps, about 18 in. tall and wide, of long, dark green leaves. The flowers and seed heads wave high above the foliage on wiry stalks up to 7 ft. tall and turn golden yellow in fall. Makes a see-through screen. If 'Windspiel' is unavailable, 'Skyracer' is a good substitute. Needs full sun, acid soil. Cut foliage to the ground in late fall or early spring. Divide every few years in spring. Page: 30.

Monarda 'Marshall's Delight'

'MARSHALL'S DELIGHT' BEE BALM OR MONARDA. A spreading perennial that forms a patch of erect stems 3 to 4 ft. tall, topped with moplike clusters of pink flowers that attract hummingbirds. Blooms for several weeks in July and August. Needs full or partial sun and fertile, moist, well-drained soil. Don't let the soil dry out in summer. Cut old stalks to the ground in fall. Divide every few years in early spring. Pages: 45, *46*, 49, 53, 77, 93, 111.

Nepeta × faassenii 'Blue Wonder'

'BLUE WONDER' CATMINT. A perennial that forms a bushy mound of soft gray foliage topped with clusters of small violet-blue flowers. Grows about 2 ft. tall and wide. Blooms most in early summer but continues or repeats throughout the season. Needs full sun and well-drained soil. Shear plants back halfway after the first blooming to keep them tidy and to promote new growth. Cut to the ground in late fall or winter. May self-sow. 'Dropmore' is a good substitute. Pages: 29, *31*, 39, 73, 105.

Nymphaea

HARDY WATER LILY. The most popular plants for pools and ponds, available from several mail-order nurseries and occasionally at large garden centers. There are two main groups of water lilies: tropical and hardy. Tropical water lilies have lovely flowers, but they need hot summers and you have to store them indoors over the winter. Hardy water lilies are easier to grow and survive outdoors from year to year. They bloom in midsummer, in shades of white, yellow, and pink. Choose dwarf or medium-size cultivars for small ponds. Water lilies need full sun. (See p. 129 for a discussion of planting water lilies.) Pages: 64, *67*.

Paeonia

PEONY. Long-lived perennials that form a bushy clump of many stems, with spectacular large, fragrant flowers in late May or June and dark glossy foliage that turns purple or gold before it dies down in fall. 'Sarah Bernhardt' (pp. 57, *58*) is an old favorite with big pink double flowers; other cultivars have white, pale pink, or rose flowers. Needs full sun and deep, well-drained, fertile soil. Plant in late summer, positioning the thick rootstock so the pink buds are no more than 1 in. deep. (If planted too deep, peonies may not bloom.) Established clumps are typically 2 to 3 ft. tall, 3 to 4 ft. wide.

Panicum virgatum

SWITCHGRASS. A handsome and adaptable native grass. Forms a dense upright clump of foliage that is bright green in summer, gold in fall, and tan in winter. Topped with a cloudlike mass of fine-textured flower stalks that are pink when they appear in late summer and fade to tan in winter. Mature clumps stand 4 to 6 ft. tall, 2 to 3 ft. wide. They last well into the winter and aren't knocked over by wind, rain, or snow. Needs full or partial sun and well-drained soil. Cut to the ground in early spring. Di-

Rhododendron
'Rosy Lights' Azalea

vide every few years in spring. If you can find it, 'Hanse Hermes' is a good cultivar with foliage that turns red in fall. Pages: 74, 93, *94*.

Parthenocissus quinquefolia var. *engelmannii*

ENGELMAN IVY. A native woody vine that can climb any fence, wall, or tree, reaching 30 ft. or taller. Deciduous leaves are dark green in summer, turning bright red in early autumn. If this variety is unavailable, substitute Virginia creeper, which is a different form of the same species, with larger leaves. Adapts to sun or shade. Prune it hard at planting to force the young vine to branch out near the base. Once it is established, prune as needed to control its shape or size. Pages: 58, *58*.

Pennisetum alopecuroides 'Hameln'

DWARF FOUNTAIN GRASS. A perennial grass that forms a hassocklike clump, about 2 ft. tall and 3 ft. wide, of arching leaves that are green in summer, gold or tan in fall. Blooms over a long season from midsummer to fall, with fluffy spikes of tiny flowers on arching stalks. Needs full sun. Cut the clump to the ground in late winter, or sooner if storms knock it apart. Can go many years without being divided. Pages: 46, *46*, 64.

Phlox carolina 'Miss Lingard'

'MISS LINGARD' PHLOX. A perennial with big clusters of fragrant white flowers in midsummer. Forms a clump or patch of erect stalks 2 to 3 ft. tall, with healthy foliage that stays green all summer. Needs full or partial sun. Cut off flowers after they fade. Divide clumps every few years in spring. Sometimes listed as *P. maculata*. Pages: 49, *51*, 111.

Phlox stolonifera

CREEPING PHLOX. A low perennial with creeping stems, small semievergreen leaves, and clusters of fragrant flowers in spring. 'Bruce's White' has white flowers. 'Blue Ridge' has blue flowers. Other cultivars are good, too. Grows only a few inches tall but can spread 1 to 2 ft. in a year. Makes a carefree ground cover for sites with partial or full shade and fertile, moist, well-drained soil. Pages: 69, 70, *86*, 87.

Picea glauca 'Conica'

DWARF ALBERTA SPRUCE. A dwarf conifer with close-set, pale green needles. Forms a dense cone that gets a few inches taller each year, eventually reaching 8 to 10 ft. or taller. Needs full sun and well-drained soil. Never requires pruning. Page: 99.

Potentilla fruticosa

POTENTILLA. A small deciduous shrub that forms a compact mound 2 to 3 ft. tall and blooms off and on all summer, with round flowers about 1 in. wide. 'Abbotswood' (pp. 54, 101, *103*) has white flowers and dark green foliage. 'Primrose Beauty' (p. 96) has pale yellow flowers and gray-green foliage. Finely divided leaves and thin brown twigs are handsome, too. Prune hard every year or two in early spring, cutting stems to the ground to promote fresh new growth. Needs full sun and well-drained soil.

Pulmonaria saccharata 'Sissinghurst White'

'SISSINGHURST WHITE' LUNGWORT. A perennial that blooms for many weeks in spring, with masses of tiny white flowers on 1-ft. stalks. The large, white-spotted leaves make a good ground cover throughout the summer and fall. Needs partial shade and rich, moist, well-drained soil. Cut off flower stalks when the petals fade. Divide every few years in late summer. Wear gloves when handling this plant, because it is covered with prickly hairs. Pages: 84, 86.

Rhododendron

NORTHERN LIGHTS AZALEAS. A group of deciduous azaleas developed at the University of Minnesota. They bloom in late spring, as or soon after the new leaves unfold, with generous clusters of fragrant flowers in shades of white, yellow, orange, pink, and rose. There are several cultivars, named by flower color. Extremely hardy and adaptable, they thrive throughout the Midwest region on sites with full or partial sun and moist, well-drained, acid soil. The bushes grow 4 to 6 ft. tall and wide. Prune young plants immediately after flowering to encourage them to branch out. Older plants need little if any pruning. Pages: 22, 62, 68, 70, 84, 96, 99, 110.

Rhododendron 'Olga Mezitt'

'OLGA MEZITT' RHODODENDRON. An evergreen shrub that blooms in early spring, with masses of clear pink flowers. The small, shiny, leathery leaves are dark green all summer, maroon in winter. Grows 4 to 5 ft. tall. Needs full or partial sun and moist, well-drained, acid soil. Amend the bed with plenty of peat moss before planting, and mulch with oak leaves, pine needles, or pine bark. Needs only minimal pruning. Pages: 24, 33, 34, **35**, 62, 66, 109.

Rhus aromatica 'Gro-Low'

'GRO-LOW' SUMAC. A deciduous shrub that spreads to form a low mounded patch under 2 ft. tall but 6 to 8 ft. wide. Scalloped leaves are glossy dark green all summer and turn scarlet in fall. Small clusters of fuzzy red fruits add interest in summer. Takes full or partial sun, any well-drained soil. Doesn't need pruning, but you can shear or shape it if you want to. Pages: 30, 36, **38**.

Ribes alpinum 'Green Mound'

'GREEN MOUND' ALPINE CURRANT. A compact deciduous shrub that naturally forms a dense mound 2 to 3 ft. tall, covered with small, lobed, bright green leaves. Doesn't call attention to itself but makes a good background or edging that looks neat all season and needs virtually no care. Adapts to sun or shade. Pages: 46, **58**, 59.

Rosa

ROSE. Fast-growing deciduous shrubs with glossy compound leaves, thorny stems or canes, and very showy, often fragrant, flowers. (See the box at right for information on specific roses.) In the spring, many garden centers stock bare-root roses, with their roots wrapped in a plastic bag and packed in a cardboard box. These are a good investment if you buy them right after they arrive in the stores and plant them promptly, but their quality deteriorates with every day in the box. Nurseries may sell bare-root roses in the spring, but they usually grow the plants in containers. If you buy a potted rose, you can plant it anytime from spring to late summer.

Many roses are propagated by grafting and have a swollen place called the bud union where the graft was inserted. When planting, place the bud union at ground level, then heap an inch or more of soil

Recommended roses

'Bonica' rose
A broad bush, about 5 ft. tall and wide, with clusters of scentless double pink flowers from early summer until hard frost.
Pages: 60, 70, **71**.

'Carefree Wonder' rose
A small rounded bush, about 3 ft. tall and wide, with fragrant double pink-and-white flowers all summer. Pages: 57, 81, **83**.

'Frau Dagmar Hartop' rose
A rugosa-type rose with fragrant single pink flowers all summer and hips the size and color of cherry tomatoes. Forms an upright or rounded bush 5 ft. tall and wide. Pages: 21, 53, **55**, 77.

Rosa 'Zéphirine Drouhin'

'Othello' rose
A vigorous shrub, 4 to 5 ft. tall and wide, with large double flowers that are a rich crimson color and very fragrant. Has dark green foliage and thorny stems.
Page: 110.

'The Fairy' rose
A low, spreading shrub, about 2 ft. tall and 3 to 4 ft. wide, with small shiny leaves and masses of small, scentless, light pink flowers from early summer until hard frost.
Pages: 46, **46**, 60.

'William Baffin' rose
A very hardy, vigorous, climbing rose with fragrant double pink flowers. Grows 8 to 10 ft. tall. This is one of several "Explorer" roses, bred in Canada for maximum cold-hardiness. 'Henry Kelsey', with red flowers, and 'John Cabot', with fuchsia flowers, are similar in habit and hardiness.
Pages: 53, 102, **103**.

'Zéphirine Drouhin' rose
An antique rose that's become very popular again, with sweet-scented semidouble rose-pink flowers on long, arching, almost thornless canes. Climbs about 12 ft. tall. Unlike most roses, this blooms well even in partial shade, starting in early summer and continuing until frost. Not reliably hardy in Zone 4; substitute 'William Baffin' there.
Pages: 88, 92, **94**.

up over it. All roses grow best in full sun and well-amended, well-drained soil topped with a few inches of mulch. Once established, the roses recommended in this book require no more care than many other shrubs. Prune them once a year in spring, before new growth starts. (See p. 162 for information on pruning roses.)

Aphids—soft-bodied insects the size of a pinhead—may attack the new growth on roses but do no serious damage. You can wash them away with plain or soapy water. Japanese beetles are a major problem in some areas, and unfortunately there isn't much you can do but go out every morning and knock them into a pail of hot soapy water, where they drown. Other beetle-control methods such as traps and sprays are more trouble and less effective. Swarms of beetles eat rosebuds, blossoms, and foliage in July and August but are fairly uncommon in June or from September onward, so early and late blossoms may be untouched. Deer eat rosebushes, despite the thorns. Where deer are a problem, consider planting lilac, spirea, clematis, or other plants instead of roses.

Rudbeckia fulgida 'Goldsturm'

'GOLDSTURM' BLACK-EYED SUSAN, CONEFLOWER. An excellent cultivar of this popular perennial prairie

Sedum 'Autumn Joy'

wildflower. Blooms for several weeks in late summer, with flowers 3 to 4 in. wide. Forms a robust clump, with large dark green leaves at the base and stiff, erect, branching flower stalks about 3 ft. tall. Adapts to most soils. Needs full or partial sun. Cut down the flower stalks in fall or spring. (They provide some interest in a snowy winter landscape.) Divide every few years in spring. May self-seed but isn't weedy. Pages: 21, 42, *43,* 72, 77.

Ruta graveolens

RUE. A shrubby perennial that forms an 18-in. mound of lacy, blue-gray foliage that looks good from early spring until very late in fall. Clusters of small yellow flowers are held above the foliage in midsummer. Needs full sun and well-drained soil. Prune hard in spring, cutting stems back halfway. Wear gloves as you do this, because some people get a rash from touching rue. Pages: 39, 109, 111, *111.*

Salix purpurea 'Nana'

DWARF PURPLE WILLOW. A deciduous shrub with thin, supple, purple-barked twigs and slender blue-gray leaves. Looks best if you prune it to the ground every year in early spring; this keeps it compact and vigorous. By midsummer it will be a dome-shaped mound with scores of unbranched stems 3 to 5 ft. long. Needs full sun. Grows fine in garden soil; also adapts to wet, poorly drained sites. Pages: 64, *67.*

Salvia superba

SALVIA. A showy perennial that forms a patch of dark green foliage topped with slender, erect spikes of small flowers. 'Blue Queen' has dark blue flowers; those of 'East Friesland' are blue-purple. Starts blooming in June and repeats off and on through summer and fall if you shear or trim off the old flower stalks from time to time. Grows 18 to 24 in. tall, spreads 2 ft. wide. Prefers full sun and well-drained soil. Divide every few years in spring or fall. Pages: 47, 72, 105, *107.*

Schizachyrium scoparius

LITTLE BLUESTEM GRASS. A native grass that forms dense clumps 2 to 3 ft. tall, with slender leaves that are dark blue-green in summer, turning cinnamon-colored in cold weather. The white seed heads are small and wispy but sparkle on sunny fall and winter days. Needs full sun. Stands up well through the winter; cut to the ground in early spring. Clumps can grow for many years before needing division. Pages: 42, *43,* 54, 59, 77, 81.

Sedum 'Autumn Joy'

'AUTUMN JOY' SEDUM. A perennial that forms a vase-shaped clump about 2 ft. tall and wide. The thick stems are lined with large, fleshy, gray-green leaves. Broad flat clusters of buds form at the top of each stem in late summer and gradually change from creamy white to pink to rust as the flowers open and mature. Needs full sun. Cut stems back partway in early summer to keep them from flopping over and to make the clump bushier. In late fall or spring, cut old stems to the ground. Divide every few years in early spring. Pages: 42, 45, 72, 105, *107.*

Sedum sieboldii

OCTOBER PLANT, SEDUM. A neat, low perennial with trailing stems. Plump, round, blue-gray leaves are arranged in groups of three. Clusters of rosy pink flowers stay colorful for several weeks in the fall. Grows 6 to 8 in. tall, 8 to 12 in. wide. Needs full sun and well-drained soil. Remove dead stems in early spring. Pages: 26, *27,* 69.

Spiraea

SPIREA. Small to medium-size deciduous shrubs with a rounded habit, fine-textured foliage, and pretty clusters of small pink or white flowers. *S. × bumalda* 'Anthony Waterer' (pp. 36, 53, *55,* 58, 96) grows about 2 ft. tall and 3 ft. wide, with dark green foliage and dark pink flowers that bloom for several weeks in July and early August. *S. × bumalda* 'Goldflame' (pp. 36, 96, 106, *107*) grows about 2 ft. tall and 3 ft. wide, with leaves that are gold in spring, chartreuse in summer, and orange-red in fall. It bears crimson flowers off and on throughout the summer. *S. japonica* 'Little Princess' (pp. 21, 70, 81, 102, *103*) grows about 18 in. tall and 2 ft. wide, with dark green foliage and pink flowers during June and July. *S. nipponica* 'Snowmound' (pp. 49, 51, *51*) grows about 4 ft. tall and wide, with blue-green foliage and clear white flowers in May. All require full or partial sun. Shear off the tops of the stems after the flowers fade. Spireas often get uneven or straggly looking after several years. When that happens, cut the bush to the ground in early spring. It will grow back right away and look better than ever.

Syringa meyeri 'Palibin'

DWARF LILAC, DWARF KOREAN LILAC. A deciduous shrub with fragrant lilac flowers in May and small, glossy dark green leaves that turn purple in fall. Forms a bushy clump with many erect stems 4 to 6 ft. tall. Needs full sun for maximum flowering. Much more compact than common lilacs, and resistant to powdery mildew, which often disfigures their foliage in midsummer. Snap off the flower clusters as soon as they fade; at the same time, do any pruning or shearing required to shape the plant. Pages: 29, 31, *31,* 93.

Syringa reticulata

JAPANESE TREE LILAC. A small deciduous tree with clusters of fragrant, creamy white flowers in June, later than other lilacs. Often trained with multiple trunks to show more of the dark, glossy, peeling bark. Neat leaves are dark green all summer with little fall color. Grows about 25 ft. tall, with an upright oval crown. 'Ivory Silk' is a popular cultivar with especially nice flowers and attractive bark. Needs full sun. Snap off the flower clusters as soon as they fade; at the same time, prune out weak or crossing stems. Pages: 60, *62.*

Taxus

YEW. Evergreen shrubs and trees with flat sprays of needlelike foliage that starts out bright green when it develops in late spring, turns dark green in summer and fall. Foliage may stay green all winter or turn bronze, depending on the cultivar and conditions. In fall, female plants produce red berries that

Spiraea japonica
'Little Princess'

Tiarella cordifolia
FOAMFLOWER

Taxus cuspidata 'Nana'
DWARF JAPANESE YEW

attract birds but are poisonous to people. Yews tolerate repeated pruning and are often sheared into formal or geometric shapes and used for specimens, hedges, and foundation plantings. Some kinds are naturally compact and don't need to be sheared.

Upright Japanese yew, *T. cuspidata* 'Capitata' (pp. 98, *99*) grows upright into a broad pyramid. Unless pruned, it eventually becomes a small tree. Dwarf Japanese yew, *T. cuspidata* 'Nana' (pp. 26, 95), is slow-growing and compact, reaching 3 to 4 ft. tall and 4 to 6 ft. wide after several years. 'Dark Green Spreader', 'Densiformis', 'Everlow', 'Sebian', and 'Tauntonii' are all compact, wider-than-tall cultivars of hybrid yew, *T. × media* (pp. 23, 33, 34, *35*, 82, *83*, 84, 98). They differ slightly in hardiness, rate of growth, and winter foliage color, but all are satisfactory, so you can use whichever is available at your local nursery.

Yews adapt to full sun, partial sun, or shade but must have well-drained soil. They are sold in containers or balled-and-burlapped. If you want fast results, large plants are readily available and transplant well. To maintain a formal look, shear back the new growth in early summer, before it has hardened. For a natural look, prune individual branches as needed to maintain the desired shape. Where deer are a problem, plant boxwood, andromeda, or other evergreens instead of yews.

Thuja occidentalis

ARBORVITAE. A native evergreen tree, source of many fine cultivars for garden use. All have fragrant foliage. Older plants sometimes bear small woody cones. 'Holmstrup' (pp. 49, *51*, 98) forms a small, dense, narrow specimen about 6 ft. tall and 2 to 3 ft. wide, with fans of glossy rich green foliage. 'Nigra' (p. 28) forms a broad, upright cone of dark green foliage. It can reach 25 ft. or taller, or you can keep it pruned as you choose. 'Rheingold' (p. 98) forms a bushy oval, usually under 5 ft. tall, of fine-textured prickly or scaly foliage that is golden yellow in summer and turns coppery or bronzy in winter. 'Techny', also called 'Mission' (pp. 29, *31*, 57, 62), has dark green foliage and forms a broad cone 10 to 15 ft. tall.

All arborvitae need full or partial sun and moist, well-drained soil. Plant container-grown or balled-and-burlapped stock in spring or fall. These plants don't need pruning, but you can prune or shear them at any time if you want to direct or control the growth. Arborvitae often have several main shoots or leaders growing side by side; use soft twine to tie them together so they don't split apart in heavy snow or ice storms. Replace the twine every year or two. Where deer are a problem, plant spruce or juniper instead of arborvitae.

Thymus serpyllum
MOTHER-OF-THYME. A creeping perennial that forms low mats of wiry stems and tiny semievergreen leaves. Tolerates light foot traffic and smells good when you step on it. Clusters of pink, lavender, or white flowers bloom over a long season in midsummer. Grows 4 to 6 in. tall, 1 to 2 ft. wide. Look in the herb department of a nursery to find this plant. There are several other kinds of creeping thymes, and they all make attractive, fragrant, hardy ground covers for sites with full sun and well-drained soil. Shear old stems close to the ground in early spring. May self-sow and pop up here and there in cracks of pavement, in gravel walks, or even in the lawn, but isn't weedy. Pages: 109, *111.*

Tiarella cordifolia
FOAMFLOWER. A perennial woodland wildflower that quickly forms a dense low patch of evergreen foliage, covered with spikes of dainty white flowers on 6-in. stalks in late spring. Leaves are typically medium green, but there are several new cultivars whose leaves are marked with red-brown spots or streaks. Prefers partial shade and moist, well-drained soil. Divide every few years in spring or fall if you want to make more plants, or if the patch has gotten crowded and stopped flowering. Pages: 78, 84.

Tricyrtis hirta 'Miyazaki'
'MIYAZAKI' TOAD LILY. An unusual perennial that blooms in fall, with freckled white-and-lilac flowers about 1 in. wide. The flowers, which resemble orchids, last for weeks in the garden and make good cut flowers. Spreads by rhizomes to form a patch of arching stems 2 to 3 ft. tall lined with fuzzy, lance-shaped leaves. Prefers partial shade and rich, moist, well-drained, acid soil. Carefree. Pages: *90,* 91.

Tsuga canadensis var. sargentii
WEEPING HEMLOCK. A selected form of this native evergreen tree, with limbs that arch gracefully out and down, forming a mounded specimen. Grows slowly and spreads wider than tall, eventually reaching up to 10 ft. tall and 20 ft. wide. Buy the largest specimen you can afford, and prune only as needed to shape its growth. Takes sun or shade but needs moist, well-drained, acid soil. Pages: 98, *99.*

Veronica 'Sunny Border Blue'
'SUNNY BORDER BLUE' VERONICA. A perennial that blooms all summer, bearing slender spikes of dark blue-purple flowers on 2-ft. stalks, above a basal mat of glossy green leaves. Needs full or partial sun. Keep cutting off the old flower stalks. Divide every few years in early spring. Page: 34.

Viburnum
VIBURNUM. Deciduous shrubs with many outstanding features — showy foliage, flowers, fruits, or all of the above. For more information on specific plants, see the box on p. 196. All of the viburnums recom-

Veronica 'Sunny Border Blue'

Recommended viburnums

Viburnum carlesii 'Compactum', Compact Korean spice viburnum
Clusters of pink buds open into spicy-scented white flowers in May. Leaves may be red or green in fall. Grows about 4 ft. tall and wide. Pages: 26, 33, 34, 94, 110.

V. dentatum, Arrowwood viburnum
A native shrub, very hardy and adaptable, with white flowers in June and blue berries in September. Glossy dark green leaves turn maroon in fall. Grows to 8 ft. or taller, with straight, erect stems. Pages: 54, 94, **94**, 96.

V. dilatatum, Linden viburnum
A broad, mounded shrub 6 ft. tall and 8 ft. wide, with flat clusters of white flowers in May, berries that ripen from green to red to coral, and large leaves that turn bright red-orange in fall. 'Erie' is an excellent and widely available cultivar. Pages: 77, **79**.

V. opulus 'Nanum', Dwarf cranberrybush viburnum
A small, twiggy shrub, growing only 2 ft. tall and wide, with maplelike leaves that are dark green in summer, red in fall. Rarely flowers or fruits. Pages: 21, **23**.

V. trilobum 'Compactum', Compact cranberrybush viburnum
A compact, rounded shrub with lacy clusters of white flowers in May or June, maplelike leaves that turn red in fall, and juicy crimson berries that ripen in late summer and hang on all winter. Grows 4 to 6 ft. tall and wide. _V. opulus_ 'Compactum', a closely related plant, is a good substitute. Pages: 70, 77, **79**, 82, 88.

V. × juddii, Judd viburnum
Related to Korean spice viburnum, this has similar fragrant flowers, but its dark green foliage is glossier and more attractive, and it grows 6 to 8 ft. tall, 4 to 6 ft. wide. Page: 93.

Viburnum carlesii 'Compactum'
COMPACT KOREAN SPICE VIBURNUM

Viburnum opulus 'Nanum'
DWARF CRANBERRYBUSH VIBURNUM

mended in this book need full or partial sun and moist, well-drained soil. Prune young plants in late winter to encourage them to branch out and become bushy. Established plants need little pruning. Aphids sometimes attack viburnum buds and foliage, but the damage is mostly cosmetic. Spray them with a solution of insecticidal soap, or just wait a few weeks and they'll go away.

Vinca minor

PERIWINKLE. An evergreen ground cover with small, glossy, leathery, dark green leaves. Gradually forms a thick mass of foliage about 6 in. tall. Blooms in late spring, typically with round lavender-blue flowers about 1 in wide. 'Alba' (p. 20) and a few other cultivars have pure white flowers. 'Bowles' has flowers that are larger and darker blue than average. There are also some pretty variegated cultivars with green-and-cream leaves. Adapts to most soils, in partial sun or shade. Once established, needs absolutely no care. Pages: 25, 96, 111, *111.*

Viola odorata

SWEET VIOLET. A low-growing perennial that spreads by seeds and runners to make a patch or ground cover. Dark green, heart-shaped leaves are evergreen in mild winters. Blooms in late fall and again in early spring, with wonderfully fragrant purple flowers that perfume the whole garden. Adapts to most soils, in sun or shade. It is invasive but is too short (under 4 in.) to be much of a problem. You can easily pull up runners and seedlings that stray too far. Pages: 78, 96, *99.*

Weigela florida 'Variegata'

VARIEGATED WEIGELA. A deciduous shrub with lovely foliage; the glossy oval leaves are green edged with creamy white. Blooms in early summer, with clusters of light pink flowers. Looks best if you cut it to the ground every few years (or every year, if you don't mind sacrificing the flowers) in early spring. The new shoots that grow back have much prettier shape and foliage than old shoots do. Pruned like this, it grows about 4 ft. tall; unpruned, it can grow 6 to 8 ft. tall but gets shabby-looking. Needs full or partial sun. Pages: 88, *90.*

Water plants

Most big garden centers have a small collection of water plants. Mail-order water-garden specialists offer several dozen kinds as well as a range of supplies for water gardening. Most water plants are fast-growing, even weedy, so you will need only one of each kind to start with. (For water lilies, see *Nymphaea,* p. 189.)

Marginal or emergent aquatic plants are planted in containers of heavy soil covered with 2 in. or more of water; their leaves and flower stalks stick up into the air. Three good hardy emergents that do well in ponds in the Midwest region are blue flag iris (*Iris versicolor*), which has lovely blue flowers in spring and slender leaves 18 to 24 in. tall; arrowhead (*Sagittaria latifolia*), which has white flowers on 3-ft. stalks in summer and large, glossy, arrowhead-shaped leaves; and golden club (*Orontium aquatica*), which has unusual yellow flowers in early spring and large elliptical leaves. Plant these in 1-gal. cans; divide and replant every year or two. (For more on planting and caring for container-grown water plants, see p. 129.)

Oxygenating or submerged aquatic plants grow underwater; they help keep the water clear and provide oxygen, food, and shelter for fish. Anacharis (*Elodea canadensis*) is a popular oxygenator with tiny, dark green leaves. Page: 64.

Viola odorata
SWEET VIOLET

Glossary

Amendments. Organic materials or minerals used to improve the soil. Peat moss, perlite, and compost are commonly used.

Annual. A plant that grows from seed, flowers, produces new seeds, and dies during a single growing season; a perennial plant treated like an annual in that it is grown for only a single season's display and then removed.

Balled-and-burlapped. Describes a tree or shrub dug out of the ground with a ball of soil intact around the roots, the ball then wrapped in burlap and tied for transport.

Bare-root. Describes a plant dug out of the ground and then shaken or washed to remove the soil from the roots.

Balled-and-burlapped

Bare-root

Compound leaf. A leaf consisting of two or more leaflets branching from the same stalk.

Container-grown. Describes a plant raised in a pot that is removed before planting.

Crown. That part of a plant where the roots and stem meet, usually at soil level.

Cultivar. A cultivated variety of a plant, often bred or selected for some special trait such as double flowers, compact growth, cold hardiness, or disease resistance.

Deadheading. Removing spent flowers during the growing season to improve a plant's appearance, prevent seed formation, and stimulate the development of new flowers.

Deciduous. Describes a tree, shrub, or vine that drops all its leaves in winter.

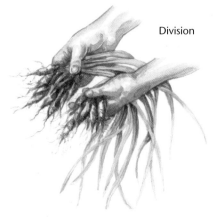

Division

Division. Propagation of a plant by separating it into two or more pieces, each piece possessing at least one bud and some roots. Plants commonly divided include perennials, bulbs, grasses, and ferns.

Drainage. Movement of water through soil. If water poured into a foot-deep hole drains completely in a few hours, the drainage is good.

Drip line. The circle of soil beneath a tree mirroring the circumference of the tree's canopy. This area benefits from direct rainfall and "drip" from leaves. Because many of the tree's feeder roots are found along the drip line and beyond, this area is the best for fertilizing and watering.

Dry-laid. Describes a masonry path or wall that is installed without mortar.

Edging. A barrier that serves as the border between lawn and a planting bed. Edgings may be shallow trenches or barriers of plastic, brick, or boards.

Exposure. The characterization of a site according to the sun, wind, and temperature acting upon it.

Formal. Describes a style of landscaping that features symmetrical layouts, with beds and walks related to adjacent buildings, and often with plants sheared to geometric or other shapes.

Foundation planting. Traditionally, a narrow border of evergreen shrubs planted around the foundation of a house. Contemporary foundation plantings often include deciduous shrubs, grasses, perennials, and other plants as well.

Frost heaving. A disturbance or uplifting of soil, pavement, or plants caused when moisture in the soil freezes and expands.

Full shade. Describes a site that receives no direct sun during the growing season.

Full sun. Describes a site that receives at least eight hours of direct sun each day during the growing season.

Garden soil. Soil specially prepared for planting to make it loose enough for roots and water to penetrate easily. Usually requires digging or tilling and the addition of some organic matter.

Grade. The angle and direction of the ground's slope in a given area.

Ground cover. A plant providing continuous cover for an area of soil. Commonly a low, spreading foliage plant such as candytuft, vinca, or ajuga.

Habit. The characteristic shape of a plant, such as upright, mounded, columnar, or vase-shaped.

Hardiness. A plant's ability to survive the winter temperatures in a given region without protection.

Hardscape. Parts of a landscape constructed from materials other than plants, such as walks, walls, and trellises made of wood, stone, or other materials.

Herbicide. A chemical used to kill plants. Preemergent herbicides are used to kill weed seeds as they sprout, and thus to prevent weed growth. Postemergent herbicides kill plants that are already growing.

Hybrid. A plant with two parents that belong to different varieties, species, or genera.

Interplant. To use plants with different bloom times or growth habits in the same bed to increase the variety and appeal of the planting.

Invasive. Describes a plant that spreads quickly, usually by runners, and mixes with or dominates adjacent plantings.

Landscape fabric. A synthetic fabric, sometimes water-permeable, spread under paths or mulch to serve as a weed barrier.

Lime, limestone. Mineral compounds applied to soil to lower its pH, rendering it less acid and thereby allowing plants to absorb nutrients better. Limestone also supplies calcium that plants need.

Loam. Soil rich in organic matter and with mineral particles in a range of sizes. Excellent for many garden plants.

Microclimate. A small-scale "system" of factors affecting plant growth on a particular site, including shade, temperature, rainfall, and so on.

Brick mowing strip

Mowing strip. A row of bricks or paving stones set flush with the soil around the edge of a bed, and wide enough to support one wheel of the lawn mower.

Mulch. A layer of organic or other materials spread several inches thick around the base of plants and over open soil in a bed. Mulch conserves soil moisture, smothers weeds, and moderates soil temperatures. Where winters are cold, mulches help protect plants from freezing. Common mulches include compost, shredded leaves, straw, lawn clippings, gravel, newspaper, and landscape fabric.

Native. Describes a plant that is or once was found in the wild in a particular region and was not imported from another area.

Nutrients. Elements needed by plants. Found in the soil and supplied by fertilizers, nutrients include nitrogen, phosphorus, potassium, calcium, magnesium, sulfur, iron, and other elements, in various forms and compounds.

Organic matter. Partially or fully decomposed plant and animal matter. Includes leaves, trimmings, and manure.

Peat moss. Partially decomposed mosses and sedges. Dug from boggy areas, peat moss is often used as an organic amendment for garden soil.

Perennial. A plant with a life span of more than one year. Woody plants such as trees and shrubs are perennials, in addition to the "herbaceous perennials" more commonly cited, which have no woody tissue that persists from year to year.

Pressure-treated lumber. Softwood lumber treated with chemicals that protect it from decay.

Propagate. To produce new plants from seeds or by vegetative means such as dividing plant parts, taking root cuttings, and grafting stems onto other plants.

Retaining wall. A wall built to stabilize a slope and keep soil from sliding or eroding downhill.

Rhizome. A horizontal underground stem from which roots and shoots emerge. Some swell to store food. Branched rhizomes (those of iris, for instance) can be divided to produce new plants.

Root ball. The mass of soil and roots dug with a plant when it is removed from the ground; the soil and roots of a plant grown in a container.

Rosette. A low, flat cluster or crown of overlapping leaves.

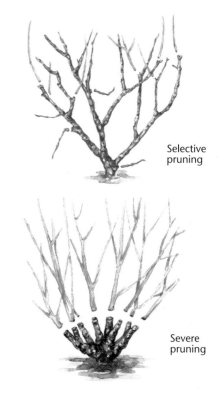

Selective pruning

Severe pruning

Selective pruning. Using pruning shears to remove or cut back individual shoots in order to refine the shape of a shrub, maintain its vigor, or limit its size.

Severe pruning. Using pruning shears or loppers to cut away most of a shrub's top growth, leaving just short stubs or a gnarly trunk.

Shearing. Using hedge shears or an electric hedge trimmer to shape the surface of a shrub, hedge, or tree and produce a smooth, solid mass of greenery.

Specimen plant. A plant placed for individual display.

Spike. An elongated flower cluster on which individual flowers are attached directly to the main stem or are on very short stalks attached to the main stem.

Tender. Describes a plant that is damaged by cold weather in a particular region.

Underplanting. Growing short plants, such as ground covers, under a taller plant, such as a shrub.

Variegated. Describes foliage with color patterns in stripes, specks, or blotches that occur naturally or result from breeding.

Photo Credits

Note: Photographs are keyed by letters corresponding to positions on the page beginning at the upper right corner of the page and proceeding clockwise.

Rita Buchanan: 27 A, E; 31 C; 35 B, D; 38 E, F; 58 D; 62 E; 67 B; 86 B, C; 90 A, E; 99 E; 111 E; 172; 177 A; 178 A; 185 C; 194 B

Karen Bussolini: 43 B; 55 C; 75 B, C, D; 94 A; 184

Ruth Rogers Clausen: 107 A

Galen Gates: 23 A; 31 A, B, D, F; 35 C; 38 D; 43 E; 46 A, F; 51 B, C; 55 E; 58 A, B; 62 C, F; 67 F; 71 B, D; 79 A, C; 83 B, C, E, G; 86 E; 90 D; 94 D; 99 A; 103 D; 107 E; 173 B; 177 B; 182; 187; 190; 196 A, B

Saxon Holt: 27 B; 46 B; 51 D; 55 A; 67 C, E; 86 A; 94 F; 107 C; 175; 178 B; 191; 194 A

Dency Kane: 79 E, F; 103 C

Charles Mann: 23 B, D; 27 C, D; 35 A, E; 38 A, C; 43 A, D; 46 E; 55 F; 58 E; 67 D, G; 71 A; 75 A; 90 F; 94 C; 99 F; 103 A, B, F; 107 F; 111 A, B, C, D; 179; 183 A, B; 192; 193

Rick Mastelli: 7; 46 D; 99 B; 180; 185 B; 197

Carole Ottesen: 83 A; 90 C; 174; 181; 188

Jerry Pavia: 23 C; 31 E; 38 B; 43 F; 46 C; 55 D; 58 C; 62 A; 67 A; 71 C, E; 79 D; 83 D, F; 86 D; 90 B; 94 B, E; 99 C, D; 103 E; 107 B, D; 176; 195

Cheryl Richter: 51 A, E; 173 A; 185 A; 186

Lauren Springer: 23 E; 43 C; 55 B; 62 B, D; 75 E; 79 B

Index

Note: Page numbers in **bold italic** refer to illustrations.

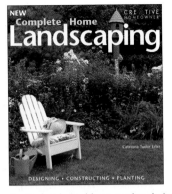

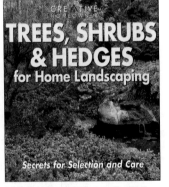
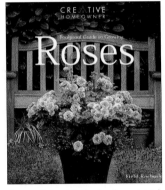
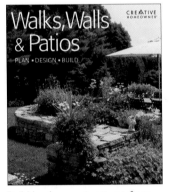
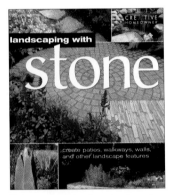
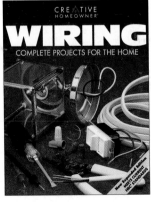
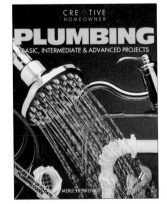
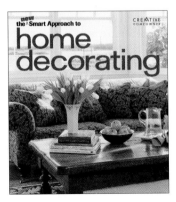
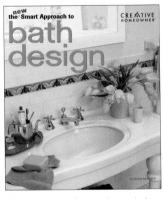